SACRED SPACE

the prayer book 2013

from the website www.sacredspace.ie

VERITAS

Acknowledgements

The publisher would like to thank Brian Grogan SJ and the Sacred Space team for their kind assistance in making this book possible. Correspondence with the Sacred Space team can be directed to feedback@sacredspace.ie where comments or suggestions relating to the book or to www.sacredspace.ie will always be welcome.

Published in 2013 by
Veritas Publications
7–8 Lower Abbey Street
Dublin 1
Ireland
Email: publications@veritas.ie
Website: www.veritas.ie

ISBN 9781 84730 387 5

A catalogue record for this book is available from the British Library.

Design and typesetting: Bernard Metcalfe, Biz Write Pty Ltd
Cover design: Luke Harris, Chameleon Print Design
Printed in Singapore by Toppan Security Printing Pte. Ltd.
International Standard Serial Number ISSN 1449-048X

How to use this book

We invite you to make a sacred space in your day and spend ten minutes praying here and now, wherever you are, with the help of a prayer guide and scripture chosen specially for each day. Every place is a sacred space so you may wish to have this book on your desk at work or available to be picked up and read at any time of the day, whilst travelling or on your bedside table, a park bench . . . Remember that God is everywhere, all around us, constantly reaching out to us, even in the most unlikely situations. When we know this, and with a bit of practice, we can pray anywhere.

The following pages will guide you through a session of prayer stages.

Something to think and pray about each day this week
The presence of God
Freedom
Consciousness
The Word (leads you to the daily scripture and provides help with the text)
Conversation
Conclusion

It is most important to come back to these pages each day of the week as they are an integral part of each day's prayer and lead to the scripture and inspiration points.

Although written in the first person the prayers are for "doing" rather than for reading out. Each stage is a kind of exercise or meditation aimed at helping you to get in touch with God and God's presence in your life.

We hope that you will join the many people around the world praying with us in our sacred space.

Open us, O Lord

Lord, open our eyes,
that we may see you in our brothers and sisters;
Lord, open our ears,
that we may hear the cries of the hungry,
the frightened, the oppressed.
Lord, open our hands,
that we may reach out to all who are in need;
Lord, open our hearts,
that we may love each other as you love us.

Canadian prayer

Contents

december 2–8

Something to think and pray about each day this week:

The coming days

Advent is in many ways the most beautiful and profound time of the Christian year.

Advent means "coming," and the season is about our *waiting* for the most mysterious and wonderful coming of all, into the heart of our lives, our needy lives. The words of St Paul are relevant: "It is full time now for you to wake from sleep. For salvation is nearer to us now than when we first believed; the night is far gone, the day is at hand. Let us then cast off the works of darkness and put on the armour of light" (Romans 13:11–12).

So over and over, from the heart of the Christian people, and down through the centuries, the prayer has gone up: "Show us, Lord, your steadfast love. And grant us your salvation." "Come, Lord, and bring us peace. Let us rejoice before you with sincere hearts." And we can pray now: "Lord, help us to wait, with patience, with longing, for your coming—your coming into our poor lives. As once your people waited, and you came in our midst as a child, to be among us—so help us now to wait, and hope, and love what we wait for: your coming, and your peace."

The Presence of God

Lord, help me to be fully alive to your holy presence.
Enfold me in your love.
Let my heart become one with yours.

Freedom

Many countries are at this moment suffering
the agonies of war.
I bow my head in thanksgiving for my freedom.
I pray for all prisoners and captives.

Consciousness

At this moment, Lord, I turn my thoughts to You.
I will leave aside my chores and preoccupations.
I will take rest and refreshment in your presence Lord.

The Word

The word of God comes down to us through the scriptures. May the Holy Spirit enlighten my mind and my heart to respond to the gospel teachings. (Please turn to your scripture on the following pages. Inspiration points are there should you need them. When you are ready, return here to continue.)

Conversation

Sometimes I wonder what I might say
if I were to meet You in person, Lord.
I might say "Thank You, Lord" for always being there for me.
I know with certainty there were times when you carried me.
When through your strength I got through the dark times in my life.

Conclusion

Glory be to the Father, and to the Son, and to the Holy Spirit,
As it was in the beginning, is now and ever shall be,
World without end. Amen

Sunday 2nd December,
First Sunday of Advent **Luke 21:25–28**

Jesus said, "There will be signs in the sun, the moon, and the stars, and on the earth distress among nations confused by the roaring of the sea and the waves. People will faint from fear and foreboding of what is coming upon the world, for the powers of the heavens will be shaken. Then they will see 'the Son of Man coming in a cloud' with power and great glory. Now when these things begin to take place, stand up and raise your heads, because your redemption is drawing near."

- Jesus is using traditional Jewish symbolism to describe what will happen when God's final judgment occurs. He says that people "will see the Son of Man coming in a cloud." The cloud is a symbol for God's presence.
- Jesus' message bursts with hope and confidence because, unlike those who have reason to fear his coming, Jesus' followers will be able to hold their heads high because their liberation is at hand.

Monday 3rd December,
St Francis Xavier **Matthew 8:5–11**

When Jesus entered Capernaum, a centurion came to him, appealing to him and saying, "Lord, my servant is lying at home paralyzed, in terrible distress." And he said to him, "I will come and cure him." The centurion answered, "Lord, I am not worthy to have you come under my roof; but only speak the word, and my servant will be healed. For I also am a man under authority, with soldiers under me; and I say to one, 'Go,' and he goes, and to another, 'Come,' and he comes, and to my slave, 'Do this,' and the slave does it." When Jesus heard him, he was amazed and said to those who followed him, "Truly I tell you, in no one in Israel have I found such faith. I tell you, many will come from east and west and will eat with Abraham and Isaac and Jacob in the kingdom of heaven."

- Every passage in the Gospel is a revelation of God. Here Jesus reveals the compassion of God. He has been sent to heal illnesses. I imagine the scene, and then I ask Jesus to come to me, to cure me and make me fully alive. I relax in the compassion he shows for me.

- I pray: "Lord, the centurion interceded for his sick servant. I now intercede for others who are unwell. More than that, I intercede for our sick world which you love so much."

Tuesday 4th December **Luke 10:21–24**

At that same hour Jesus rejoiced in the Holy Spirit and said, "All things have been handed over to me by my Father; and no one knows who the Son is except the Father, or who the Father is except the Son and anyone to whom the Son chooses to reveal him." Then turning to the disciples, Jesus said to them privately, "Blessed are the eyes that see what you see! For I tell you that many prophets and kings desired to see what you see, but did not see it, and to hear what you hear, but did not hear it."

- I watch Jesus at his prayer. What is it like to see him rejoicing in the Holy Spirit and thanking his Father? At this moment as I pray, the three divine Persons are present with me, and the Spirit is praying in me. Awareness of this can transform my prayer.
- I pray: "Jesus, so many people have never heard your Good News. But I have heard it, and I have seen you through the pages of the Gospels. Let your Word never become boring or stale for me, but fresh, creative, and challenging."

Wednesday 5th December **Matthew 15:29–37**

After Jesus had left that place, he passed along the Sea of Galilee, and he went up the mountain, where he sat down. Great crowds came to him, bringing with them the lame, the maimed, the blind, the mute, and many others. They put them at his feet, and he cured them, so that the crowd was amazed when they saw the mute speaking, the maimed whole, the lame walking, and the blind seeing. And they praised the God of Israel. Then Jesus called his disciples to him and said, "I have compassion for the crowd, because they have been with me now for three days and have nothing to eat; and I do not want to send them away hungry, for they might faint on the way." The disciples said to him, "Where are we to get enough bread in the desert to feed so great a crowd?" Jesus asked them, "How many loaves have you?" They said, "Seven, and a few small fish." Then ordering the crowd to sit down on the ground, he took the seven loaves and the fish; and after giving thanks he broke them and gave them to the disciples, and the disciples gave them to the crowds. And all of them ate and were filled; and they took up the broken pieces left over, seven baskets full.

- Jesus had compassion for the crowds. He sees me among them and knows my needs. I tell him where I am most challenged and listen for his word.
- Fullness of life and ability were offered to the sick and to those in need. Jesus calls me to full life, forgiving and healing any lack of capacity or effort that I have, inviting me to be a fuller sign of God's presence.

Thursday 6th December **Matthew 7:21, 24–27**

Jesus said to the people, "Not everyone who says to me, 'Lord, Lord,' will enter the kingdom of heaven, but only one who does the will of my Father in heaven." "Everyone then who hears these words of mine and acts on them will be like a wise man who built his house on rock. The rain fell, the floods came, and the winds blew and beat on that house, but it did not fall, because it had been founded on rock. And everyone who hears these words of mine and does not act on them will be like a foolish man who built his house on sand. The rain fell, and the floods came, and the winds blew and beat against that house, and it fell—and great was its fall!"

- Hearing or reading the Word is important, but is not the end. I take time to let the Word of God settle into the shape of my life. I take care not to let it merely stay in my mind, but to let it touch my heart and desires.
- I ask God to help me be present to the Word. I ask for sincerity and integrity, that my words do not just remain sounds but that they are backed up by my way of living.

Friday 7th December **Matthew 9:27–31**

As Jesus went on his way, two blind men followed him, crying loudly, "Have mercy on us, Son of David!" When he entered the house, the blind men came to him; and Jesus said to them, "Do you believe that I am able to do this?" They said to him, "Yes, Lord." Then he touched their eyes and said, "According to your faith let it be done to you." And their eyes were opened. Then Jesus sternly ordered them, "See that no one knows of this." But they went away and spread the news about him throughout that district.

- The blind men remind me of the need to be persistent in my prayer. Is what I ask God for now in my mind during the day? Do I look with expectation and hope to see how God is answering me? If I don't, what might my lack of perseverance say?
- I give thanks to God for those times when my eyes have been opened and ask God to lead me to appreciate truth.

Saturday 8th December,
The Immaculate Conception of the
Blessed Virgin Mary **Luke 1:30–33**

The angel said to her, "Do not be afraid, Mary, for you have found favor with God. And now, you will conceive in your womb and bear a son, and you will name him Jesus. He will be great, and will be called the Son of the Most High, and the Lord God will give to him the throne of his ancestor David. He will reign over the house of Jacob forever, and of his kingdom there will be no end."

- We know this encounter between God's messenger and Mary changed the world; and our world too. Whatever hopes she held for her life, she let go in this moment.
- Can we look beyond this momentous event to delve into our own responses? Can we let go our wishes and fears, and embrace hope? Can we say, "I don't know what this all means, but I trust that good things will happen."

december 9–15

Something to think and pray about each day this week:

The waiting days

Waiting takes up a large part of our life. Often we see waiting as "non-productive", as waste of time, and are frustrated. But waiting, and indeed the helplessness of it, can be more meaningful and fruitful than all the achieving we feel will give us status and fulfillment. A mother waits the birth of her child. I wait for the homecoming of someone I cherish and love. I wait, when all human efforts run out, for what is right and just.

Advent shows how beautiful waiting is. Years ago W.H. Vanstone wrote *The Stature of Waiting*, on the meaning and fruitfulness of waiting. And much further back John Henry Newman preached one of his most evocative Oxford sermons for Advent, entitled "Watching," on how we as Christians are called in all things to "look out" for Christ, to "watch," and be alert for his coming, in the midst of our daily lives, as well as at the end. Our prayer especially can have that element to it, of "being on the watch" as Jesus puts it in the Gospel. Lord, let me be prayerful, and watchful, this Advent.

The Presence of God
God is with me, but more,
God is within me, giving me existence.
Let me dwell for a moment on God's life-giving presence
in my body, my mind, my heart
and in the whole of my life.

Freedom
God is not foreign to my freedom.
Instead the Spirit breathes life into my most intimate desires,
gently nudging me towards all that is good.
I ask for the grace to let myself be enfolded by the Spirit.

Consciousness
Help me, Lord, to be more conscious of your presence.
Teach me to recognize your presence in others.
Fill my heart with gratitude for the times your love
has been shown to me through the care of others.

The Word
I read the Word of God slowly, a few times over, and I listen to what God is saying to me. (Please turn to your scripture on the following pages. Inspiration points are there should you need them. When you are ready, return here to continue.)

Conversation
How has God's Word moved me? Has it left me cold?
Has it consoled me or moved me to act in a new way?
I imagine Jesus standing or sitting beside me,
I turn and share my feelings with him.

Conclusion
Glory be to the Father, and to the Son, and to the Holy Spirit,
As it was in the beginning, is now and ever shall be,
World without end. Amen

Sunday 9th December,
Second Sunday of Advent **Luke 3:1–6**

In the fifteenth year of the reign of Emperor Tiberius, when Pontius Pilate was governor of Judea, and Herod was ruler of Galilee, and his brother Philip ruler of the region of Ituraea and Trachonitis, and Lysanias ruler of Abilene, during the high priesthood of Annas and Caiaphas, the word of God came to John son of Zechariah in the wilderness. He went into all the region around the Jordan, proclaiming a baptism of repentance for the forgiveness of sins, as it is written in the book of the words of the prophet Isaiah, "The voice of one crying out in the wilderness: 'Prepare the way of the Lord, make his paths straight. Every valley shall be filled, and every mountain and hill shall be made low, and the crooked shall be made straight, and the rough ways made smooth; and all flesh shall see the salvation of God.'"

- John the Baptist was an independent Jewish prophet active around 28 AD. He quotes the prophet Isaiah, "Prepare the way of the Lord; make his paths straight." The image John uses is that of a road engineer, shouting out orders for the construction of the "royal road" of the Lord.
- In Advent, I am called upon to open up the royal road to my own heart so that Jesus may be re-birthed in me.

Monday 10th December **Luke 5:17–20**

One day, while he was teaching, Pharisees and teachers of the law were sitting near by (they had come from every village of Galilee and Judea and from Jerusalem); and the power of the Lord was with him to heal. Just then some men came, carrying a paralyzed man on a bed. They were trying to bring him in and lay him before Jesus; but finding no way to bring him in because of the crowd, they went up on the roof and let him down with his bed through the tiles into the middle of the crowd in front of Jesus. When he saw their faith, he said, "Friend, your sins are forgiven you."

- The patient is not stretchered on the corridor, as sometimes happens in hospitals today, but lowered through the roof, a helpless paralytic.
- Lord, you do not want us to be helpless, immobile, or dependent on others for our every movement. You give us energy and dynamism, tell us to rise, take up our bed, and walk. No room for self-pity or learned helplessness. You ask each of us to take charge of our own life.

Tuesday 11th December **Isaiah 40:3–5**

A voice cries out: "In the wilderness prepare the way of the Lord, make straight in the desert a highway for our God. Every valley shall be lifted up, and every mountain and hill be made low; the uneven ground shall become level, and the rough places a plain. Then the glory of the Lord shall be revealed, and all people shall see it together, for the mouth of the Lord has spoken."

- "Prepare the way of the Lord." This is the essence of this season of Advent. As Isaiah sees it, the earth-shaking preparations of the revealing of the Glory of God are themselves the gift of God.
- Can I apply this to myself and my own preparations to meet the Lord? Do the obstacles between me and new life—small or great—seem very immovable, beyond my efforts?

Wednesday 12th December **Matthew 11:28–30**

Jesus said, "Come to me, all you that are weary and are carrying heavy burdens, and I will give you rest. Take my yoke upon you, and learn from me; for I am gentle and humble in heart, and you will find rest for your souls. For my yoke is easy, and my burden is light."

- For many people Christmas is a time of stress—dealing with concerns about costs, food preparations, or long-standing family compromises and conflicts.
- Lord, open our hearts to your love, to know the security and depth of belonging, to recognize how we all belong in Jesus the Christ.

Thursday 13th December **Matthew 11:11–15**

Truly I tell you, among those born of women no one has arisen greater than John the Baptist; yet the least in the kingdom of heaven is greater than he. From the days of John the Baptist until now the kingdom of heaven has suffered violence, and the violent take it by force. For all the prophets and the law prophesied until John came; and if you are willing to accept it, he is Elijah who is to come. Let anyone with ears listen!

- John may be the greatest figure of the past but, from Jesus' perspective—now that the Messiah has appeared—whoever believes in Jesus and accepts his teaching about God's kingdom is greater than John.
- Jesus remains entwined with John the Baptist as he does with Elijah; and as he will be with the apostles and the women who follow him.
- In the same way we are entwined with Jesus, and with all those who are part of the journey with Jesus to God.

Friday 14th December **Matthew 11:16–19**

Jesus spoke to the crowds, "But to what will I compare this generation? It is like children sitting in the marketplaces and calling to one another, 'We played the flute for you, and you did not dance; we wailed, and you did not mourn.' For John came neither eating nor drinking, and they say, 'He has a demon'; the Son of Man came eating and drinking, and they say, 'Look, a glutton and a drunkard, a friend of tax collectors and sinners!' Yet wisdom is vindicated by her deeds."

- Jesus illustrates two negative responses to the ministries of both himself and of John the Baptist.
- John is too severe for them, he "has a demon"; Jesus is too lax, he is "a friend of tax collectors and sinners."
- Jesus' ministry may disturb us because he preaches a God of compassion, which may not be what we expect. How do we try to make God "fit in" with what we want?

Saturday 15th December **Matthew 17:10–13**

And the disciples asked him, "Why, then, do the scribes say that Elijah must come first?" He replied, "Elijah is indeed coming and will restore all things; but I tell you that Elijah has already come, and they did not recognize him, but they did to him whatever they pleased. So also the Son of Man is about to suffer at their hands." Then the disciples understood that he was speaking to them about John the Baptist.

- The Jews expected Elijah to come as a great and terrible reformer, making the world perfect before the Messiah would arrive. Jesus insists that God works not through a powerful cleansing fire, but through sacrificial love.
- Jesus was always aware that he was to suffer; the crib is most realistic when the cross is in the background, close by. Lord, teach me to follow you, to accept this challenge, to understand love and suffering.

december 16–22

Something to think and pray about each day this week:

Becoming a little one

In the Bible, it was the poor who were especially conscious of God's working in their lives. Called the *anawim* in Hebrew, they were often just a remnant, a small number, "a humble and lowly people" (Zephaniah 3:12), who took refuge in God alone.

In the Gospel of Luke, people like Elizabeth and Zechariah, John the Baptist, Simeon and Anna, and above all Joseph and Mary, are portrayed as belonging to the *anawim.* They are not the great people walking the earth, but the hidden ones, living with faith, with humanity, and in truth. It is to them God comes, and especially to Mary. Mary, in response to the Angel, says in effect: "Let what God wants come about in my life" (cf Luke 1:38). And Elizabeth would then say to her cousin: "Yes, blessed is she who believed that the promise made her by the Lord would be fulfilled" (Luke 1:45).

Lord, help me in the poverty of my heart to be open to you—to your coming, your love, blessing, and peace. Help me to depend on you, for you are Lord of my heart, my deepest peace, and the surest guide along the path of my life. Lord, place me among the *anawim,* to be blessed by you through the gift of believing.

The Presence of God

What is present to me is what has a hold on my becoming.
I reflect on the presence of God always there in love,
amidst the many things that have a hold on me.
I pause and pray that I may let God
affect my becoming in this precise moment.

Freedom

There are very few people
who realize what God would make of them
if they abandoned themselves into his hands,
and let themselves be formed by his grace. (St Ignatius)
I ask for the grace to trust myself totally to God's love.

Consciousness

In the presence of my loving Creator,
I look honestly at my feelings over the last day,
the highs, the lows and the level ground.
Can I see where the Lord has been present?

The Word

God speaks to each one of us individually. I need to listen to hear what he is saying to me. Read the text a few times, then listen. (Please turn to your scripture on the following pages. Inspiration points are there should you need them. When you are ready, return here to continue.)

Conversation

What is stirring in me as I pray?
Am I consoled, troubled, left cold?
I imagine Jesus himself standing or sitting at my side,
and share my feelings with him.

Conclusion

Glory be to the Father, and to the Son, and to the Holy Spirit,
As it was in the beginning, is now and ever shall be,
World without end. Amen

Sunday 16th December,
Third Sunday of Advent **Luke 3:10–14**

And the crowds asked John the Baptist, "What then should we do?" In reply he said to them, "Whoever has two coats must share with anyone who has none; and whoever has food must do likewise." Even tax collectors came to be baptized, and they asked him, "Teacher, what should we do?" He said to them, "Collect no more than the amount prescribed for you." Soldiers also asked him, "And we, what should we do?" He said to them, "Do not extort money from anyone by threats or false accusation, and be satisfied with your wages."

- Preparing the way for the Messiah is not simply a matter of belonging to the Jewish nation, John insists, but comes about through repentance, through changing the way one thinks, and changing one's lifestyle in practical ways.
- What does my lifestyle say about my faith in Christ? Do I hoard, or do I share what I have with others, especially those who are poor and on the margins of society?

Monday 17th December **Genesis 49:2, 8–10**

Jacob called his sons, and said to them, "Assemble and hear, O sons of Jacob; listen to Israel your father. Judah, your brothers shall praise you; your hand shall be on the neck of your enemies; your father's sons shall bow down before you. Judah is a lion's whelp; from the prey, my son, you have gone up. He crouches down, he stretches out like a lion, like a lioness—who dares rouse him up? The scepter shall not depart from Judah, nor the ruler's staff from between his feet, until tribute comes to him; and the obedience of the peoples is his."

- As Jacob was dying he called his twelve sons around him to give his testament and tell them what lay in store for them.
- "The scepter shall not pass from Judah . . . until he come to whom it belongs." In the words of the old man we Christians hear the promise of the "one who is to come."
- Can I begin to let myself feel some of the hope and expectation of those who wait for a promised Messiah?

Tuesday 18th December **Matthew 21:18–25**

Now the birth of Jesus the Messiah took place in this way. When his mother Mary had been engaged to Joseph, but before they lived together, she was found to be with child from the Holy Spirit. Her husband Joseph, being a righteous man and unwilling to expose her to public disgrace, planned to dismiss her quietly. But just when he had resolved to do this, an angel of the Lord appeared to him in a dream and said, "Joseph, son of David, do not be afraid to take Mary as your wife, for the child conceived in her is from the Holy Spirit. She will bear a son, and you are to name him Jesus, for he will save his people from their sins." All this took place to fulfill what had been spoken by the Lord through the prophet: "Look, the virgin shall conceive and bear a son, and they shall name him Emmanuel," which means, "God is with us." When Joseph awoke from sleep, he did as the angel of the Lord commanded him; he took her as his wife, but had no marital relations with her until she had borne a son; and he named him Jesus.

- Joseph often seems to be in the shadows of the nativity scene. I spend some time with him today, appreciating his integrity, valuing his ability to discern and recognizing that God gave him a message of encouragement.
- Joseph, although he had made up his mind, was prepared to let his dream speak. I ask for the grace to be able to bring my decisions before God, allowing my heart to be shaped and my mind to be changed.

Wednesday 19th December **Psalm 70 (71):3–6, 16–17**

Be to me a rock of refuge, a strong fortress, to save me, for you are my rock and my fortress. Rescue me, O my God, from the hand of the wicked, from the grasp of the unjust and cruel. For you, O Lord, are my hope, my trust, O Lord, from my youth. Upon you I have leaned from my birth; it was you who took me from my mother's womb. I will come praising the mighty deeds of the Lord God, I will praise your righteousness, yours alone. O God, from my youth you have taught me, and I still proclaim your wondrous deeds.

- The Psalms express this most fundamental hope; that our refuge, our rest and security lie in God alone.
- Lord, teach us to speak with the clear voice of the Psalmist, to acknowledge that God is with each of us from the moment of our birth; today, yesterday and tomorrow.

Thursday 20th December **Luke 1:26–29**

In the sixth month the angel Gabriel was sent by God to a town in Galilee called Nazareth, to a virgin whose name was Mary. And he came to her and said, "Greetings, favored one! The Lord is with you." But she was much perplexed by his words and pondered what sort of greeting this might be.

- "The Lord is with you." This encounter between God's messenger and Mary is full of mystery. In her response Mary shows us how to pray, and how to seek the will of God in our daily encounters.
- As the end of the Advent season brings the promise of God's incarnate Son, Jesus, what can we learn from Mary response?

Friday 21st December **Luke 1:39–45**

In those days Mary set out and went with haste to a Judean town in the hill country, where she entered the house of Zechariah and greeted Elizabeth. When Elizabeth heard Mary's greeting, the child leapt in her womb. And Elizabeth was filled with the Holy Spirit and exclaimed with a loud cry, "Blessed are you among women, and blessed is the fruit of your womb. And why has this happened to me, that the mother of my Lord comes to me? For as soon as I heard the sound of your greeting, the child in my womb leapt for joy. And blessed is she who believed that there would be a fulfillment of what was spoken to her by the Lord."

- Mary has just learned that she is to be the mother of God. She does not bask in being the celebrity of all celebrities, but puts on sandals and cloak and walks to Judea to help her pregnant cousin.

- Think of occasions when I served and took joy in it: not as a paid job but as a labor of love, and the delight that comes from thinking more about others than about myself. Saint Paul quotes Jesus as saying, "There is more happiness in giving than in receiving" (Acts 20:35).

Saturday 22nd December **Luke 1:46–56**

And Mary said, "My soul magnifies the Lord, and my spirit rejoices in God my Savior, for he has looked with favor on the lowliness of his servant. Surely, from now on all generations will call me blessed; for the Mighty One has done great things for me, and holy is his name. His mercy is for those who fear him from generation to generation. He has shown strength with his arm; he has scattered the proud in the thoughts of their hearts. He has brought down the powerful from their thrones, and lifted up the lowly; he has filled the hungry with good things, and sent the rich away empty. He has helped his servant Israel, in remembrance of his mercy, according to the promise he made to our ancestors, to Abraham and to his descendants forever." And Mary remained with Elizabeth about three months and then returned to her home.

- The *Magnificat*, with some minor interpolations, is clearly patterned on the hymn of Hannah, the mother of Samuel (1 Sam 2:1–10). Having heard that her son is to be son of David and Son of God, Mary translates this into good news for the lowly and the hungry people of the world. At the same time it is a warning for the rich and powerful.
- Jesus will reinforce this message in his public life. Mary's radical canticle demonstrates what God will do: he will scatter the arrogant, pull down the mighty, send the rich away empty. God also exalts the lowly, fills the hungry, and leads his people by the hand. This is exactly the reversal that Jesus announces in the Beatitudes.
- Do I find myself on the side of the lowly or, without openly admitting it, on the side of the arrogant?

december 23–29

Something to think and pray about each day this week:

Wait no more

Coming closer to Christmas, there is naturally a greater focus in Christian prayer and liturgy on the historical waiting of Mary, and of her people, for the promised Messiah. Above all, Mary's waiting, in her pregnancy, can be mingled with ours this Advent. For Mary is not far away, but close—her expectation, her prayer, being joined with ours.

And then deep from the heart of history a great prayer arises and joins with ours too. For from the eight century, the great "O Antiphon" prayers ring out for us now in the Christian liturgy. "O Wisdom," "O Adonai and leader of Israel," "O stock of Jesse," "O key of David," "O Rising Sun," "O King whom all the nations desire," and finally "O Emmanuel": "O come!". Come and save us, free all those in darkness, and do not delay.

Our prayer now, our deep hunger, is joined to that crying from the heart of history—and therefore too from the depths of a needy world today. And it all rises to the living God, who is truly coming to us, in the little Child to be born of Mary.

The Presence of God

God is with me, but more, God is within me.
Let me dwell for a moment on God's life-giving presence
in my body, in my mind, in my heart,
as I sit here, right now.

Freedom

A thick and shapeless tree-trunk would never believe
that it could become a statue, admired as a miracle of sculpture,
and would never submit itself to the chisel of the sculptor,
who sees by her genius what she can make of it. (St Ignatius)
I ask for the grace to let myself be shaped by my loving Creator.

Consciousness

Knowing that God loves me unconditionally,
I can afford to be honest about how I am.
How has the last day been, and how do I feel now?
I share my feelings openly with the Lord.

The Word

I read the Word of God slowly, a few times over, and I listen to what God is saying to me. (Please turn to your scripture on the following pages. Inspiration points are there should you need them. When you are ready, return here to continue.)

Conversation

Do I notice myself reacting as I pray with the Word of God?
Do I feel challenged, comforted, angry?
Imagining Jesus sitting or standing by me,
I speak out my feelings, as one trusted friend to another.

Conclusion

Glory be to the Father, and to the Son, and to the Holy Spirit,
As it was in the beginning, is now and ever shall be,
World without end. Amen

Sunday 23rd December,
Fourth Sunday of Advent **Luke 1:39–45**

In those days Mary set out and went with haste to a Judean town in the hill country, where she entered the house of Zechariah and greeted Elizabeth. When Elizabeth heard Mary's greeting, the child leaped in her womb. And Elizabeth was filled with the Holy Spirit and exclaimed with a loud cry, "Blessed are you among women, and blessed is the fruit of your womb. And why has this happened to me, that the mother of my Lord comes to me? For as soon as I heard the sound of your greeting, the child in my womb leaped for joy. And blessed is she who believed that there would be a fulfilment of what was spoken to her by the Lord."

- Elizabeth's statement is astounding. She greets Mary as "the mother of my Lord," a title normally reserved for God. So Elizabeth seems to know dimensions of Mary's condition and Jesus' status that only become clear to the Apostles after the Resurrection.
- When I encounter someone for the first time do I perceive and respect that person as a son or daughter of God? What about the people I meet on a day-to-day basis?

Monday 24th December **Luke 1:67–79**

Then his father Zechariah was filled with the Holy Spirit and spoke this prophecy: "Blessed be the Lord God of Israel, for he has looked favorably on his people and redeemed them. He has raised up a mighty savior for us in the house of his servant David, as he spoke through the mouth of his holy prophets from of old, that we would be saved from our enemies and from the hand of all who hate us. Thus he has shown the mercy promised to our ancestors, and has remembered his holy covenant, the oath that he swore to our ancestor Abraham, to grant us that we, being rescued from the hands of our enemies, might serve him without fear, in holiness and righteousness before him all our days. And you, child, will be called the prophet of the Most High; for you will go before the Lord to prepare his ways, to give knowledge of salvation to his people by the forgiveness of their sins. By the tender mercy of our God, the dawn from on high will break upon us, to give light to those who sit in darkness and in the shadow of death, to guide our feet into the way of peace."

- Allow this psalm of thanks and praise to be made for you, your *Benedictus*. Zechariah made this prayer for his son. It was a prayer grown and made in love. We are now the ones who go before the Lord; our love and care can be the dawn breaking into the lives of others, giving light to all in darkness.
- Take what is suitable from this great prayer, said each morning throughout the church, and let it link you with the living Christ.

Tuesday 25th December,
Feast of the Nativity of the Lord **John 1:1–5**

In the beginning was the Word, and the Word was with God, and the Word was God. He was in the beginning with God. All things came into being through him, and without him not one thing came into being. What has come into being in him was life, and the life was the light of all people. The light shines in the darkness, and the darkness did not overcome it.

- The Word lives among us. I let this truth sink in more deeply, giving time to allow joy and gratitude to be my response to God's act of faith in me.
- Among all the lights of this Christmas, I cherish the light that prayer brings to me. I am reassured by the assertion that darkness does not overcome the light and pray that all who celebrate this feast may experience light and joy.

Wednesday 26th December,
St Stephen, the first Martyr **Matthew 10:17–22**

Jesus said to his apostles, "Beware of them, for they will hand you over to councils and flog you in their synagogues; and you will be dragged before governors and kings because of me, as a testimony to them and the Gentiles. When they hand you over, do not worry about how you are to speak or what you are to say; for what you are to say will be given to you at that time; for it is not you who speak, but the Spirit of your Father speaking through you. Brother will betray brother to death, and a father his child, and children will rise against parents and have them put to death; and you will be hated by all because of my name. But the one who endures to the end will be saved."

- St Stephen, in the midst of his sufferings, placed his trust in God. Jesus' words may well have echoed in his ears: "When they hand you over, do not worry about how you are to speak or what you are to say. You will be given at that moment what you are to say."
- Wisdom, it is said, is making peace with the unchangeable. Do I make peace with any suffering that comes my way?

Thursday 27th December,
St John, Evangelist **John 20:1a, 2–8**

Early on the first day of the week, while it was still dark, Mary Magdalene came to the tomb and saw that the stone had been removed from the tomb. So she ran and went to Simon Peter and the other disciple, the one whom Jesus loved, and said to them, "They have taken the Lord out of the tomb, and we do not know where they have laid him." Then Peter and the other disciple set out and went toward the tomb. The two were running together, but the other disciple outran Peter and reached the tomb first. He bent down to look in and saw the linen wrappings lying there, but he did not go in. Then Simon Peter came, following him, and went into the tomb. He saw the linen wrappings lying there, and the cloth that had been on Jesus' head, not lying with the linen wrappings but rolled up in a place by itself. Then the other disciple, who reached the tomb first, also went in, and he saw and believed.

- The memory of St John links the end of Jesus' passion and death with the new life of the resurrection; it links Christmas with Easter. We know by faith that the Christ child is the risen Lord. Christmas is the feast of glory, the glory of God hidden in the child who would rise from death.

- The glory of God is hidden in each of God's people. In prayer we can allow our faith in the mystery of the risen Emmanuel to grow and to reach out to embrace all, so that we see the incarnate and risen God in each person we meet.

Friday 28th December,
The Holy Innocents **Matthew 2:16–18**

When Herod saw that he had been tricked by the wise men, he was infuriated, and he sent and killed all the children in and around Bethlehem who were two years old or under, according to the time that he had learned from the wise men. Then was fulfilled what had been spoken through the prophet Jeremiah: "A voice was heard in Ramah, wailing and loud lamentation, Rachel weeping for her children; she refused to be consoled, because they are no more."

- Matthew uses Old Testament parallels to show how salvation history unfolds. Just as Joseph, of multi-coloured dream-coat fame, interprets dreams, so does Joseph, Mary's husband. Pharaoh tried to slay all the male children of the Hebrews, only to have one of them, Moses, escape and become the savior of his people. The tyrant Herod, not wanting any rivals, orders the massacre of all male children two years and under in Bethlehem and its vicinity. But Jesus escapes and he, in his turn, becomes the new savior of his people.
- While we don't know the number of children killed, there would certainly have been "sobbing and lamentation" by the children's parents. We pray for all parents who know the pain of burying their child.

Saturday 29th December **Luke 2:22–24**

When the time came for their purification according to the law of Moses, they brought him up to Jerusalem to present him to the Lord (as it is written in the law of the Lord, "Every firstborn male shall be designated as holy to the Lord"), and they offered a sacrifice according to what is stated in the law of the Lord, "a pair of turtle-doves or two young pigeons."

- Modern minds find the notion of "purification" very strange. To the Israelite mind certain profane and sacred things, including childbirth, possessed mysterious qualities that communicated themselves to anyone who came in contact with them, and set such people in a class apart from the ordinary. In order to return to the everyday world and activity, such people had to be "purified."
- Purification set the Israelites apart from other nations and gave them a greater sense of their own identity. Can we look behind familiar religious rituals to deepen our own understanding, to know how they enrich our life with God?

Sacred Space

Something to think and pray about each day this week:

Building from nothing

If Jesus were to appear in our world, he would be born unnoticed, to a good, struggling family in Ecuador, Uzbekistan or some place usually out of the news. People would be puzzled, "Where is that place?" He would not be on television, nor would he occupy a center of power or wealth. He would be pushed around, slandered and criticized. He would speak simple truths and some would listen to him and recognize the voice of God. The good news would spread slowly, as it did two thousand years ago. It would graft onto whatever was good in the world. The brokers of power and wealth would not notice it, nor offer their sponsorship.

The happy irony of today is that after the first two thousand years, the good news is so widespread that, whether they know it or not, the whole human race is richer for Jesus' birthday.

The Presence of God
As I sit here, the beating of my heart,
the ebb and flow of my breathing, the movements of my mind
are all signs of God's ongoing creation of me.
I pause for a moment, and become aware
of this presence of God within me.

Freedom
I ask for the grace
to let go of my own concerns
and be open to what God is asking of me,
to let myself be guided and formed by my loving Creator.

Consciousness
In the presence of my loving Creator,
I look honestly at my feelings over the last day,
the highs, the lows and the level ground.
Can I see where the Lord has been present?

The Word
I take my time to read the Word of God, slowly, a few times, allowing myself to dwell on anything that strikes me. (Please turn to your scripture on the following pages. Inspiration points are there should you need them. When you are ready, return here to continue.)

Conversation
Remembering that I am still in God's presence,
I imagine Jesus himself standing or sitting beside me,
and say whatever is on my mind, whatever is in my heart,
speaking as one friend to another.

Conclusion
Glory be to the Father, and to the Son, and to the Holy Spirit,
As it was in the beginning, is now and ever shall be,
World without end. Amen

Sunday 30th December,
The Holy Family **Luke 2:41–52**

Now every year his parents went to Jerusalem for the festival of the Passover. And when he was twelve years old, they went up as usual for the festival. When the festival was ended and they started to return, the boy Jesus stayed behind in Jerusalem, but his parents did not know it. Assuming that he was in the group of travelers, they went a day's journey. Then they started to look for him among their relatives and friends. When they did not find him, they returned to Jerusalem to search for him. After three days they found him in the temple, sitting among the teachers, listening to them and asking them questions. And all who heard him were amazed at his understanding and his answers. When his parents saw him they were astonished; and his mother said to him, "Child, why have you treated us like this? Look, your father and I have been searching for you in great anxiety." He said to them, "Why were you searching for me? Did you not know that I must be in my Father's house?" But they did not understand what he said to them.

- I imagine that I'm young and I live near Joseph's house; he and Mary often invite me to come over, and they welcome me. I love to be there, and to play with their son, their child.
- Let me sit with my thoughts, with what I feel in this moment.

Monday 31st December **John 1:16–18**

From his fullness we have all received, grace upon grace. The law indeed was given through Moses; grace and truth came through Jesus Christ. No one has ever seen God. It is God the only Son, who is close to the Father's heart, who has made him known.

- Taking time to pray provides me with a way to receive the truth and grace that God wants to offer me. I prepare myself to receive blessings from the very heart of God.
- "Grace upon grace"; I picture an abundance of blessing, a cascade of goodness. This is what God desires for me. I ask that I not be content with less.

Tuesday 1st January,
Solemnity of Mary, Mother of God **Luke 2:16–21**

So they went with haste and found Mary and Joseph, and the child lying in the manger. When they saw this, they made known what had been told them about this child; and all who heard it were amazed at what the shepherds told them. But Mary treasured all these words and pondered them in her heart. The shepherds returned, glorifying and praising God for all they had heard and seen, as it had been told them. After eight days had passed, it was time to circumcise the child; and he was called Jesus, the name given by the angel before he was conceived in the womb.

- Shepherds were not commonly regarded as ideal witnesses, given the marginal, nomadic nature of their lives. Yet we see them as among the first to announce Jesus who would proclaim himself "shepherd." I ask God to help me to receive the Gospel from unexpected sources.
- On the threshold of this new year, I prepare to receive words and memories to treasure and to ponder. I ask for God's blessing.

Wednesday 2nd January **John 1:19–28**

This is the testimony given by John when the Jews sent priests and Levites from Jerusalem to ask him, "Who are you?" He confessed and did not deny it, but confessed, "I am not the Messiah." And they asked him, "What then? Are you Elijah?" He said, "I am not." "Are you the prophet?" He answered, "No." Then they said to him, "Who are you? Let us have an answer for those who sent us. What do you say about yourself?" He said, "I am the voice of one crying out in the wilderness, 'Make straight the way of the Lord,'" as the prophet Isaiah said. Now they had been sent from the Pharisees. They asked him, "Why then are you baptizing if you are neither the Messiah, nor Elijah, nor the prophet?" John answered them, "I baptize with water. Among you stands one whom you do not know, the one who is coming after me; I am not worthy to untie the thong of his sandal." This took place in Bethany across the Jordan where John was baptizing.

- In prayer God speaks words of comfort and assurance into the wildernesses of our lives—our bad moments of guilt, fears, anxieties, resentment. God speaks words which help us put ourselves into a bigger world, the world of the love of God.
- In prayer God calls each of us to be voices in the wilderness for others in their search for love, for meaning, for faith and for God.

Thursday 3rd January **John 1:29**

The next day John saw Jesus coming toward him and declared, "Here is the Lamb of God who takes away the sin of the world!

- Jesus commended John the Baptist highly. Here John shows his ability to recognize Jesus and point others to him.
- I think of how I might live more in this way.

Friday 4th January **John 1:35–39**

The next day John again was standing with two of his disciples, and as he watched Jesus walk by, he exclaimed, "Look, here is the Lamb of God!" The two disciples heard him say this, and they followed Jesus. When Jesus turned and saw them following, he said to them, "What are you looking for?" They said to him, "Rabbi" (which translated means Teacher), "where are you staying?" He said to them, "Come and see." They came and saw where he was staying, and they remained with him that day.

- John is a signpost, drawing attention to the presence of God. He is content not to be the object of attention.
- I hear Jesus ask me. "What are you looking for?" I take time to answer with what is deep in my heart. I listen for his invitation to draw closer, "Come and see."

Saturday 5th January **John 1:43–51**

The next day Jesus decided to go to Galilee. He found Philip and said to him, "Follow me." Now Philip was from Bethsaida, the city of Andrew and Peter. Philip found Nathanael and said to him, "We have found him about whom Moses in the law and also the prophets wrote, Jesus son of Joseph from Nazareth." Nathanael said to him, "Can anything good come out of Nazareth?" Philip said to him, "Come and see." When Jesus saw Nathanael coming toward him, he said of him, "Here is truly an Israelite in whom there is no deceit!" Nathanael asked him, "Where did you get to know me?" Jesus answered, "I saw you under the fig tree before Philip called you." Nathanael replied, "Rabbi, you are the Son of God! You are the King of Israel!" Jesus answered, "Do you believe because I told you that I saw you under the fig tree? You will see greater things than these." And he said to him, "Very truly, I tell you, you will see heaven opened and the angels of God ascending and descending upon the Son of Man."

- Philip's invitation echoes Jesus' words, "Come and see." I notice myself growing in discipleship when my reactions and communication reflects how Jesus is.
- Jesus saw something in Nathanael that surprised him. My hidden actions and desires are evident to Jesus. I hear him acknowledge and affirm the goodness in me that others may not notice.

Something to think and pray about each day this week:

Our new start

The greatest sale of self-help books takes place every year around the end of December and beginning of January. We see the New Year as a time to turn over a new leaf, to make a new beginning. Our best intentions, and the books we buy, can easily become something of a reproach as the year progresses and we see ourselves making little progress. Perhaps we need to be careful about the scale against which we measure ourselves. Growing in patience, self-awareness and in proper love of oneself are tasks that deserve time—even if we cannot always measure or prove our progress. Allowing ourselves to be open to the work of God within us will remain a call to all of us during 2013. God won't give up but waits for us to awaken to the wonder and joy of knowing ourselves to be always in the presence of God.

The Presence of God

I pause for a moment
and reflect on God's life-giving presence
in every part of my body, in everything around me,
in the whole of my life.

Freedom

Many countries are at this moment suffering
the agonies of war.
I bow my head in thanksgiving for my freedom.
I pray for all prisoners and captives.

Consciousness

Knowing that God loves me unconditionally,
I look honestly over the last day, its events and my feelings.
Do I have something to be grateful for? Then I give thanks.
Is there something I am sorry for? Then I ask forgiveness.

The Word

God speaks to each one of us individually. I need to listen to hear what he is saying to me. Read the text a few times, then listen. (Please turn to your scripture on the following pages. Inspiration points are there should you need them. When you are ready, return here to continue.)

Conversation

How has God's Word moved me? Has it left me cold?
Has it consoled me or moved me to act in a new way?
I imagine Jesus standing or sitting beside me,
I turn and share my feelings with him.

Conclusion

Glory be to the Father, and to the Son, and to the Holy Spirit,
As it was in the beginning, is now and ever shall be,
World without end. Amen

Sunday 6th January,
The Epiphany of the Lord **Matthew 2:1–6**

In the time of King Herod, after Jesus was born in Bethlehem of Judea, wise men from the East came to Jerusalem, asking, "Where is the child who has been born king of the Jews? For we observed his star at its rising, and have come to pay him homage." When King Herod heard this, he was frightened, and all Jerusalem with him; and calling together all the chief priests and scribes of the people, he inquired of them where the Messiah was to be born. They told him, "In Bethlehem of Judea; for so it has been written by the prophet: 'And you, Bethlehem, in the land of Judah, are by no means least among the rulers of Judah; for from you shall come a ruler who is to shepherd my people Israel.'"

- Herod was interested in Jesus in an intellectual way, careful that his own position not be affected. I realize that my prayer draws me into a relationship and ask that I be ready to accept the consequences that may come to light.
- The comfortable and established did not recognize Jesus but the travellers and strangers appreciated who he was. I ask that I be open to the voices of the stranger and to wisdom from other traditions.

Monday 7th January **Matthew 4:17, 23–25**

From that time Jesus began to proclaim, "Repent, for the kingdom of heaven has come near." Jesus went throughout Galilee, teaching in their synagogues and proclaiming the good news of the kingdom and curing every disease and every sickness among the people. So his fame spread throughout all Syria, and they brought to him all the sick, those who were afflicted with various diseases and pains, demoniacs, epileptics, and paralytics, and he cured them. And great crowds followed him from Galilee, the Decapolis, Jerusalem, Judea, and from beyond the Jordan.

- Jesus calls us to change. With Jesus, I allow aspects of my way of living that are in need of change to come to light. I ask for the help I need.

- Jesus is willing and able to heal. I pray for those in need. I acknowledge my own neediness and humbly ask for healing.

Tuesday 8th January **Mark 6:34–44**

As he went ashore, he saw a great crowd; and he had compassion for them, because they were like sheep without a shepherd; and he began to teach them many things. When it grew late, his disciples came to him and said, "This is a deserted place, and the hour is now very late; send them away so that they may go into the surrounding country and villages and buy something for themselves to eat." But he answered them, "You give them something to eat." They said to him, "Are we to go and buy two hundred denarii worth of bread, and give it to them to eat?" And he said to them, "How many loaves have you? Go and see." When they had found out, they said, "Five, and two fish." Then he ordered them to get all the people to sit down in groups on the green grass. So they sat down in groups of hundreds and of fifties. Taking the five loaves and the two fish, he looked up to heaven, and blessed and broke the loaves, and gave them to his disciples to set before the people; and he divided the two fish among them all. And all ate and were filled; and they took up twelve baskets full of broken pieces and of the fish. Those who had eaten the loaves numbered five thousand men.

- The compassion of Jesus is represented in his heart, the Sacred Heart, that longs for our good. I consider that Jesus opens his heart to me generously, vulnerable and in a life-giving way.
- The disciples wanted something to be done; Jesus showed them what they might do. I ask for strengthening in the spirit of Jesus able to see and respond to the needs around me.

Wednesday 9th January **Mark 6:45–52**

Immediately he made his disciples get into the boat and go on ahead to the other side, to Bethsaida, while he dismissed the crowd. After saying farewell to them, he went up on the mountain to pray. When evening came, the boat was out on the sea, and he was alone on the land. When he saw that they were straining at the oars against an adverse wind, he came towards them early in the morning, walking on the sea. He intended to pass them by. But when they saw him walking on the sea, they thought it was a ghost and cried out; for they all saw him and were terrified. But immediately he spoke to them and said, "Take heart, it is I; do not be afraid." Then he got into the boat with them and the wind ceased. And they were utterly astounded, for they did not understand about the loaves, but their hearts were hardened.

- Jesus' words "It is I," or simply "I Am," recall the name God gave himself when requested to do so by Moses in the Book of Exodus. Here Mark is hinting at Jesus' divine status.
- The boat can be taken as a symbol for Mark's little church, and the storm as a symbol for the persecution suffered by his Christian community. Jesus' words, "Do not be afraid," surely resonate with all Christians today who often live in an indifferent or hostile world.

Thursday 10th January **Luke 4:14–22**

Then Jesus, filled with the power of the Spirit, returned to Galilee, and a report about him spread through all the surrounding country. He began to teach in their synagogues and was praised by everyone. When he came to Nazareth, where he had been brought up, he went to the synagogue on the sabbath day, as was his custom. He stood up to read, and the scroll of the prophet Isaiah was given to him. He unrolled the scroll and found the place where it was written: "The Spirit of the Lord is upon me, because he has anointed me to bring good news to the poor. He has sent me to proclaim release to the captives and recovery of sight to the blind, to let the oppressed go free, to proclaim the year of the Lord's favor." And he rolled up the scroll, gave it back to the attendant, and sat down. The eyes of all in the synagogue were fixed on him. Then he began to say to them, "Today this scripture has been fulfilled in your hearing."

- For Luke, this passage marks the beginning of Jesus' public ministry in a scene which takes place in Jesus' local synagogue at Nazareth.

- Filled with the Spirit, Jesus is to "bring the good news to the poor," to fulfill the program set out centuries earlier by Isaiah. It is already underway. The time is "today."
- How can we put Jesus' mission into practice today?

Friday 11th January **Luke 5:12–16**

Once, when Jesus was in one of the cities, there was a man covered with leprosy. When he saw Jesus, he bowed with his face to the ground and begged him, "Lord, if you choose, you can make me clean." Then Jesus stretched out his hand, touched him, and said, "I do choose. Be made clean." Immediately the leprosy left him. And he ordered him to tell no one. "Go," he said, "and show yourself to the priest, and, as Moses commanded, make an offering for your cleansing, for a testimony to them." But now more than ever the word about Jesus spread abroad; many crowds would gather to hear him and to be cured of their diseases. But he would withdraw to deserted places and pray.

- An energy-point for Jesus was his prayer, and we find that very often as part of his life he went to quiet places to pray. His ministry needed the support and life-giving energy of his relationship with his Father.
- With us our life of love needs the energy of prayer. When we bring the love and commitments of our lives to prayer, something happens to being us deeper into the source of our convictions and commitments to God and others.

Saturday 12th January **John 3:25–30**

Now a discussion about purification arose between John's disciples and a Jew. They came to John and said to him, "Rabbi, the one who was with you across the Jordan, to whom you testified, here he is baptizing, and all are going to him." John answered, "No one can receive anything except what has been given from heaven. You yourselves are my witnesses that I said, 'I am not the Messiah, but I have been sent ahead of him.' He who has the bride is the bridegroom. The friend of the bridegroom, who stands and hears him, rejoices greatly at the bridegroom's voice. For this reason my joy has been fulfilled. He must increase, but I must decrease."

- John the Baptist knew who he was in the sight of God. He knew his strengths and his weaknesses, and knew that his life was to be centred on the one to come. This was not a drudge or burden for him: he rejoiced in the coming of Jesus and in his place in the mission and life of Jesus.
- John knew he was the announcer of good news, but not the good news itself. Something in him faded into insignificance when Jesus arrived; but this sense that he was second to another has made him first among many.
- In being humble we are big in the sight of God. Prayer can be an offering of self totally to God, giving and receiving life and love.

Sacred Space

Something to think and pray about each day this week:

Joy into the world

Life can move from sheltered intimacy into open and perhaps threatening spaces. Not just at our birth, but perhaps often in life. Sometimes we try to draw back, thinking the earlier security is better. But, hopefully, we also know that to go forward and outwards is to be open to the wider world of new life, new people, where we can grow and fulfil the promise within us.

Much of the Christian world celebrates the Baptism of the Lord this Sunday. So soon after the intimacy of the new-born Child and its Mother at Christmas! Yet the Feast of Epiphany has been about light shining forth into all nations. And now the adult Jesus is baptized at the Jordan; he is being sent out. "This is my Son, the Beloved" (Matthew 3:17). "He is my chosen one in whom my soul delights . . . I have made you a covenant of the people, and light to the nations" (Isaiah 42:1, 6).

Chosen, delighted in, sent forth: this is the truth and meaning in each of our lives. Lord, that I may know this.

The Presence of God

The world is charged with the grandeur of God (Gerard Manley Hopkins).
I dwell for a moment on the presence of God
around me, in every part of my body,
and deep within my being.

Freedom

"In these days, God taught me
as a schoolteacher teaches a pupil" (St Ignatius).
I remind myself that there are things God has to teach me yet,
and ask for the grace to hear them and let them change me.

Consciousness

How do I find myself today?
Where am I with God? With others?
Do I have something to be grateful for? Then I give thanks.
Is there something I am sorry for? Then I ask forgiveness.

The Word

I read the Word of God slowly, a few times over, and I listen to what God is saying to me. (Please turn to your scripture on the following pages. Inspiration points are there should you need them. When you are ready, return here to continue.)

Conversation

Sometimes I wonder what I might say
if I were to meet You in person, Lord.
I might say "Thank You, Lord" for always being there for me.
I know with certainty there were times when you carried me.
When through your strength I got through the dark times in my life.

Conclusion

Glory be to the Father, and to the Son, and to the Holy Spirit,
As it was in the beginning, is now and ever shall be,
World without end. Amen

Sunday 13th January,
The Baptism of the Lord **Luke 3:15–16, 21–22**

As the people were filled with expectation, and all were questioning in their hearts concerning John, whether he might be the Messiah, John answered all of them by saying, "I baptize you with water; but one who is more powerful than I is coming; I am not worthy to untie the thong of his sandals. He will baptize you with the Holy Spirit and fire." Now when all the people were baptized, and when Jesus also had been baptized and was praying, the heaven was opened, and the Holy Spirit descended upon him in bodily form like a dove. And a voice came from heaven, 'You are my Son, the Beloved; with you I am well pleased.'

- To be baptized with the Holy Spirit and fire is to be baptized with the purifying fire of Divine Love.
- As brothers and sisters of Christ, we are all *beloved* sons and daughters of God. Do I really believe this? If not, what are the obstacles preventing me from doing so?

Monday 14th January **Mark 1:14–20**

Now after John was arrested, Jesus came to Galilee, proclaiming the good news of God, and saying, "The time is fulfilled, and the kingdom of God has come near; repent, and believe in the good news." As Jesus passed along the Sea of Galilee, he saw Simon and his brother Andrew casting a net into the sea—for they were fishermen. And Jesus said to them, "Follow me and I will make you fish for people." And immediately they left their nets and followed him. As he went a little farther, he saw James son of Zebedee and his brother John, who were in their boat mending the nets. Immediately he called them; and they left their father Zebedee in the boat with the hired men, and followed him.

- As Jesus called people, he recognized their skills and spoke to them in their own language. I consider how Jesus might speak to me as I listen for his invitation to follow.

- The disciples were able to leave everything to follow. I pray for the freedom to be able to leave behind or to stay with, whichever way brings serves God.

Tuesday 15th January **Mark 1:21–28**

Jesus entered the synagogue and taught. They were astounded at his teaching, for he taught them as one having authority, and not as the scribes. Just then there was in their synagogue a man with an unclean spirit, and he cried out, "What have you to do with us, Jesus of Nazareth? Have you come to destroy us? I know who you are, the Holy One of God." But Jesus rebuked him, saying, "Be silent, and come out of him!" And the unclean spirit, convulsing him and crying with a loud voice, came out of him. They were all amazed, and they kept on asking one another, "What is this? A new teaching—with authority! He commands even the unclean spirits, and they obey him." At once his fame began to spread throughout the surrounding region of Galilee.

- The man with the unclean spirit was in the midst of the people. When life is tidied to remove such people, Jesus may be also put out of sight.
- The authority of Jesus' teaching was distinctive: his is the authority on which I need to rely.

Wednesday 16th January **Mark 1:35–39**

In the morning, while it was still very dark, he got up and went out to a deserted place, and there he prayed. And Simon and his companions hunted for him. When they found him, they said to him, "Everyone is searching for you." He answered, "Let us go on to the neighboring towns, so that I may proclaim the message there also; for that is what I came out to do." And he went throughout Galilee, proclaiming the message in their synagogues and casting out demons.

- I do what Jesus did: I take time to be with God. Jesus did not spend time in prayer despite the busyness of life but because of it. The more people wanted from him, the more he was drawn to confirm what it was that his father asked.

- Jesus did not stay where he was popular, where there was work to be done. His vision had a wider breadth than was evident to the disciples. In prayer, I can discern where my mission might lie.

Thursday 17th January **Mark 1:40–41**

A leper came to Jesus begging him, and kneeling he said to him, "If you choose, you can make me clean." Moved with pity, Jesus stretched out his hand and touched him, and said to him, "I do choose. Be made clean!"

- Jesus affirms the desire of the man with leprosy: his "I do choose," is his response to our desire for what is truly for our growth and wellbeing.
- The leper knew his need and trusted that Jesus could help him. I pray with the same attitude—not hiding my neediness, not hesitant about bringing it before Jesus, listening for Jesus' encouraging response.

Friday 18th January **Mark 2:1–5**

When he returned to Capernaum after some days, it was reported that he was at home. So many gathered around that there was no longer room for them, not even in front of the door; and he was speaking the word to them. Then some people came, bringing to him a paralyzed man, carried by four of them. And when they could not bring him to Jesus because of the crowd, they removed the roof above him; and after having dug through it, they let down the mat on which the paralytic lay. When Jesus saw their faith, he said to the paralytic, "Son, your sins are forgiven."

- The man who was paralyzed had to rely utterly on his friends to bring him to Jesus; and they were imaginative in the way they chose. I think of the trust he must have had in them and consider the trust I have in those close to me.
- Despite the evident need of the man brought for healing, Jesus first told him of forgiveness. I listen to Jesus speak to me, forgiving my sins.

Saturday 19th January **Mark 2:15–17**

And as he sat at dinner in Levi's house, many tax collectors and sinners were also sitting with Jesus and his disciples—for there were many who followed him. When the scribes of the Pharisees saw that he was eating with sinners and tax collectors, they said to his disciples, "Why does he eat with tax collectors and sinners?" When Jesus heard this, he said to them, "Those who are well have no need of a physician, but those who are sick; I have come to call not the righteous but sinners."

- The crowds who listened to Jesus were made up of many different kinds of people, many of whom had little in common with each other, some of whom despised others. I pray that Christians may be tolerant of diversity in the way that Jesus was.
- The sick and those in need usually approach Jesus boldly and directly; the seemly Pharisees approached the disciples. Much as I rely on others, I an reminded always to bring my needs and questions to Jesus, who has all the time in the world for me.

Something to think and pray about each day this week:

Called by name, always

The poetry of Isaiah can speak to our hearts. "He is my chosen one in whom my soul delights . . ." (Isaiah 42:1ff); and "You are my servant . . . in whom I shall be glorified . . . I will make you the light of the nations" (Isaiah 49:3,6). In this second poem there is a weariness, a sense of uselessness: "But I said, 'My toil has been futile, I have exhausted myself for nothing, to no purpose'" (Isaiah 49: 4).

That sense of *ennui*, weariness, when we ask, "what's the point of it all?" or, "Have I anything to show for my life?" can infiltrate our consciousness at times, or even almost overwhelm us. We are affected like this if something does not work out. But also, strange as it may seem, when something we try to do is supremely worthwhile. So how good to recall Isaiah, and hear in those profound scriptural words the loving Word of God whispering in the heart. It is good to hear these other words too: "Do not be afraid, for I have redeemed you; I have called you by your name, you are mine. Should you pass through the waters, I shall be with you" (Isaiah 43:1-2). God is always with us, calling us by name, protecting and guiding us.

The Presence of God
As I sit here, God is present,
breathing life into me and into everything around me.
For a few moments, I sit silently,
and become aware of God's loving presence.

Freedom
If God were trying to tell me something, would I know?
If God were reassuring me or challenging me, would I notice?
I ask for the grace to be free of my own preoccupations
and open to what God may be saying to me.

Consciousness
In God's loving presence I unwind the past day,
starting from now and looking back, moment by moment.
I gather in all the goodness and light, in gratitude.
I attend to the shadows and what they say to me,
seeking healing, courage, forgiveness.

The Word
I take my time to read the Word of God, slowly, a few times, allowing myself to dwell on anything that strikes me. (Please turn to your scripture on the following pages. Inspiration points are there should you need them. When you are ready, return here to continue.)

Conversation
What is stirring in me as I pray?
Am I consoled, troubled, left cold?
I imagine Jesus himself standing or sitting at my side,
and share my feelings with him.

Conclusion
Glory be to the Father, and to the Son, and to the Holy Spirit,
As it was in the beginning, is now and ever shall be,
World without end. Amen

Sunday 20th January,
Second Sunday in Ordinary Time **John 2:1–12**

On the third day there was a wedding in Cana of Galilee, and the mother of Jesus was there. Jesus and his disciples had also been invited to the wedding. When the wine gave out, the mother of Jesus said to him, "They have no wine." And Jesus said to her, "Woman, what concern is that to you and to me? My hour has not yet come." His mother said to the servants, "Do whatever he tells you." Now standing there were six stone water jars for the Jewish rites of purification, each holding twenty or thirty gallons. Jesus said to them, "Fill the jars with water." And they filled them up to the brim. He said to them, "Now draw some out, and take it to the chief steward." So they took it. When the steward tasted the water that had become wine, and did not know where it came from (though the servants who had drawn the water knew), the steward called the bridegroom and said to him, "Everyone serves the good wine first, and then the inferior wine after the guests have become drunk. But you have kept the good wine until now." Jesus did this, the first of his signs, in Cana of Galilee, and revealed his glory; and his disciples believed in him. After this he went down to Capernaum with his mother, his brothers, and his disciples; and they remained there a few days.

- John's Gospel speaks of Jesus' miracles as "signs" because they always point to something deeper than the merely miraculous. They inform us about Jesus, and the purpose of his mission.
- So in the Cana story, for example, Jesus replaces the water prescribed for Jewish purifications with more than one hundred and twenty gallons of wine! According to the Jewish Scriptures, when the Messiah comes there shall be an abundance of new wine, a symbol for God's abundant goodness towards his people.
- That Jesus turns so much water into the best of wines is a "sign" that he is in fact the long awaited Messiah.

Monday 21st January **Mark 2:18–22**

Now John's disciples and the Pharisees were fasting; and people came and said to him, "Why do John's disciples and the disciples of the Pharisees fast, but your disciples do not fast?" Jesus said to them, "The wedding-guests cannot fast while the bridegroom is with them, can they? As long as they have the bridegroom with them, they cannot fast. The days will come when the bridegroom is taken away from them, and then they will fast on that day. "No one sews a piece of unshrunk cloth on an old cloak; otherwise, the patch pulls away from it, the new from the old, and a worse tear is made. And no one puts new wine into old wineskins; otherwise, the wine will burst the skins, and the wine is lost, and so are the skins; but one puts new wine into fresh wineskins."

- The life of religious people is always open to scrutiny and examination from outside. I pray that my way of living communicates gospel values. I take care not to come to uncharitable judgments about the way others live.
- God calls me to growth and new life. May I receive the goodness God has to offer me, and be made anew in the image of God.

Tuesday 22nd January **Mark 2:23–28**

One sabbath Jesus was going through the grainfields; and as they made their way his disciples began to pluck heads of grain. The Pharisees said to him, "Look, why are they doing what is not lawful on the sabbath?" And he said to them, "Have you never read what David did when he and his companions were hungry and in need of food? He entered the house of God, when Abiathar was high priest, and ate the bread of the Presence, which it is not lawful for any but the priests to eat, and he gave some to his companions." Then he said to them, "The sabbath was made for humankind, and not humankind for the sabbath; so the Son of Man is lord even of the sabbath."

- The Pharisees were skilful at pointing out deficiencies in others. Before God I review my thoughts and words to take care but I do not measure the world by my own small scale.

- Jesus calls me to live in responsible freedom, being neither slavish nor careless. As I ask God to guide me, I give thanks as I realize that I am already guided by God.

Wednesday 23rd January **Mark 3:1–6**

Again he entered the synagogue, and a man was there who had a withered hand. They watched him to see whether he would cure him on the sabbath, so that they might accuse him. And he said to the man who had the withered hand, "Come forward." Then he said to them, "Is it lawful to do good or to do harm on the sabbath, to save life or to kill?" But they were silent. He looked around at them with anger; he was grieved at their hardness of heart and said to the man, "Stretch out your hand." He stretched it out, and his hand was restored. The Pharisees went out and immediately conspired with the Herodians against him, how to destroy him.

- Jesus was being watched to see what he might do, yet it did not stop him from doing good, from bringing life. I ask God for the courage I need to do what I know to be the right thing.
- The anger of Jesus is passion for life. I let myself imagine how Jesus wants to brush away whatever it is that holds me back from living fully as he calls me to life. For my part I ask for the strength I need to stretch out whatever ails me for healing.

Thursday 24th January **Mark 3:7–12**

Jesus departed with his disciples to the sea, and a great multitude from Galilee followed him; hearing all that he was doing, they came to him in great numbers from Judea, Jerusalem, Idumea, beyond the Jordan, and the region around Tyre and Sidon. He told his disciples to have a boat ready for him because of the crowd, so that they would not crush him; for he had cured many, so that all who had diseases pressed upon him to touch him. Whenever the unclean spirits saw him, they fell down before him and shouted, "You are the Son of God!" But he sternly ordered them not to make him known.

- Jesus recognized that there is a time for silence. I ask God to guide me to know when I might speak and when silence is my better witness.
- People came to Jesus for healing; in his presence the attraction of light and wholeness was evident. As I spend this time with Jesus, I let him quell any spirits in me that are not for my good.

Friday 25th January,
Conversion of St Paul, Apostle **Mark 16:15**

Jesus said to the disciples, "Go into all the world and proclaim the good news to the whole creation."

- I proclaim the good news to the whole of creation by the way I live, by being a blessing to the world that God has made.
- I pray for healing for those parts of creation that are wounded and damaged, that have yet to learn of the good news that Jesus sends us to proclaim.

Saturday 26th January **Mark 3:20–21**

And the crowd came together again, so that they could not even eat. When his family heard it, they went out to restrain him, for people were saying, "He has gone out of his mind."

- Those who knew Jesus well seemed to be surprised by how he lived and acted. I pray for the freedom that I need not to be hemmed in by my habits or by the expectations of others.
- To live freely is to challenge those who accept constraints. I pray for the courage that I may need to let myself be led more by the spirit of God.

Something to think and pray about each day this week:

This great light

One of the most evocative and atmospheric portraits of Jesus is drawn in Matthew 4:12–17. There, we see him as he leaves Nazareth and settles in Capernaum, on the shores of the lake of Galilee. We hear him, as he calls us to a change of heart, so we can be open to the living and real kingdom of heaven, which is close upon us.

But what makes this Matthean scene so atmospheric is the quotation from Isaiah 9:1, foretelling what was to occur in that very region, "The people that lived in darkness has seen a great light; on those who dwell in the land and shadow of death, a light has dawned." Look then at the whole quotation in Isaiah 8:23–9:3. We are, in a way, back to Epiphany again! A great light, manifested in the little child, is now shining over the nations as Jesus begins his ministry and preaching.

A great light, that of "the loving-kindness of the heart of our God, which visits us like the dawn from on high" (Luke 1:78). That light always there for me, in Jesus, in his presence to me, in his words and healing.

The Presence of God
As I sit here with my book, God is here.
Around me, in my sensations, in my thoughts and deep within me.
I pause for a moment, and become aware
of God's life-giving presence.

Freedom
I need to close out the noise, to rise above the noise;
The noise that interrupts, that separates,
The noise that isolates.
I need to listen to God again.

Consciousness
I remind myself that I am in the presence of the Lord.
I will take refuge in His loving heart.
He is my strength in times of weakness.
He is my comforter in times of sorrow.

The Word
God speaks to each one of us individually. I need to listen to what he is saying to me. (Please turn to your scripture on the following pages. Inspiration points are there should you need them. When you are ready, return here to continue.)

Conversation
Do I notice myself reacting as I pray with the Word of God?
Do I feel challenged, comforted, angry?
Imagining Jesus sitting or standing by me,
I speak out my feelings, as one trusted friend to another.

Conclusion
Glory be to the Father, and to the Son, and to the Holy Spirit,
As it was in the beginning, is now and ever shall be,
World without end. Amen

Sunday 27th January,
Third Sunday in Ordinary Time **Luke 4:14–21**

Then Jesus stood up to read in the synagogue, and the scroll of the prophet Isaiah was given to him. He unrolled the scroll and found the place where it was written: "The Spirit of the Lord is upon me, because he has anointed me to bring good news to the poor. He has sent me to proclaim release to the captives and recovery of sight to the blind, to let the oppressed go free, to proclaim the year of the Lord's favor." And he rolled up the scroll, gave it back to the attendant, and sat down. The eyes of all in the synagogue were fixed on him. Then he began to say to them, "Today this scripture has been fulfilled in your hearing."

- Jesus' good news is that we are all loved unconditionally by God, no ifs, no buts.
- When I accept that, truly believe and live by it, I gain true freedom and a new insight into the ways God works in our lives.

Monday 28th January **Mark 3:22–30**

And the scribes who came down from Jerusalem said, "He has Beelzebul, and by the ruler of the demons he casts out demons." And he called them to him, and spoke to them in parables, "How can Satan cast out Satan? If a kingdom is divided against itself, that kingdom cannot stand. And if a house is divided against itself, that house will not be able to stand. And if Satan has risen up against himself and is divided, he cannot stand, but his end has come. But no one can enter a strong man's house and plunder his property without first tying up the strong man; then indeed the house can be plundered. "Truly I tell you, people will be forgiven for their sins and whatever blasphemies they utter; but whoever blasphemes against the Holy Spirit can never have forgiveness, but is guilty of an eternal sin"—for they had said, "He has an unclean spirit."

- Jesus is scathing of those who cannot recognize goodness and who see only evil. If I wish to listen for the voice of God, I need to turn from voices that speak only negatively or in condemnation.

- The image of the house with its strong occupant is a picture of integrity and wholeness. I take some time to tidy the house that is my heart, to allow it to be a home for the spirit of Jesus.

Tuesday 29th January **Mark 3:31–35**

Then the mother and brothers of Jesus came; and standing outside, they sent to him and called him. A crowd was sitting around him; and they said to him, "Your mother and your brothers and sisters are outside, asking for you." And he replied, "Who are my mother and my brothers?" And looking at those who sat around him, he said, "Here are my mother and my brothers! Whoever does the will of God is my brother and sister and mother."

- Another awkward meeting point of Jesus and his family. They stay outside, no longer part of those around him.
- The word of God is deeper than any biological tie Jesus has; Mary knew that and was not offended but affirmed by what Jesus said here. Our deepest belonging is to God; all other belongings in life flow from that. We come from God and go to God, in prayer.

Wednesday 30th January **Mark 4:2–9**

Jesus began to teach them many things in parables, and in his teaching he said to them: "Listen! A sower went out to sow. And as he sowed, some seed fell on the path, and the birds came and ate it up. Other seed fell on rocky ground, where it did not have much soil, and it sprang up quickly, since it had no depth of soil. And when the sun rose, it was scorched; and since it had no root, it withered away. Other seed fell among thorns, and the thorns grew up and choked it, and it yielded no grain. Other seed fell into good soil and brought forth grain, growing up and increasing and yielding thirty and sixty and a hundredfold." And he said, "Let anyone with ears to hear listen!"

- The seed has been scattered by Jesus in my life, but the story is not over. Full of hope and desire, Jesus continually offers me life.
- I take care not to focus on the scorched and rocky areas, but acknowledge with thanks that God is working in me, bringing life, growth and fruit.

Thursday 31st January **Mark 4:21–25**

He said to them, "Is a lamp brought in to be put under the bushel basket, or under the bed, and not on the lampstand? For there is nothing hidden, except to be disclosed; nor is anything secret, except to come to light. Let anyone with ears to hear listen!" And he said to them, "Pay attention to what you hear; the measure you give will be the measure you get, and still more will be given you. For to those who have, more will be given; and from those who have nothing, even what they have will be taken away."

- "Listen!" "Pay attention!" Who does Jesus think I am? He knows that it is easy for people to become inattentive even to the very things that bring them life. I take this time to be attuned to my life and circumstances, listening for what God is saying to me.
- In listening, hearing and following Jesus, I grow in familiarity with his voice and hear more as to what I have, more is added. I give thanks and I pray for those who have nothing, that they might take time with God who has such time for them.

Friday 1st February **Mark 4:26–29**

Jesus said to the crowd, "The kingdom of God is as if someone would scatter seed on the ground, and would sleep and rise night and day, and the seed would sprout and grow, he does not know how. The earth produces of itself, first the stalk, then the head, then the full grain in the head. But when the grain is ripe, at once he goes in with his sickle, because the harvest has come."

- Seeds grows quietly, inexorably; tiny yet powerful. The fruit is hinted at, becomes more evident and is finally ready. God's ways come to growth in me in similar ways as I see traces in the past of what emerges later.
- Jesus wondered at small, ordinary realities. I take time to notice what is about me and let my surroundings speak to me of where God may be moving in my life.

Saturday 2nd February,
Presentation of the Lord **Luke 2:36–40**

There was also a prophet, Anna the daughter of Phanuel, of the tribe of Asher. She was of a great age, having lived with her husband for seven years after her marriage, then as a widow to the age of eighty-four. She never left the temple but worshipped there with fasting and prayer night and day. At that moment she came, and began to praise God and to speak about the child to all who were looking for the redemption of Jerusalem. When they had finished everything required by the law of the Lord, they returned to Galilee, to their own town of Nazareth. The child grew and became strong, filled with wisdom; and the favor of God was upon him.

- Anna, the daughter of Phanuel, appears and disappears in this incident. She is recorded as somebody who faithfully waited and watched for the movement of God in her life; and she did not miss the moment.
- As Joseph and Mary brought the child Jesus for blessing they realized that he would bring questions to their lives and challenge their comforts. I pray that all parents be ready to accept the questions that each life brings.

february 3–9

Something to think and pray about each day this week:

The blessed ones

We meet the *anawim*, the poor of God, in the scriptures: "the humble of the earth" (Zephaniah 2:3); "the poor in spirit, the gentle, the merciful, the pure in heart, the peacemakers" (Matthew 5:3,4,7–9). Jesus's words in the Beatitudes come out of the heart of the Old Testament, where in the prophet Zephaniah and elsewhere the *anawim* are the small remnant, often oppressed, who faithfully look to God. Jesus himself came from such in his own family, and lived and worked among people like this, in Nazareth.

Perhaps almost endlessly in our lives, a struggle goes on. In my insecurity, I look for status, achievement. I try to exercise power of some kind, over others around, or over the person or persons nearest to me. But in my heart I know there is another way, which is that of humility, kindness, forgiveness and dependence on God. This way, I will meet the true regard of other good people, and receive God's blessing and guidance. Loving Lord, in the struggles that beset me, help me always to find the right way, or, having lost it, come back to you. Only your grace and love can accomplish that. Only in that way do I know blessedness and peace of heart.

The Presence of God
At any time of the day or night we can call on Jesus.
He is always waiting, listening for our call.
What a wonderful blessing.
No phone needed, no emails, just a whisper.

Freedom
I will ask God's help,
to be free from my own preoccupations,
to be open to God in this time of prayer,
to come to love and serve him more.

Consciousness
How am I really feeling? Light-hearted? Heavy-hearted?
I may be very much at peace, happy to be here.
Equally, I may be frustrated, worried or angry.
I acknowledge how I really am. It is the real me that the Lord loves.

The Word
I read the Word of God slowly, a few times over, and I listen to what God is saying to me. (Please turn to your scripture on the following pages. Inspiration points are there should you need them. When you are ready, return here to continue.)

Conversation
Remembering that I am still in God's presence,
I imagine Jesus himself standing or sitting beside me,
and say whatever is on my mind, whatever is in my heart,
speaking as one friend to another.

Conclusion
Glory be to the Father, and to the Son, and to the Holy Spirit,
As it was in the beginning, is now and ever shall be,
World without end. Amen

Sunday 3rd February,
Fourth Sunday in Ordinary Time **Luke 4:21–30**

Then he began to say to them, "Today this scripture has been fulfilled in your hearing." All spoke well of him and were amazed at the gracious words that came from his mouth. They said, "Is not this Joseph's son?" He said to them, "Doubtless you will quote to me this proverb, 'Doctor, cure yourself!' And you will say, 'Do here also in your hometown the things that we have heard you did at Capernaum.'" And he said, "Truly I tell you, no prophet is accepted in the prophet's hometown. But the truth is, there were many widows in Israel in the time of Elijah, when the heaven was shut up three years and six months, and there was a severe famine over all the land; yet Elijah was sent to none of them except to a widow at Zarephath in Sidon. There were also many lepers in Israel in the time of the prophet Elisha, and none of them was cleansed except Naaman the Syrian." When they heard this, all in the synagogue were filled with rage. They got up, drove him out of the town, and led him to the brow of the hill on which their town was built, so that they might hurl him off the cliff. But he passed through the midst of them and went on his way.

- Why did the assembly turn on Jesus? Simply because what he said about the prophets Elijah and Elisha implied that God's offer of salvation was no longer restricted to Jews but extended to Gentiles as well. Such an implication was anathema to those who thought of themselves as God's "chosen people."
- Is my Christian belief so restricted that I fail to see that God's choice is wider than mine?

Monday 4th February **Mark 5:18–20**

As he was getting into the boat, the man who had been possessed by demons begged him that he might be with him. But Jesus refused, and said to him, "Go home to your friends, and tell them how much the Lord has done for you, and what mercy he has shown you." And he went away and began to proclaim in the Decapolis how much Jesus had done for him; and everyone was amazed.

- There are different ways of serving Jesus. As he listened, the man realized that what appealed to him was not what Jesus wanted. I bring my desires before Jesus to hear what he has to say. I pray that I may be ready to change my plans.
- I picture Jesus speaking with compassion to the man who had been healed. He sent him among his friends with a mission to speak of God's goodness. I ask that I may do this too in the way that serves Jesus best.

Tuesday 5th February **Mark 5:21, 25–34**

When Jesus had crossed again in the boat to the other side, a great crowd gathered around him; and he was by the sea. Now there was a woman who had been suffering from hemorrhages for twelve years. She had endured much under many physicians, and had spent all that she had; and she was no better, but rather grew worse. She had heard about Jesus, and came up behind him in the crowd and touched his cloak, for she said, "If I but touch his clothes, I will be made well." Immediately her hemorrhage stopped; and she felt in her body that she was healed of her disease. Immediately aware that power had gone forth from him, Jesus turned about in the crowd and said, "Who touched my clothes?" And his disciples said to him, "You see the crowd pressing in on you; how can you say, 'Who touched me?'" He looked all round to see who had done it. But the woman, knowing what had happened to her, came in fear and trembling, fell down before him, and told him the whole truth. He said to her, "Daughter, your faith has made you well; go in peace, and be healed of your disease."

- We can identify with people who know what we really want from the Lord. The woman was desperate for a cure; she did not plead or beg but we sense how single-minded she was.
- In prayer we can be afraid to be really honest and hopeful in asking God for what we want. Ask now this day for God's real and strong intervention where you really want this in your life.

Wednesday 6th February **Mark 6:1–6**

Jesus went on to his hometown, and his disciples followed him. On the sabbath he began to teach in the synagogue, and many who heard him were astounded. They said, "Where did this man get all this? What is this wisdom that has been given to him? What deeds of power are being done by his hands! Is not this the carpenter, the son of Mary and brother of James and Joses and Judas and Simon, and are not his sisters here with us?" And they took offence at him. Then Jesus said to them, "Prophets are not without honor, except in their hometown, and among their own kin, and in their own house." And he could do no deed of power there, except that he laid his hands on a few sick people and cured them. And he was amazed at their unbelief. Then he went about among the villages teaching.

- Opposition never stopped Jesus. Even when they resisted his message and sought to bring him down, he went ahead, going to other small villages; his message possessed him.
- The wisdom of Jesus came from heaven and earth. He had a calm way of seeing the meaning in things and events. This was born of earth and of his divine origin in heaven.

Thursday 7th February **Mark 6:7–13**

He called the twelve and began to send them out two by two, and gave them authority over the unclean spirits. He ordered them to take nothing for their journey except a staff; no bread, no bag, no money in their belts; but to wear sandals and not to put on two tunics. He said to them, "Wherever you enter a house, stay there until you leave the place. If any place will not welcome you and they refuse to hear you, as you leave, shake off the dust that is on your feet as a testimony against them." So they went out and proclaimed that all should repent. They cast out many demons, and anointed with oil many who were sick and cured them.

- Jesus told the disciples to shake the dust off their feet, they were not to be held back by those who are unreceptive or unwelcoming. I ask God to help me not to let negative "dust" cling to me and slow me down.

- Jesus wanted his disciples to realize that they could not depend on human possessions but might trust in him alone. Are there things that I hang onto that I might be better off letting go?

Friday 8th February **Mark 6:14–20**

King Herod heard of it, for Jesus' name had become known. Some were saying, "John the baptizer has been raised from the dead; and for this reason these powers are at work in him." But others said, "It is Elijah." And others said, "It is a prophet, like one of the prophets of old." But when Herod heard of it, he said, "John, whom I beheaded, has been raised." For Herod himself had sent men who arrested John, bound him, and put him in prison on account of Herodias, his brother Philip's wife, because Herod had married her. For John had been telling Herod, "It is not lawful for you to have your brother's wife." And Herodias had a grudge against him, and wanted to kill him. But she could not, for Herod feared John, knowing that he was a righteous and holy man, and he protected him. When he heard him, he was greatly perplexed; and yet he liked to listen to him.

- The jealousy, vanity and pride of Herod's circle stand in contrast to the simplicity of John's lifestyle and message.
- Herod liked to listen to John the Baptist, despite not understand John's message. There may be people who seem to reject what I believe but I don't know what goes on in their hearts.

Saturday 9th February **Mark 6:30–32**

The apostles gathered around Jesus, and told him all that they had done and taught. He said to them, "Come away to a deserted place all by yourselves and rest a while." For many were coming and going, and they had no leisure even to eat. And they went away in the boat to a deserted place by themselves.

- Jesus recognized the need to withdraw, to rest, to return refreshed and with renewed energy.
- To rest isn't to do nothing; it is not laziness, but relaxation. It refreshes us in body and spirit so we can come closer to God.

Something to think and pray about each day this week:

Bringing light

"Your light will rise in the darkness" (Isaiah 58:10). *My* life will be a light? My life, my person, who I am? How can that be? Sometimes I look around, and see someone whose life is a light; or I remember a person I knew, perhaps a grandparent, who radiated light. Nelson Mandela has been a light, and so too has Gandhi. And the movie *Of Gods and Men* portrays a group of Cistercian monks who elect to stay among Algeria's poor people, Muslim villagers. Despite mortal threats they decide to do so together, in fear but with consolation in their hearts. They can do no other. In consequence they give their lives.

But I myself, in my modest circumstances? "If you do away with the yoke, the clenched fist, the wicked word, if you give your bread to the hungry, and relief to the oppressed, your light will rise in the darkness, and your shadows become like noon" (Isaiah 58:9–10). My hidden life, with my continual effort to be just and upright, to overcome failure, and live with humanity and faith, will be a light. Thankfully, I will not see that myself; yet the light *will* shine. And Jesus's words will be my guarantee and strength: "You are the light of the world" (Matthew 5:14).

The Presence of God
I pause for a moment
and think of the love and the grace that God showers on me, creating me in his image and likeness, making me his temple.

Freedom
Lord, grant me the grace to be free from the excesses of this life.
Let me not get caught up with the desire for wealth.
Keep my heart and mind free to love and serve you.

Consciousness
In the presence of my loving Creator,
I look honestly at my feelings over the last day,
the highs, the lows and the level ground.
Can I see where the Lord has been present?

The Word
God speaks to each one of us individually. I need to listen to what he is saying to me. (Please turn to your scripture on the following pages. Inspiration points are there should you need them. When you are ready, return here to continue.)

Conversation
Sometimes I wonder what I might say
if I were to meet You in person, Lord.
I might say "Thank You, Lord" for always being there for me.
I know with certainty there were times when you carried me.
When through your strength I got through the dark times in my life.

Conclusion
Glory be to the Father, and to the Son, and to the Holy Spirit,
As it was in the beginning, is now and ever shall be,
World without end. Amen

Sunday 10th February,
Fifth Sunday in Ordinary Time **Luke 5:1–11**

Once while Jesus was standing beside the lake of Gennesaret, and the crowd was pressing in on him to hear the word of God, he saw two boats there at the shore of the lake; the fishermen had gone out of them and were washing their nets. He got into one of the boats, the one belonging to Simon, and asked him to put out a little way from the shore. Then he sat down and taught the crowds from the boat. When Jesus had finished speaking, he said to Simon, "Put out into the deep water and let down your nets for a catch." Simon answered, "Master, we have worked all night long but have caught nothing. Yet if you say so, I will let down the nets." When they had done this, they caught so many fish that their nets were beginning to break. So they signaled their partners in the other boat to come and help them. And they came and filled both boats, so that they began to sink. But when Simon Peter saw it, he fell down at Jesus' knees, saying, "Go away from me, Lord, for I am a sinful man!" When they had brought their boats to shore, they left everything and followed him.

- Nowhere else in the Gospels is a confession of one's sinfulness the first reaction of someone who meets Jesus and is called to discipleship. By contrast, Levi threw a party! (Luke 5:29)
- Could it be that the story of the catch of fish (John 21:1-14) has been projected back by Mark into Jesus' ministry, and that Peter's awareness of his sinfulness arose from his having denied Jesus three times during the Passion?

Monday 11th February **Mark 6:53–56**

When Jesus and the disciples had crossed over, they came to land at Gennesaret and moored the boat. When they got out of the boat, people at once recognized him, and rushed about that whole region and began to bring the sick on mats to wherever they heard he was. And wherever he went, into villages or cities or farms, they laid the sick in the marketplaces, and begged him that they might touch even the fringe of his cloak; and all who touched it were healed.

- Having withdrawn for some quiet time apart, Jesus is ready to answer the needs of the people.
- The people rushed to Jesus with their needs and their hopes. Maybe I need to follow their example—recognizing Jesus and bringing to him what in me is in need of healing.

Tuesday 12th February **Mark 7:1–2, 5–8**

Now when the Pharisees and some of the scribes who had come from Jerusalem gathered around him, they noticed that some of his disciples were eating with defiled hands, that is, without washing them. So the Pharisees and the scribes asked him, "Why do your disciples not live according to the tradition of the elders, but eat with defiled hands?" He said to them, "Isaiah prophesied rightly about you hypocrites, as it is written, 'This people honors me with their lips, but their hearts are far from me; in vain do they worship me, teaching human precepts as doctrines.' You abandon the commandment of God and hold to human tradition."

- As physically clean as the Pharisees hands were, they often used them to pick and point, to finger and accuse.
- Jesus invites me to consider how I follow God in my heart and cautions me against being distracted by human traditions. I review my habits and patterns of activity, asking God to help me to recognize where they lead me to life.

Wednesday 13th February,
Ash Wednesday **Matthew 6:1–6**

"Beware of practicing your piety before others in order to be seen by them; for then you have no reward from your Father in heaven. So whenever you give alms, do not sound a trumpet before you, as the hypocrites do in the synagogues and in the streets, so that they may be praised by others. Truly I tell you, they have received their reward. But when you give alms, do not let your left hand know what your right hand is doing, so that your alms may be done in secret; and your Father who sees in secret will reward you. And whenever you pray, do not be like the hypocrites; for they love to stand and pray in the synagogues and at the street corners, so that they may be seen by others. Truly I tell you, they have received their reward. But whenever you pray, go into your room and shut the door and pray to your Father who is in secret; and your Father who sees in secret will reward you."

- There may be outward actions that I have in mind for this Lent; I invite God to do the inward work on my heart, bringing me to conversion, healing and growth.
- I pray for the humility I may need to act quietly and discretely this Lent. How might I experience the conversion that God desires for me and learn of my need for God?

Thursday 14th February **Luke 9:23–25**

Jesus said to them all, "If any want to become my followers, let them deny themselves and take up their cross daily and follow me. For those who want to save their life will lose it, and those who lose their life for my sake will save it. What does it profit them if they gain the whole world, but lose or forfeit themselves?"

- Lent invites me to consider what I am really looking for as I hear Jesus say that it is possible to gain the world and lose oneself. I ask God to help me, through my time of quiet and prayer, to recognize how I am being called to life.
- There are many ways in which I can enjoy the gains and benefits of the world. How do these distract me from what is for my lasting good? For what wisdom might I ask?

Friday 15th February **Matthew 9:14–15**

Then the disciples of John came to him, saying, "Why do we and the Pharisees fast often, but your disciples do not fast?" And Jesus said to them, "The wedding guests cannot mourn as long as the bridegroom is with them, can they? The days will come when the bridegroom is taken away from them, and then they will fast."

- The disciples of John compared their religious observation to that of Jesus and his followers.
- Do I sometimes contrast my practice with that of others? Am I drawn either to pride or to despair? Lent calls me to walk humbly with God in company with and in prayer for others.

Saturday 16th February **Luke 5:27–32**

After this he went out and saw a tax collector named Levi, sitting at the tax booth; and he said to him, "Follow me." And he got up, left everything, and followed him. Then Levi gave a great banquet for him in his house; and there was a large crowd of tax collectors and others sitting at the table with them. The Pharisees and their scribes were complaining to his disciples, saying, "Why do you eat and drink with tax collectors and sinners?" Jesus answered, "Those who are well have no need of a physician, but those who are sick; I have come to call not the righteous but sinners to repentance."

- I need never feel unworthy of being in the presence of Jesus; I can be all the more ready to receive his word when I know my need. It was for the needy that he came, finding a home among the poor.
- The Pharisees strove to live good lives but went astray when they used their own lives as the measure against which to judge everyone else. How judgemental am I if I consider others have gone astray—as I see it? I pray for compassion and quietly ask for God's blessing for those in need.

Something to think and pray about each day this week:

The getting of wisdom

Wisdom is a great yet elusive gift. It may be that I often I see, in retrospect, how I was more foolish than wise. I may have been worked up over something, and thought I was in the right, motivated by high ideals. Yet the end result was an unsettling one, leaving me and others more dispirited than at peace.

Yet often it is from the failures that wisdom comes. How? When I recover from the attendent blackness and in a spirit of peace reflect back on what has happened. I learn something about myself and about life, something I had not seen before or else had not held onto at the crucial time. I gain more self-understanding, the ability to see the wider picture, and the courage to be patient in difficult circumstances.

And the openness of my heart to God's presence and teaching leads me along the path of wisdom. "Lord, make me know your ways. Lord, teach me your paths. Make me walk in your truth and teach me: for you are God my Saviour" (Psalm 25:4–5). In God's presence, then, let me reflect on life, on what is happening. And in a spirit of blessing and hope, let me go forward, and gain wisdom of heart.

The Presence of God
Jesus waits silent and unseen to come into my heart.
I will respond to His call.
He comes with His infinite power and love
May I be filled with joy in His presence.

Freedom
I ask for the grace
to let go of my own concerns
and be open to what God is asking of me,
to let myself be guided and formed by my loving Creator.

Consciousness
Knowing that God loves me unconditionally,
I can afford to be honest about how I am.
How has the last day been, and how do I feel now?
I share my feelings openly with the Lord.

The Word
I read the Word of God slowly, a few times over, and I listen to what God is saying to me. (Please turn to your scripture on the following pages. Inspiration points are there should you need them. When you are ready, return here to continue.)

Conversation
Remembering that I am still in God's presence,
I imagine Jesus himself standing or sitting beside me,
and say whatever is on my mind, whatever is in my heart,
speaking as one friend to another.

Conclusion
Glory be to the Father, and to the Son, and to the Holy Spirit,
As it was in the beginning, is now and ever shall be,
World without end. Amen

Sunday 17th February,
First Sunday of Lent **Luke 4:1–8, 13**

Jesus, full of the Holy Spirit, returned from the Jordan and was led by the Spirit in the wilderness, where for forty days he was tempted by the devil. He ate nothing at all during those days, and when they were over, he was famished. The devil said to him, "If you are the Son of God, command this stone to become a loaf of bread." Jesus answered him, "It is written, 'One does not live by bread alone.'" Then the devil led him up and showed him in an instant all the kingdoms of the world. And the devil said to him, "To you I will give their glory and all this authority; for it has been given over to me, and I give it to anyone I please. If you, then, will worship me, it will all be yours." Jesus answered him, "It is written, 'Worship the Lord your God, and serve only him.'" When the devil had finished every test, he departed from him until an opportune time.

- Jesus, like Moses before him, retreats into the wilderness where he fasts for forty days. Each temptation involves a seizure of power: power over the elements of creation; political and military power; and the power to force God's.
- How are we tempted today? I pray for the courage to turn to God for protection each day.

Monday 18th February **Matthew 25:37–40**

"The righteous will answer him, 'Lord, when was it that we saw you hungry and gave you food, or thirsty and gave you something to drink? And when was it that we saw you a stranger and welcomed you, or naked and gave you clothing? And when was it that we saw you sick or in prison and visited you?' And the king will answer them, 'Truly I tell you, just as you did it to one of the least of these who are members of my family, you did it to me.'"

- Jesus does not tell this parable to make us afraid but to encourage us in our Christian lives.
- I may not do all these actions, but I pray for those who carry them out in Jesus' name.

Tuesday 19th February **Matthew 6:7–15**

Jesus said, "When you are praying, do not heap up empty phrases as the Gentiles do; for they think that they will be heard because of their many words. Do not be like them, for your Father knows what you need before you ask him. Pray then in this way: 'Our Father in heaven, hallowed be your name. Your kingdom come. Your will be done, on earth as it is in heaven. Give us this day our daily bread. And forgive us our debts, as we also have forgiven our debtors. And do not bring us to the time of trial, but rescue us from the evil one. For if you forgive others their trespasses, your heavenly Father will also forgive you; but if you do not forgive others, neither will your Father forgive your trespasses.'"

- I am reminded by Jesus not to let my prayer time become too wordy, I might use a favourite phrase from the Our Father and let it guide me through this day.
- Jesus' prayer brings God into the centre. I am reminded that my prayer is time given to God and is not to be measured by how well I feel afterwards or what insights my mind may have received.

Wednesday 20th February **Luke 11:29–30**

When the crowds were increasing, he began to say, "This generation is an evil generation; it asks for a sign, but no sign will be given to it except the sign of Jonah. For just as Jonah became a sign to the people of Nineveh, so the Son of Man will be to this generation."

- Jesus recognized the human tendency to look for results, to seek identifiable signs. God has already blessed me with many signs of grace.
- I take some time to recognize them and ask God's help that I may not miss the messages that may be around me every day.

Thursday 21st February **Matthew 7:7–12**

Jesus said to the disciples, "Ask, and it will be given you; search, and you will find; knock, and the door will be opened for you. For everyone who asks receives, and everyone who searches finds, and for everyone who knocks, the door will be opened. Is there anyone among you who, if your child asks for bread, will give a stone? Or if the child asks for a fish, will give a snake? If you then, who are evil, know how to give good gifts to your children, how much more will your Father in heaven give good things to those who ask him! In everything do to others as you would have them do to you; for this is the law and the prophets."

- In the very act of praying we receive something from God. As we open our hearts to God in prayer, God's hands are open to give us good gifts. We leave a time of prayer with an increase of faith, hope and love, which is the consolation of God.
- No time of prayer is wasted; all prayer is in the service of love, and prayer increases within us our capacity to love.

Friday 22nd February,
Chair of St Peter, Apostle **Matthew 16:13–19**

Now when Jesus came into the district of Caesarea Philippi, he asked his disciples, "Who do people say that the Son of Man is?" And they said, "Some say John the Baptist, but others Elijah, and still others Jeremiah or one of the prophets." He said to them, "But who do you say that I am?" Simon Peter answered, "You are the Messiah, the Son of the living God." And Jesus answered him, "Blessed are you, Simon son of Jonah! For flesh and blood has not revealed this to you, but my Father in heaven. And I tell you, you are Peter, and on this rock I will build my church, and the gates of Hades will not prevail against it. I will give you the keys of the kingdom of heaven, and whatever you bind on earth will be bound in heaven, and whatever you loose on earth will be loosed in heaven."

- Jesus speaks as a builder, seeking a strong foundation for his construction. Peter is loving, impulsive, generous and in his own way, weak. Jesus is to build his church on such people, who do their best but trust more in God's strength than their own.
- Here I am, Lord. It is only your power that gives me the courage to carry on your work.

Saturday 23rd February **Matthew 5:43–48**

Jesus said to the disciples, "You have heard that it was said, 'You shall love your neighbour and hate your enemy.' But I say to you, Love your enemies and pray for those who persecute you, so that you may be children of your Father in heaven; for he makes his sun rise on the evil and on the good, and sends rain on the righteous and on the unrighteous. For if you love those who love you, what reward do you have? Do not even the tax collectors do the same? And if you greet only your brothers and sisters, what more are you doing than others? Do not even the Gentiles do the same? Be perfect, therefore, as your heavenly Father is perfect."

- Words of love and tolerance to our enemies and to all who hurt us are difficult.
- Jesus has died for all; in our place at the death of Jesus we meet all for whom he died. God knows also that we only slowly bring deep hurts to light. God is with us in love in the hurts and in the enmities of our lives.

Something to think and pray about each day this week:

Perfection, in God's way

Some things put forward in scripture, as ideals for us, seem utterly impossible to attain. "Be holy, for I, the Lord your God, am holy" (Leviticus 19:2). "You must therefore be perfect, just as your heavenly Father is perfect" (Matthew 5:48).

Perfection, utter holiness. And Jesus's words about loving our enemies, and praying for them (Matthew 5: 44), can seem beyond our reach. Yet, we must learn a way of understanding the highest ideals of scripture. So, for instance, when Jesus says, "when anyone hits you on the right cheek, offer him the other one as well" (Matthew 5:39), that saying has to be related to the time when Jesus himself was struck on the cheek, and his own response was, "If there is some offence in what I said, point it out; but if not, why do you strike me?" (John 18:23).

We reach the holiness of loving, and the perfection of being utterly upright, only in God's way, and in God's time. We reach it while still being frail and failing. And, in fact, *we* do not *reach* that ideal at all. Rather, it is something *done* in us, by *God's* doing and blessing. Lord, sow in the depths of my being your goodness and holiness, and in the ways you know best. Let me rely on you, and not on my own efforts. Let me be in your hands, and trust you, in childlike faith.

The Presence of God
For a few moments, I think of God's veiled presence in things:
in the elements, giving them existence;
in plants, giving them life; in animals, giving them sensation;
and finally, in me, giving me all this and more,
making me a temple, a dwelling-place of the Spirit.

Freedom
God is not foreign to my freedom.
Instead the Spirit breathes life into my most intimate desires,
gently nudging me towards all that is good.
I ask for the grace to let myself be enfolded by the Spirit.

Consciousness
Knowing that God loves me unconditionally,
I can afford to be honest about how I am.
How has the last day been, and how do I feel now?
I share my feelings openly with the Lord.

The Word
The word of God comes down to us through the scriptures. May the Holy Spirit enlighten my mind and my heart to respond to the gospel teachings. (Please turn to your scripture on the following pages. Inspiration points are there should you need them. When you are ready, return here to continue.)

Conversation
How has God's Word moved me? Has it left me cold?
Has it consoled me or moved me to act in a new way?
I imagine Jesus standing or sitting beside me,
I turn and share my feelings with him.

Conclusion
Glory be to the Father, and to the Son, and to the Holy Spirit,
As it was in the beginning, is now and ever shall be,
World without end. Amen

Sunday 24th February,
Second Sunday of Lent **Luke 9:28–36**

Now about eight days after these sayings Jesus took with him Peter and John and James, and went up on the mountain to pray. And while he was praying, the appearance of his face changed, and his clothes became dazzling white. Suddenly they saw two men, Moses and Elijah, talking to him. They appeared in glory and were speaking of his departure, which he was about to accomplish at Jerusalem. Now Peter and his companions were weighed down with sleep; but since they had stayed awake, they saw his glory and the two men who stood with him. Just as they were leaving him, Peter said to Jesus, "Master, it is good for us to be here; let us make three dwellings, one for you, one for Moses, and one for Elijah"—not knowing what he said. While he was saying this, a cloud came and overshadowed them; and they were terrified as they entered the cloud. Then from the cloud came a voice that said, "This is my Son, my Chosen; listen to him!" When the voice had spoken, Jesus was found alone. And they kept silent and in those days told no one any of the things they had seen.

- The disciples were encouraged as they saw Jesus as he really is. Accompanied by Moses and Elijah he was guided by the law and by the prophets. I seek this balance too, drawing on the wisdom that comes from tradition and from vision.
- Peter wanted to stay with the glorious moment. I pray that I might appreciate the blessings that I have received, even as I try to not to get stuck in the past.

Monday 25th February **Luke 6:36–38**

Jesus said to the disciples, "Be merciful, just as your Father is merciful. Do not judge, and you will not be judged; do not condemn, and you will not be condemned. Forgive, and you will be forgiven; give, and it will be given to you. A good measure, pressed down, shaken together, running over, will be put into your lap; for the measure you give will be the measure you get back."

- I consider whether my capacity to receive is increasing as I become more generous. As I give of what I have, I realize that it really does not belong to me but has been given to me on trust. Being able to receive gifts graciously—from God and from others—is a sign of my growing freedom.
- Jesus sees compassion as a hallmark of how God works. I pray that I may be compassionate, not so much in imitation of God as in being open to being a channel of God's very presence.

Tuesday 26th February **Matthew 23:1–12**

Then Jesus said to the crowds and to his disciples, "The scribes and the Pharisees sit on Moses' seat; therefore, do whatever they teach you and follow it; but do not do as they do, for they do not practice what they teach. They tie up heavy burdens, hard to bear, and lay them on the shoulders of others; but they themselves are unwilling to lift a finger to move them. They do all their deeds to be seen by others; for they make their phylacteries broad and their fringes long. They love to have the place of honor at banquets and the best seats in the synagogues, and to be greeted with respect in the marketplaces, and to have people call them rabbi. But you are not to be called rabbi, for you have one teacher, and you are all students. And call no one your father on earth, for you have one Father—the one in heaven. Nor are you to be called instructors, for you have one instructor, the Messiah. The greatest among you will be your servant. All who exalt themselves will be humbled, and all who humble themselves will be exalted."

- Jesus cautions the disciples against an easy rejection of the Pharisees; you are not to reject them outright but are to be discerning and wise. I ask God to help me to resist any fundamentalist rejection of others and to help me to appreciate good wherever I find it.
- There may seem to be a contradiction between obedience and independence. I pray that I may have the humility to imitate, to receive instruction and to follow even as I accept the dignity that God gives me by speaking in love directly to my heart.

Wednesday 27th February **Matthew 20:20–23**

Then the mother of the sons of Zebedee came to Jesus with her sons, and kneeling before him, she asked a favour of him. And he said to her, "What do you want?" She said to him, "Declare that these two sons of mine will sit, one at your right hand and one at your left, in your kingdom." But Jesus answered, "You do not know what you are asking. Are you able to drink the cup that I am about to drink?" They said to him, "We are able." He said to them, "You will indeed drink my cup, but to sit at my right hand and at my left, this is not mine to grant, but it is for those for whom it has been prepared by my Father."

- Although James and John allowed their mother to speak for them, it was to them that Jesus directed his reply.
- As I pray for others, asking for their good, I pray also that they will notice God's action in their lives and be drawn more deeply into conversation with God.
- I ask for what I need, but allow God to answer. God knows my abilities and will give me what I need, even if not always what I want.

Thursday 28th February **Luke 16:19–31**

Jesus said to the Pharisees, "There was a rich man who was dressed in purple and fine linen and who feasted sumptuously every day. And at his gate lay a poor man named Lazarus, covered with sores, who longed to satisfy his hunger with what fell from the rich man's table; even the dogs would come and lick his sores. The poor man died and was carried away by the angels to be with Abraham. The rich man also died and was buried. In Hades, where he was being tormented, he looked up and saw Abraham far away with Lazarus by his side. He called out, 'Father Abraham, have mercy on me, and send Lazarus to dip the tip of his finger in water and cool my tongue; for I am in agony in these flames.' But Abraham said, 'Child, remember that during your lifetime you received your good things, and Lazarus in like manner evil things; but now he is comforted here, and you are in agony. Besides all this, between you and us a great chasm has been fixed, so that those who might want to pass from here to you cannot do so, and no one can cross from there to us.' He said, 'Then, father, I beg you to send him to my father's house—for I have five brothers—that he may warn them, so that they will not also come into this place of torment.' Abraham replied, 'They have Moses and the prophets; they should listen to them.' He said, 'No, father Abraham; but if someone goes to them from the dead, they will repent.' He said to him, 'If they do not listen to Moses and the prophets, neither will they be convinced even if someone rises from the dead.'"

- The rich man had some feeling for his brothers, if little for the poor man at his gate. I pray that my sense of fellowship be broader than any limits of class, country or religion that the world teaches me to observe.
- God's message is abundantly clear, Jesus says. I ask God to help me to perceive, attend and follow God's word in this day.

Friday 1st March **Matthew 21:33–43**

Jesus said, "Listen to another parable. There was a landowner who planted a vineyard, put a fence around it, dug a wine press in it, and built a watch-tower. Then he leased it to tenants and went to another country. When the harvest time had come, he sent his slaves to the tenants to collect his produce. But the tenants seized his slaves and beat one, killed another, and stoned another. Again he sent other slaves, more than the first; and they treated them in the same way. Finally he sent his son to them, saying, 'They will respect my son.' But when the tenants saw the son, they said to themselves, 'This is the heir; come, let us kill him and get his inheritance.' So they seized him, threw him out of the vineyard, and killed him. Now when the owner of the vineyard comes, what will he do to those tenants?" They said to him, "He will put those wretches to a miserable death, and lease the vineyard to other tenants who will give him the produce at the harvest time. Jesus said to them, "Have you never read in the scriptures: 'The stone that the builders rejected has become the cornerstone; this was the Lord's doing, and it is amazing in our eyes.' Therefore I tell you, the kingdom of God will be taken away from you and given to a people that produces the fruits of the kingdom."

- In prayer we often see things in a new way. Like the rejected stone which becomes the central or corner stone, some of our weaknesses and sins can be stepping stones to fuller and deeper life.
- There is a side to prayer which of itself strengthens and heals us; we know that nothing of the worst of life need be final. The Lord can turn weakness into compassion for others, and can bring us through darkness into light. God heals the broken-hearted.

Saturday 2nd March **Luke 15:25–32**

Now his elder son was in the field; and when he came and approached the house, he heard music and dancing. He called one of the slaves and asked what was going on. He replied, "Your brother has come, and your father has killed the fatted calf, because he has got him back safe and sound." Then he became angry and refused to go in. His father came out and began to plead with him. But he answered his father, "Listen! For all these years I have been working like a slave for you, and I have never disobeyed your command; yet you have never given me even a young goat so that I might celebrate with my friends. But when this son of yours came back, who has devoured your property with prostitutes, you killed the fatted calf for him!" Then the father said to him, "Son, you are always with me, and all that is mine is yours. But we had to celebrate and rejoice, because this brother of yours was dead and has come to life; he was lost and has been found."

- Maybe the older son reminds me of people I know who are distracted from what is good by judging others things better; I know that I am like this sometimes. I ask God to help me to appreciate my relationships and the gifts I have been given.
- The older son had fallen out of familiarity with the ways of his father; he served him faithfully but did not know his heart. God invites me to keep my prayer time as a time when we converse heart to heart, growing in love and knowledge of one another.

Sacred Space

march 3–9

Something to think and pray about each day this week:

Seeing into the heart
"What is essential is invisible to the eye," says the fox in *The Little Prince* by Antoine de Saint-Exupéry. Yes indeed. But many things in modern life may lead us to rely on outward appearances. Those appearances may satisfy for a while but there is in fact a deeper seeing, where what is invisible to the ordinary eye will be noticed.

For instance, the prophet Samuel heard the words, "God does not see as people see; people look at appearances but the Lord looks at the heart" (1 Samuel 16:7).

Perhaps a project this Lent might be to cultivate a way of seeing which is deeper than normal. It is a way of seeing which involves my own heart—where I do not rely on outward appearances, but can look inwardly, into myself, and into others. "Indeed you love truth in the heart. Then in the secret of my heart teach me wisdom" (Psalm 51:6). Then I can see more clearly into life, and with something of the eyes and wisdom of God. Lord, clear away my blindness, heal me and free me, and let me see clearly.

The Presence of God
Dear Jesus, today I call on you in a special way.
Mostly I come asking for favors.
Today I'd like just to be in Your presence.
Let my heart respond to Your Love.

Freedom
'I am free.'
When I look at these words in writing
They seem to create in me a feeling of awe.
Yes, a wonderful feeling of freedom.
Thank You, God.

Consciousness
Lord, You gave me the night to rest in sleep.
In my waking hours may I not forget your goodness to me.
Guide me to share your blessings with others.

The Word
I read the Word of God slowly, a few times over, and I listen to what God is saying to me. (Please turn to your scripture on the following pages. Inspiration points are there should you need them. When you are ready, return here to continue.)

Conversation
Dear Jesus, I can open up my heart to you.
I can tell you everything that troubles me.
I know You care about all the concerns in my life.
Teach me to live in the knowledge
that You who care for me today,
will care for me tomorrow and all the days of my life.

Conclusion
Glory be to the Father, and to the Son, and to the Holy Spirit,
As it was in the beginning, is now and ever shall be,
World without end. Amen

Sunday 3rd March,
Third Sunday of Lent **Luke 13:6–9**

Jesus told this parable: "A man had a fig tree planted in his vineyard; and he came looking for fruit on it and found none. So he said to the gardener, "See here! For three years I have come looking for fruit on this fig tree, and still I find none. Cut it down! Why should it be wasting the soil?' He replied, 'Sir, let it alone for one more year, until I dig around it and put manure on it. If it bears fruit next year, well and good; but if not, you can cut it down.'"

- The owner looked at the tree as property, judging the investment by its return. The gardener saw an opportunity for growth and recognized that effort, nourishment and time were called for.
- I consider how God looks on me lovingly, "digs around me" and is patient with me. I humbly lay the fruit of my life before God.

Monday 4th March **Luke 4:24–30**

And he said, "Truly I tell you, no prophet is accepted in the prophet's hometown. But the truth is, there were many widows in Israel in the time of Elijah, when the heaven was shut up three years and six months, and there was a severe famine over all the land; yet Elijah was sent to none of them except to a widow at Zarephath in Sidon. There were also many lepers in Israel in the time of the prophet Elisha, and none of them was cleansed except Naaman the Syrian." When they heard this, all in the synagogue were filled with rage. They got up, drove him out of the town, and led him to the brow of the hill on which their town was built, so that they might hurl him off the cliff. But he passed through the midst of them and went on his way.

- The people who listened to Jesus' message were able to accept it only if it did not reflect badly on them. I allow myself to hear any message from God that calls me to growth. I accept that I am on a journey and have not arrived yet.
- Jesus' hearers did not seem to like the reminder of the importance of other nations; perhaps they had grown to think themselves superior. I ask God to help me to correct any false notions I have about myself or about my people.

Tuesday 5th March **Matthew 18:21–22**

Then Peter came and said to him, "Lord, if another member of the church sins against me, how often should I forgive? As many as seven times?" Jesus said to him, "Not seven times, but, I tell you, seventy-seven times."

- Peter had an idea that faith might be about counting and calculating but Jesus thinks otherwise.
- It is easy to be led to give attention to numbers and to measure the wrong things on the wrong scales. I ask for God's help as I try to figure out what Jesus' message means to me.

Wednesday 6th March **Matthew 5:17–19**

Jesus said to his disciples, "Do not think that I have come to abolish the law or the prophets; I have come not to abolish but to fulfill. For truly I tell you, until heaven and earth pass away, not one letter, not one stroke of a letter, will pass from the law until all is accomplished. Therefore, whoever breaks one of the least of these commandments, and teaches others to do the same, will be called least in the kingdom of heaven; but whoever does them and teaches them will be called great in the kingdom of heaven."

- Jesus saw the continuity of God's message; he spoke as had the prophets of old. I realize that I too have a history and tradition.
- I ask God to continue to bless me and to lead me into the wisdom that Jesus had. I pray in respect for all who teach the faith that has come to us from the apostles.

Thursday 7th March **Luke 11:14–20**

Jesus was casting out a demon that was mute; when the demon had gone out, the one who had been mute spoke, and the crowds were amazed. But some of them said, "He casts out demons by Beelzebul, the ruler of the demons." Others, to test him, kept demanding from him a sign from heaven. But he knew what they were thinking and said to them, "Every kingdom divided against itself becomes a desert, and house falls on house. If Satan also is divided against himself, how will his kingdom stand? —for you say that I cast out the demons by Beelzebul. Now if I cast out the demons by Beelzebul, by whom do your exorcists cast them out? Therefore they will be your judges. But if it is by the finger of God that I cast out the demons, then the kingdom of God has come to you.

- Even the best of actions are open to misjudgement. I pray that I may seek out the best interpretation of the events around me and ask for the inspiration of God's spirit as I do.
- Where I notice good, I give thanks to God who is at work in the world. In thought, I gather what is good and life-giving now and offer thanks to God.

Friday 8th March **Mark 12:28–34**

One of the scribes came near and heard them disputing with one another, and seeing that he answered them well, he asked him, "Which commandment is the first of all?" Jesus answered, "The first is, 'Hear, O Israel: the Lord our God, the Lord is one; you shall love the Lord your God with all your heart, and with all your soul, and with all your mind, and with all your strength.' The second is this, 'You shall love your neighbor as yourself.' There is no other commandment greater than these." Then the scribe said to him, "You are right, Teacher; you have truly said that 'he is one, and besides him there is no other'; and 'to love him with all the heart, and with all the understanding, and with all the strength,' and 'to love one's neighbor as oneself,'—this is much more important than all whole burnt offerings and sacrifices." When Jesus saw that he answered wisely, he said to him, "You are not far from the kingdom of God." After that no one dared to ask him any question.

- The text, "Hear, O Israel", would have been one that Jesus learned to pray from an early age. I might count it among the prayers that I know by heart and return to it from time to time asking God to help me to use all my energies—heart, soul, mind and strength—in God's service.

Saturday 9th March **Luke 18:9–14**

He also told this parable to some who trusted in themselves that they were righteous and regarded others with contempt: "Two men went up to the temple to pray, one a Pharisee and the other a tax collector. The Pharisee, standing by himself, was praying thus, 'God, I thank you that I am not like other people: thieves, rogues, adulterers, or even like this tax collector. I fast twice a week; I give a tenth of all my income.' But the tax collector, standing far off, would not even look up to heaven, but was beating his breast and saying, 'God, be merciful to me, a sinner!' I tell you, this man went down to his home justified rather than the other; for all who exalt themselves will be humbled, but all who humble themselves will be exalted."

- I place myself with the humble tax collector, asking God for mercy as I realize that I am a sinner. I ask God to help me to know my need without becoming disheartened.
- The Pharisee did not just think well of himself but did so at the expense of other people, looking down on them from the height to which she had exalted himself. Are there ways in which I promote myself?

Something to think and pray about each day this week:

Open to mystery

The psalms are wonderful poems and songs for prayer. We can, of course, use our own words or even simply go beyond words into a silence, a communion beyond what can be spoken. Yet often a phrase from a psalm can catch our mood, or sum up all that our own words are trying to utter. So it is, following from last week's words, "In God alone my soul can find its rest and peace" (Psalm 62), we might find it helpful to say over and over: "In you, O Lord, I take refuge. Let me never be put to shame. In your justice, set me free, hear me and speedily rescue me" (Psalm 31).

We need that protection always, that lifting up which comes from God. It is true, we need it in human and tangible form too—from a friend, a person who cares, a spouse, a neighbor. And we in turn offer it to others too. But the *source* of it all is God. How good, then, when we turn in the depths of our hearts, in the quiet of our being, to prayer before the mystery of God. Especially, if we feel bound, imprisoned in some way, we can reach out to the God who saves: "In your justice, set me free, hear me and speedily rescue me."

The Presence of God

I pause for a moment
and think of the love and the grace that God showers on me,
creating me in his image and likeness, making me his temple.

Freedom

Everything has the potential to draw forth from me a fuller love and life.
Yet my desires are often fixed, caught, on illusions of fulfillment.
I ask that God, through my freedom, may orchestrate
my desires in a vibrant loving melody rich in harmony.

Consciousness

In the presence of my loving Creator,
I look honestly at my feelings over the last day,
the highs, the lows and the level ground.
Can I see where the Lord has been present?

The Word

God speaks to each one of us individually. I need to listen to what he is saying to me. (Please turn to your scripture on the following pages. Inspiration points are there should you need them. When you are ready, return here to continue.)

Conversation

What feelings are rising in me
as I pray and reflect on God's Word?
I imagine Jesus himself sitting or standing beside me,
and open my heart to him.

Conclusion

Glory be to the Father, and to the Son, and to the Holy Spirit,
As it was in the beginning, is now and ever shall be,
World without end. Amen

Sunday 10th March,
Fourth Sunday of Lent **Luke 15:25–32**

The elder son was in the field; and when he came and approached the house, he heard music and dancing. He called one of the slaves and asked what was going on. He replied, "Your brother has come, and your father has killed the fatted calf, because he has got him back safe and sound." Then he became angry and refused to go in. His father came out and began to plead with him. But he answered his father, "Listen! For all these years I have been working like a slave for you, and I have never disobeyed your command; yet you have never given me even a young goat so that I might celebrate with my friends. But when this son of yours came back, who has devoured your property with prostitutes, you killed the fatted calf for him!" Then the father said to him, "Son, you are always with me, and all that is mine is yours. But we had to celebrate and rejoice, because this brother of yours was dead and has come to life; he was lost and has been found."

- The son who stayed at home seemed to have lost sight of his father's generous character. I ask God to bless me with a life-giving understanding of our relationship.
- God has a heart full of love for me; for what do I ask?
- I rejoice with God at signs of life, at the rediscovery of what has been lost or forgotten.

Monday 11th March **John 4:47–50**

Now there was a royal official whose son lay ill in Capernaum. When he heard that Jesus had come from Judea to Galilee, he went and begged him to come down and heal his son, for he was at the point of death. Then Jesus said to him, "Unless you see signs and wonders you will not believe." The official said to him, "Sir, come down before my little boy dies." Jesus said to him, "Go; your son will live." The man believed the word that Jesus spoke to him and started on his way.

- The request that the official made of Jesus was simple and direct. I try to be as clear and as almost as I express my desire in prayer.

- The man went on his way confident that Jesus would do as he said. I ask God's help to face the next day with confidence and trust in the word of God given to me.

Tuesday 12th March **John 5:2–9**

Now in Jerusalem by the Sheep Gate there is a pool, called in Hebrew Beth-zatha, which has five porticoes. In these lay many invalids—blind, lame, and paralyzed. One man was there who had been ill for thirty-eight years. When Jesus saw him lying there and knew that he had been there a long time, he said to him, "Do you want to be made well?" The sick man answered him, "Sir, I have no one to put me into the pool when the water is stirred up; and while I am making my way, someone else steps down ahead of me." Jesus said to him, "Stand up, take your mat and walk." At once the man was made well, and he took up his mat and began to walk.

- It was evident to Jesus that the man had been beside the pool for a long time; he must have looked as if he was settled in, familiar with the place. As Jesus looks at me, he may see that I am comfortable—even in the limits about which I complain. Do I have the courage to ask Jesus to heal me?
- I pray with compassion for all who believe themselves to be incurable or irredeemable.

Wednesday 13th March **John 5:17–23**

Jesus said to the Jews, "My Father is still working, and I also am working." For this reason the Jews were seeking all the more to kill him, because he was not only breaking the sabbath, but was also calling God his own Father, thereby making himself equal to God. Jesus said to them, "Very truly, I tell you, the Son can do nothing on his own, but only what he sees the Father doing; for whatever the Father does, the Son does likewise. The Father loves the Son and shows him all that he himself is doing; and he will show him greater works than these, so that you will be astonished. Indeed, just as the Father raises the dead and gives them life, so also the Son gives life to whomsoever he wishes. The Father judges no one but has given all judgment to the Son, so that all may honor the Son just as they honor the Father. Anyone who does not honor the Son does not honor the Father who sent him."

- Jesus' relationship to God was threatening to those who saw God differently. He spoke of God as a loving father with whom he related closely confidently. I think of the relationships that have helped me to understand what Jesus meant. I relax in the presence of God who loves me deeply.
- Such was the unity of the Father and Jesus that the work of one is the work of the other. Jesus trusts me enough to call me into the same closeness. He reminds me that whatever I do I do with him, and that what I do to others, I do to him.

Thursday 14th March **John 5:39–47**

Jesus said to the Jews "You search the scriptures because you think that in them you have eternal life; and it is they that testify on my behalf. Yet you refuse to come to me to have life. I do not accept glory from human beings. But I know that you do not have the love of God in you. I have come in my Father's name, and you do not accept me; if another comes in his own name, you will accept him. How can you believe when you accept glory from one another and do not seek the glory that comes from the one who alone is God? Do not think that I will accuse you before the Father; your accuser is Moses, on whom you have set your hope. If you believed Moses, you would believe me, for he wrote about me. But if you do not believe what he wrote, how will you believe what I say?"

- Our churches rely on structures, on theology, liturgy and human organisation. Jesus puts all of these in perspective by reminding us of our need to come to him for life; only when we do this will our structures have meaning.
- Jesus placed little value on human acclaim. Do I seek the approval of others too much, forgetting were my true value lies?

Friday 15th March **John 7:1–2, 10, 25–30**

Jesus went about in Galilee. He did not wish to go about in Judea because the Jews were looking for an opportunity to kill him. Now the Jewish festival of Booths was near. But after his brothers had gone to the festival, then he also went, not publicly but as it were in secret. Now some of the people of Jerusalem were saying, "Is not this the man whom they are trying to kill? And here he is, speaking openly, but they say nothing to him! Can it be that the authorities really know that this is the Messiah? Yet we know where this man is from; but when the Messiah comes, no one will know where he is from." Then Jesus cried out as he was teaching in the temple, "You know me, and you know where I am from. I have not come on my own. But the one who sent me is true, and you do not know him. I know him, because I am from him, and he sent me." Then they tried to arrest him, but no one laid hands on him, because his hour had not yet come.

- The arguments go to and fro about Jesus: some say that they know nothing about him, others that they know everything. It sometimes seems like that nowadays too, that there are experts on every side.
- I realize that Lent calls me, not to be convinced in my mind, but to accept Jesus in my heart. This is the kind of knowledge that Jesus values.
- No matter how much I know about somebody there always remains much of which is hidden and known only to God. I pray for a deeper reverence of those around me—especially for those I think I know well.

Saturday 16th March **John 7:50–53**

Nicodemus, who had gone to Jesus before, and who was one of them, asked, "Our law does not judge people without first giving them a hearing to find out what they are doing, does it?" They replied, "Surely you are not also from Galilee, are you? Search and you will see that no prophet is to arise from Galilee." Then each of them went home.

- Nicodemus is an honest man, ready to speak up for truth. I ask God for courage to speak for truth, even at the risk of rejection.
- Those with power are always tempted to use the law to preserve their own comfort. I pray for the integrity of all those in decision-making positions and for the courage of those who resist wrong-doing. I think of what I may need to do to stand for justice.

Sacred Space

Something to think and pray about each day this week:

The living God

The scholar John L. McKenzie SJ describes how the roots of Christian (and Jewish and Muslim) faith grew in "the desert wastes of Syria and Arabia, which seem to stretch into infinity." The Chosen People were in those wastes for forty years. Jesus himself recapitulated that experience of his people, by going into the wilderness for forty days. And Christians, following him, starting out on the forty days of Lent each year enter that desert experience too. But, in truth, our own day-to-day mundane lives often have something of that desert reality about them. What happens out there, in the real, or in the man-made deserts of today? Between the desert floor and the desert sky, life is stripped of all its artificial props, brought down to its essentials, in the effort to remain alive and avoid death. Vulnerable and exposed in that setting, we might also feel particularly threatened or tempted, as if surrounded by malignant forces in the swirling windswept sands. Such was the actual desert experience.

But, more than this and above all, it was the place where the Chosen People experienced God: at Mount Sinai they were drawn into a Covenant relationship. They could never forget that. In the desert—our illusions taken away, leaving us exposed and vulnerable—we find, not nothingness, but the living God. God before us, God with us, the God of fidelity, and truth, and love.

The Presence of God

I reflect for a moment on God's presence around me and in me.
Creator of the universe, the sun and the moon, the earth, every molecule, every atom, everything that is:
God is in every beat of my heart. God is with me, now.

Freedom

A thick and shapeless tree-trunk would never believe
that it could become a statue, admired as a miracle of sculpture,
and would never submit itself to the chisel of the sculptor,
who sees by her genius what she can make of it. (St Ignatius)
I ask for the grace to let myself be shaped by my loving Creator.

Consciousness

Knowing that God loves me unconditionally,
I look honestly over the last day, its events and my feelings.
Do I have something to be grateful for? Then I give thanks.
Is there something I am sorry for? Then I ask forgiveness.

The Word

I read the Word of God slowly, a few times over, and I listen to what God is saying to me. (Please turn to your scripture on the following pages. Inspiration points are there should you need them. When you are ready, return here to continue.)

Conversation

What is stirring in me as I pray?
Am I consoled, troubled, left cold?
I imagine Jesus himself standing or sitting at my side,
and share my feelings with him.

Conclusion

Glory be to the Father, and to the Son, and to the Holy Spirit,
As it was in the beginning, is now and ever shall be,
World without end. Amen

Sunday 17th March,
Fifth Sunday of Lent **John 8:1–7**

Early in the morning Jesus came again to the temple. All the people came to him and he sat down and began to teach them. The scribes and the Pharisees brought a woman who had been caught in adultery; and making her stand before all of them, they said to him, "Teacher, this woman was caught in the very act of committing adultery. Now in the law Moses commanded us to stone such women. Now what do you say?" They said this to test him, so that they might have some charge to bring against him. Jesus bent down and wrote with his finger on the ground. When they kept on questioning him, he straightened up and said to them, "Let anyone among you who is without sin be the first to throw a stone at her."

- Jesus knew that there were times when many words might be spoken and times when words would not help. I pray for the wisdom to know when my words need to be fewer and for God's inspiration to choose the right ones.
- The people asked a question for which they wanted to hear only one answer. Jesus did not engage in a dialogue with them. As I come to pray, I am reminded to listen for the voice of Jesus in dialogue with me, not saying only what I want to hear.

Monday 18th March **John 8:7–12**

When they kept on questioning him, he straightened up and said to them, "Let anyone among you who is without sin be the first to throw a stone at her." And once again he bent down and wrote on the ground. When they heard it, they went away, one by one, beginning with the elders; and Jesus was left alone with the woman standing before him. Jesus straightened up and said to her, "Woman, where are they? Has no one condemned you?" She said, "No one, sir." And Jesus said, "Neither do I condemn you. Go your way, and from now on do not sin again."

- This story often invites people to heap criticism on the Pharisees; we can become critical, judgemental and superior just as we notice these traits in the Pharisees. "Don't look out," Jesus says, "look in." I look in to my heart and become aware of my own need for forgiveness.

- What Jesus said to the woman he says to me, "I don't condemn you. Go on your way and don't sin." I am before Jesus, not condemned but being sent on my way, loved and trusted.
- If Jesus were to write a quiet message on the ground for me, what would it be?

Tuesday 19th March,
St Joseph **Matthew 1:18–25**

Now the birth of Jesus the Messiah took place in this way. When his mother Mary had been engaged to Joseph, but before they lived together, she was found to be with child from the Holy Spirit. Her husband Joseph, being a righteous man and unwilling to expose her to public disgrace, planned to dismiss her quietly. But just when he had resolved to do this, an angel of the Lord appeared to him in a dream and said, "Joseph, son of David, do not be afraid to take Mary as your wife, for the child conceived in her is from the Holy Spirit. She will bear a son, and you are to name him Jesus, for he will save his people from their sins." All this took place to fulfill what had been spoken by the Lord through the prophet: "Look, the virgin shall conceive and bear a son, and they shall name him Emmanuel," which means, "God is with us." When Joseph awoke from sleep, he did as the angel of the Lord commanded him; he took her as his wife, but had no marital relations with her until she had borne a son; and he named him Jesus.

- Joseph showed discretion even though he might well have felt wronged. I think of how he waited, considering what God had to say before he acted.
- I pray for the restraint I need when I am tempted to act impulsively.

Wednesday 20th March **John 8:31–42**

Then Jesus said to the Jews who had believed in him, "If you continue in my word, you are truly my disciples; and you will know the truth, and the truth will make you free." They answered him, "We are descendants of Abraham and have never been slaves to anyone. What do you mean by saying, 'You will be made free'?" Jesus answered them, "Very truly, I tell you, everyone who commits sin is a slave to sin. The slave does not have a permanent place in the household; the son has a place there forever. So if the Son makes you free, you will be free indeed. I know that you are descendants of Abraham; yet you look for an opportunity to kill me, because there is no place in you for my word. I declare what I have seen in the Father's presence; as for you, you should do what you have heard from the Father." They answered him, "Abraham is our father." Jesus said to them, "If you were Abraham's children, you would be doing what Abraham did, but now you are trying to kill me, a man who has told you the truth that I heard from God. This is not what Abraham did. You are indeed doing what your father does." They said to him, "We are not illegitimate children; we have one father, God himself." Jesus said to them, "If God were your Father, you would love me, for I came from God and now I am here. I did not come on my own, but he sent me."

- Jesus wants to lead me into truth so that I may be free. If I truly desire freedom, I need to be ready to accept the truth. There is nothing threatening or accusatory here—it is about being known fully and loved deeply.
- John shows the people who listened to Jesus as being prickly and precious, quick to defend their religion and righteousness. Jesus' replies show them that they have forgotten love and relationship.

Thursday 21st March **John 8:51–56**

Jesus said, "Very truly, I tell you, whoever keeps my word will never see death." The Jews said to him, "Now we know that you have a demon. Abraham died, and so did the prophets; yet you say, 'Whoever keeps my word will never taste death.' Are you greater than our father Abraham, who died? The prophets also died. Who do you claim to be?" Jesus answered, "If I glorify myself, my glory is nothing. It is my Father who glorifies me, he of whom you say, 'He is our God,' though you do not know him. But I know him; if I were to say that I do not know him, I would be a liar like you. But I do know him and I keep his word. Your ancestor Abraham rejoiced that he would see my day; he saw it and was glad."

- Lent helps me to recover my sincerity, to restoring my relationship with God. Jesus calls me to conversion, to leave aside any images or notions to which I have become attached.
- Jesus promises me life if I keep his word. What is his word for me today?

Friday 22nd March **John 10:31–38**

The Jews took up stones again to stone him. Jesus replied, "I have shown you many good works from the Father. For which of these are you going to stone me?" The Jews answered, "It is not for a good work that we are going to stone you, but for blasphemy, because you, though only a human being, are making yourself God." Jesus answered, "Is it not written in your law, 'I said, you are gods'? If those to whom the word of God came were called 'gods'—and the scripture cannot be annulled—can you say that the one whom the Father has sanctified and sent into the world is blaspheming because I said, 'I am God's Son'? If I am not doing the works of my Father, then do not believe me. But if I do them, even though you do not believe me, believe the works, so that you may know and understand that the Father is in me and I am in the Father."

- The message of Jesus was threatening to the people of his time and remains threatening today. What might have to change for me if I were to accept what Jesus proclaims?
- Jesus asserts the dignity that I have in being a child of God. I pray for people who suffer injustice.
- I think of what I might do to express the vision that Jesus gives me.

Saturday 23rd March **John 11:45–48**

Many of the Jews therefore, who had come with Mary and had seen what Jesus did, believed in him. But some of them went to the Pharisees and told them what he had done. So the chief priests and the Pharisees called a meeting of the council, and said, "What are we to do? This man is performing many signs. If we let him go on like this, everyone will believe in him, and the Romans will come and destroy both our holy place and our nation."

- The leaders saw that believing in Jesus would threaten much of the security that they knew. It may be so with me; I might have to correct comfortable habits or give up patterns that I have settled into. I ask Jesus to show them to me and to help me to leave them behind.
- It is not possible to believe in Jesus and to let life be unchanged. I acknowledge that my way of living shows the signs of my following Jesus and ask for the strength and courage I need to be a calm and confident disciple.

Sacred Space

march 24–30

Something to think and pray about each day this week:

Staying the journey

In this Holy Week, now upon us, we see Jesus entering the dark realm of his suffering and death. The whole course of his earthly life has led to this—to the brief applause and "hosannas" when entering Jerusalem, to the Passover Supper with his disciples, to the agony of Gethsemane, the betrayal and arrest, followed by his condemnation by the religious and civil authorities, and his being done to death by crucifixion outside the city walls.

We, however, try to stay with him these days—even though that staying seemed impossible for his disciples then: "And they all deserted him and ran away" (Mark 14:50). Only the women, including his mother, and the beloved disciple, stood by him (John 19:25).

All his life, surely, from his infancy by Mary's side, was moving towards this place. And dimly we can see, in it all, the momentum of a great unending love, by which "God so loved the world, that he gave his own beloved Son" (John 3:16). So we look towards him, and at that love. We look too at the faces of people stricken by natural disaster, death and war. And all of us, in turn, are looked upon by the Father, and through the eyes of the beloved Son . . . *This* is God's way, in vulnerable brokenness, into our hearts, and drawing us into eternal life. This is God's deepest meaning.

The Presence of God
In the silence of my innermost being,
in the fragments of my yearned-for wholeness,
can I hear the whispers of God's presence?
Can I remember when I felt God's nearness?
When we walked together and I let myself be embraced by God's love.

Freedom
There are very few people
who realize what God would make of them
if they abandoned themselves into his hands,
and let themselves be formed by his grace. (St Ignatius)
I ask for the grace to trust myself totally to God's love.

Consciousness
How do I find myself today?
Where am I with God? With others?
Do I have something to be grateful for? Then I give thanks.
Is there something I am sorry for? Then I ask forgiveness.

The Word
I take my time to read the Word of God, slowly, a few times, allowing myself to dwell on anything that strikes me. (Please turn to your scripture on the following pages. Inspiration points are there should you need them. When you are ready, return here to continue.)

Conversation
Do I notice myself reacting as I pray with the Word of God?
Do I feel challenged, comforted, angry?
Imagining Jesus sitting or standing by me,
I speak out my feelings, as one trusted friend to another.

Conclusion
Glory be to the Father, and to the Son, and to the Holy Spirit,
As it was in the beginning, is now and ever shall be,
World without end. Amen

Sunday 24th March,
Palm Sunday of the Lord's Passion **Luke 22:24–27**

A dispute also arose among the disciples as to which one of them was to be regarded as the greatest. But Jesus said to them, "The kings of the Gentiles lord it over them; and those in authority over them are called benefactors. But not so with you; rather the greatest among you must become like the youngest, and the leader like one who serves. For who is greater, the one who is at the table or the one who serves? Is it not the one at the table? But I am among you as one who serves."

- Jesus makes us think again about what it means to be a leader as he shows us new meanings of "friend" and "servant." I take time with these words, considering what they mean for me.
- In the presence of God, I look at how I lead, serve and befriend.

Monday 25th March **John 12:1–6**

Six days before the Passover Jesus came to Bethany, the home of Lazarus, whom he had raised from the dead. There they gave a dinner for him. Martha served, and Lazarus was one of those at the table with him. Mary took a pound of costly perfume made of pure nard, anointed Jesus' feet, and wiped them with her hair. The house was filled with the fragrance of the perfume. But Judas Iscariot, one of his disciples (the one who was about to betray him), said, "Why was this perfume not sold for three hundred denarii and the money given to the poor?" (He said this not because he cared about the poor, but because he was a thief; he kept the common purse and used to steal what was put into it.)

- Breathe deeply in and imagine the smell of a precious scent filling the house. It was an extravagant, wasteful and indulgent thing to do but speaks of a human reality: some opportunities need to be grasped as they arise, some moments need to be honoured, friendship cannot always be calculating.
- Holy Week invites me to spend time with Jesus not for any logical reason but simply to accompany a loved friend.

Tuesday 26th March **John 13:31–33, 36–38**

When Judas had gone out, Jesus said, "Now the Son of Man has been glorified, and God has been glorified in him. If God has been glorified in him, God will also glorify him in himself and will glorify him at once. Little children, I am with you only a little longer. You will look for me; and as I said to the Jews so now I say to you, 'Where I am going, you cannot come.'" Simon Peter said to him, "Lord, where are you going?" Jesus answered, "Where I am going, you cannot follow me now; but you will follow afterwards." Peter said to him, "Lord, why can I not follow you now? I will lay down my life for you." Jesus answered, "Will you lay down your life for me? Very truly, I tell you, before the cock crows, you will have denied me three times."

- Following Jesus requires recognizing how he chooses, where he goes, what he might do or say. I take time during these days to consider deeply what is in Jesus' heart and how, even when he is in turmoil, his thoughts are for his friends.
- Peter's best intentions were not matched by his performance. I know what that is like. I allow myself to be forgiven by God and to be trusted still to act in Jesus name.

Wednesday 27th March **Matthew 26:14–16, 20–25**

Then one of the twelve, who was called Judas Iscariot, went to the chief priests and said, "What will you give me if I betray him to you?" They paid him thirty pieces of silver. And from that moment he began to look for an opportunity to betray him. When it was evening, Jesus took his place with the twelve; and while they were eating, he said, "Truly I tell you, one of you will betray me." And they became greatly distressed and began to say to him one after another, "Surely not I, Lord?" He answered, "The one who has dipped his hand into the bowl with me will betray me. The Son of Man goes as it is written of him, but woe to that one by whom the Son of Man is betrayed! It would have been better for that one not to have been born." Judas, who betrayed him, said, "Surely not I, Rabbi?" He replied, "You have said so."

- Thirty pieces of silver was a high price; Jesus has often been betrayed for less. The deal does not always involve money; the currencies of comfort, popularity, influence and power are often acceptable forms of payment.
- Although he saw that he might be betrayed, Jesus did not turn from the disciples or from giving himself to them. He did not let their distress silence him but spoke the truth to them, knowing it would be unwelcome.

Thursday 28th March,
Holy Thursday **John 13:2–15**

During supper Jesus, knowing that the Father had given all things into his hands, and that he had come from God and was going to God, got up from the table, took off his outer robe, and tied a towel around himself. Then he poured water into a basin and began to wash the disciples' feet and to wipe them with the towel that was tied around him. He came to Simon Peter, who said to him, "Lord, are you going to wash my feet?" Jesus answered, "You do not know now what I am doing, but later you will understand." Peter said to him, "You will never wash my feet." Jesus answered, "Unless I wash you, you have no share with me." Simon Peter said to him, "Lord, not my feet only but also my hands and my head!" Jesus said to him, "One who has bathed does not need to wash, except for the feet, but is entirely clean. And you are clean, though not all of you." For he knew who was to betray him; for this reason he said, "Not all of you are clean." After Jesus had washed their feet, had put on his robe, and had returned to the table, he said to them, "Do you know what I have done to you? You call me Teacher and Lord—and you are right, for that is what I am. So if I, your Lord and Teacher, have washed your feet, you also ought to wash one another's feet. For I have set you an example, that you also should do as I have done to you."

- John the Evangelist communicates to us what is at the heart of the Eucharist, not by describing the action with bread and wine, but by giving us a lingering look at the servant heart of Jesus.
- I humbly give thanks for my opportunities to be of service to others. I pray that even my small acts of service may be for the good of the world and for the glory of God.

Friday 29th March,
Good Friday **John 18:1–5**

After Jesus had spoken these words, he went out with his disciples across the Kidron valley to a place where there was a garden, which he and his disciples entered. Now Judas, who betrayed him, also knew the place, because Jesus often met there with his disciples. So Judas brought a detachment of soldiers together with police from the chief priests and the Pharisees, and they came there with lanterns and torches and weapons. Then Jesus, knowing all that was to happen to him, came forward and asked them, "For whom are you looking?" They answered, "Jesus of Nazareth." Jesus replied, "I am he." Judas, who betrayed him, was standing with them.

- The betrayal of Jesus happened in a garden, reminding us of the earlier rejection of God's ways in the Garden of Eden. God can be forgotten even when we are surrounded by natural goodness.
- When I see a cross or crucifix I think, "For me" as I recall Jesus' love for me. I think of how I might create some space this day to remember Jesus' going to the cross. I ask for the help I need as I take up the crosses that I find in my life.

Saturday 30th March,
Holy Saturday **Matthew 27:57–66**

When it was evening, there came a rich man from Arimathea, named Joseph, who was also a disciple of Jesus. He went to Pilate and asked for the body of Jesus; then Pilate ordered it to be given to him. So Joseph took the body and wrapped it in a clean linen cloth and laid it in his own new tomb, which he had hewn in the rock. He then rolled a great stone to the door of the tomb and went away. Mary Magdalene and the other Mary were there, sitting opposite the tomb. The next day, that is, after the day of Preparation, the chief priests and the Pharisees gathered before Pilate and said, "Sir, we remember what that impostor said while he was still alive, 'After three days I will rise again.' Therefore command that the tomb be made secure until the third day; otherwise his disciples may go and steal him away, and tell the people, 'He has been raised from the dead', and the last deception would be worse than the first." Pilate said to them, "You have a guard of soldiers; go, make it as secure as you can." So they went with the guard and made the tomb secure by sealing the stone.

- This quiet day of waiting at the tomb draws me into a compassion for all who are waiting, uncertain or who hold on to fragile hope. I think of those who await medical results, of people in prison, of those whose dreams have been crushed.
- I wait for the Lord, drawing strength from the company of others and from the memory of the God's goodness and in hope of God's goodness in the future.

Sacred Space

march 31–april 6

Something to think and pray about each day this week:

Into the new light

Can light come from deepest darkness? Many women cry out from their desolation on behalf of "the disappeared"—their husbands and their children—who have been violently taken away to be no more. "Death and the hells of dereliction and abandonment eat up men and women, exhaust them, scrape them out and bring them to nothing" (Rowan Williams, *Open to Judgement*).

But on this Easter day, the women who have waited in that most dreadful darkness, have found a light dawning. It was "still dark" (John 20:1), indeed, when Mary of Magdala came to the tomb, where the body of Jesus had been laid. Next, the beloved disciple, who had been with the women by the Cross, came to a dawning of faith as he looked into the empty tomb: "He saw, and he believed," even though he saw no person. And then Mary, in the beautiful garden scene, finds herself called by name, "Mary!"—and *there* is Jesus, before her, alive, risen, the One for whom her heart yearned. And all is changed, utterly. For us, too, that transforming Easter faith is offered to us.

And that dawning faith can change everything.

The Presence of God
God is with me, but more,
God is within me, giving me existence.
Let me dwell for a moment on God's life-giving presence
in my body, my mind, my heart
and in the whole of my life.

Freedom
Many countries are at this moment suffering
the agonies of war.
I bow my head in thanksgiving for my freedom.
I pray for all prisoners and captives.

Consciousness
I remind myself that I am in the presence of the Lord.
I will take refuge in His loving heart.
He is my strength in times of weakness.
He is my comforter in times of sorrow.

The Word
I read the Word of God slowly, a few times over, and I listen to what God is saying to me. (Please turn to your scripture on the following pages. Inspiration points are there should you need them. When you are ready, return here to continue.)

Conversation
How has God's Word moved me? Has it left me cold?
Has it consoled me or moved me to act in a new way?
I imagine Jesus standing or sitting beside me,
I turn and share my feelings with him.

Conclusion
Glory be to the Father, and to the Son, and to the Holy Spirit,
As it was in the beginning, is now and ever shall be,
World without end. Amen

Sunday 31st March,
Easter Sunday **John 20:1–9**

Early on the first day of the week, while it was still dark, Mary Magdalene came to the tomb and saw that the stone had been removed from the tomb. So she ran and went to Simon Peter and the other disciple, the one whom Jesus loved, and said to them, "They have taken the Lord out of the tomb, and we do not know where they have laid him." Then Peter and the other disciple set out and went toward the tomb. The two were running together, but the other disciple outran Peter and reached the tomb first. He bent down to look in and saw the linen wrappings lying there, but he did not go in. Then Simon Peter came, following him, and went into the tomb. He saw the linen wrappings lying there, and the cloth that had been on Jesus' head, not lying with the linen wrappings but rolled up in a place by itself. Then the other disciple, who reached the tomb first, also went in, and he saw and believed; for as yet they did not understand the scripture, that he must rise from the dead.

- When Jesus raised Lazarus, Lazarus had to be freed from his grave-clothes. Jesus' grave-clothes are rolled up and lying on the side, a reflection of his mastery over death.
- I stand in the doorway beside the entrance and stare into that empty tomb. Do I grasp the difference between this resurrection and that of Lazarus?

Monday 1st April **Matthew 28:8–10**

So the women left the tomb quickly with fear and great joy, and ran to tell his disciples. Suddenly Jesus met them and said, "Greetings!" And they came to him, took hold of his feet, and worshiped him. Then Jesus said to them, "Do not be afraid; go and tell my brothers to go to Galilee; there they will see me."

- I ask God to help me in this Easter season to leave behind what does not lead me to life. I think of how baptism saves me and points me in a new direction.
- The women were sent, at Jesus' instruction, to tell the disciples where they might meet with him. I listen for the voice of the Lord this Easter so that I may point others to life.

Tuesday 2nd April **John 20:11–18**

But Mary stood weeping outside the tomb. As she wept, she bent over to look into the tomb; and she saw two angels in white, sitting where the body of Jesus had been lying, one at the head and the other at the feet. They said to her, "Woman, why are you weeping?" She said to them, "They have taken away my Lord, and I do not know where they have laid him." When she had said this, she turned around and saw Jesus standing there, but she did not know that it was Jesus. Jesus said to her, "Woman, why are you weeping? Whom are you looking for?" Supposing him to be the gardener, she said to him, "Sir, if you have carried him away, tell me where you have laid him, and I will take him away." Jesus said to her, "Mary!" She turned and said to him in Hebrew, "Rabbouni!" (which means Teacher). Jesus said to her, "Do not hold on to me, because I have not yet ascended to the Father. But go to my brothers and say to them, 'I am ascending to my Father and your Father, to my God and your God.'" Mary Magdalene went and announced to the disciples, "I have seen the Lord"; and she told them that he had said these things to her.

- Mary "turned around" and saw Jesus. I ask God to give me the strength I need always to be ready to turn around, to look again, that I may see and recognize Jesus' presence in my life.
- The angels asked Mary, "why are you weeping?" Even as, in Easter, I pray in hope, I bring myself fully before God, expressing my needs and my difficulties. I look for signs of resurrection in places where life might not seem likely to be found.

Wednesday 3rd April **Luke 24:30–35**

When Jesus was at the table with the disciples, he took bread, blessed and broke it, and gave it to them. Then their eyes were opened, and they recognized him; and he vanished from their sight. They said to each other, "Were not our hearts burning within us while he was talking to us on the road, while he was opening the scriptures to us?" That same hour they got up and returned to Jerusalem; and they found the eleven and their companions gathered together. They were saying, "The Lord has risen indeed, and he has appeared to Simon!" Then they told what had happened on the road, and how he had been made known to them in the breaking of the bread.

- It was only when they stopped to reflect that the disciples recognized that their hearts had been burning. I ask God to guide me as I look over recent days that I may see where I have been called to life, and recognize where I have walked with Jesus.
- I give thanks to God for the meals that I have shared, for the company I have enjoyed. I pray for all of those with whom I have broken bread.

Thursday 4th April **Luke 24:35–40**

Then the disciples told what had happened on the road, and how he had been made known to them in the breaking of the bread. While they were talking about this, Jesus himself stood among them and said to them, "Peace be with you." They were startled and terrified, and thought that they were seeing a ghost. He said to them, "Why are you frightened, and why do doubts arise in your hearts? Look at my hands and my feet; see that it is I myself. Touch me and see; for a ghost does not have flesh and bones as you see that I have." And when he had said this, he showed them his hands and his feet.

- I take some time to listen to Jesus say to me, "Peace be with you." He repeats his greeting as he notices my reaction, my hesitations and my doubts.
- I think of the relationships and situations with which I am concerned and, with Jesus, pray, "Peace be with you." I imagine them blossoming and being the best they can be. I prepare myself to be a blessing.

Friday 5th April **John 21:1–7**

After these things Jesus showed himself again to the disciples by the Sea of Tiberias; and he showed himself in this way. Gathered there together were Simon Peter, Thomas called the Twin, Nathanael of Cana in Galilee, the sons of Zebedee, and two others of his disciples. Simon Peter said to them, "I am going fishing." They said to him, "We will go with you." They went out and got into the boat, but that night they caught nothing. Just after daybreak, Jesus stood on the beach; but the disciples did not know that it was Jesus. Jesus said to them, "Children, you have no fish, have you?" They answered him, "No." He said to them, "Cast the net to the right side of the boat, and you will find some." So they cast it, and now they were not able to haul it in because there were so many fish. That disciple whom Jesus loved said to Peter, "It is the Lord!"

- Even though somewhat bereft, the disciples kept themselves occupied and were open to the wisdom of a stranger.
- A night's fruitless labor did not prevent the disciples having another try.

Saturday 6th April **Mark 16:9–15**

Now after he rose early on the first day of the week, he appeared first to Mary Magdalene, from whom he had cast out seven demons. She went out and told those who had been with him, while they were mourning and weeping. But when they heard that he was alive and had been seen by her, they would not believe it. After this he appeared in another form to two of them, as they were walking into the country. And they went back and told the rest, but they did not believe them. Later he appeared to the eleven themselves as they were sitting at the table; and he upbraided them for their lack of faith and stubbornness, because they had not believed those who saw him after he had risen. And he said to them, "Go into all the world and proclaim the good news to the whole creation."

- Mary Magdalene might not have seemed the most likely of witnesses to those who would not believe. I draw inspiration from her as a witness to life, an announcer of truth.
- The lack of faith that the disciples had was a disappointment to Jesus yet he sent them to proclaim the good news. Jesus knows my failures but trusts me.

Something to think and pray about each day this week:

My Lord and God

How strange are many of the gospel post-resurrection scenes! Especially the one where the disciples have locked themselves away in a room, and are fearful, despite Mary of Magdala's testimony about her encounter with the living Jesus. They are withdrawn, paralysed, immobile. Yet Jesus himself comes *through* the barriers they have erected, comes to them *precisely where they are,* and *as they are.* And extraordinary too is the gift he offers: "Peace be with you," and repeated, "Peace be with you." And that peace is offered a third time when Jesus comes among them once more, to help the disciple we call "Doubting Thomas" receive the gift of Easter faith."'My Lord and my God!" he exclaims (John 20:28), in words which are perhaps the climax of all those uttered in faith in John's Gospel. And all this strangeness and mystery is immediately there for me, for us now. Someone comes to us, just where we are, and as we are. "Behold, I am standing at the door knocking!" (Revelation 3:20). He will come in, to the house of my heart, and sit down to share a meal with me. And from that encounter I can go out, with courage in my heart, to radiate the gift of Easter faith.

The Presence of God

To be present is to arrive as one is and open up to the other.
At this instant, as I arrive here, God is present waiting for me.
God always arrives before me, desiring to connect with me
even more than my most intimate friend.
I take a moment and greet my loving God.

Freedom

"In these days, God taught me
as a schoolteacher teaches a pupil" (St Ignatius).
I remind myself that there are things God has to teach me yet,
and ask for the grace to hear them and let them change me.

Consciousness

How am I really feeling? Light-hearted? Heavy-hearted?
I may be very much at peace, happy to be here.
Equally, I may be frustrated, worried or angry.
I acknowledge how I really am. It is the real me that the Lord loves.

The Word

I take my time to read the Word of God, slowly, a few times, allowing myself to dwell on anything that strikes me. (Please turn to your scripture on the following pages. Inspiration points are there should you need them. When you are ready, return here to continue.)

Conversation

What feelings are rising in me
as I pray and reflect on God's Word?
I imagine Jesus himself sitting or standing beside me,
and open my heart to him.

Conclusion

Glory be to the Father, and to the Son, and to the Holy Spirit,
As it was in the beginning, is now and ever shall be,
World without end. Amen

Sunday 7th April,
Second Sunday of Easter **John 20:19–23**

When it was evening on that day, the first day of the week, and the doors of the house where the disciples had met were locked for fear of the Jews, Jesus came and stood among them and said, "Peace be with you." After he said this, he showed them his hands and his side. Then the disciples rejoiced when they saw the Lord. Jesus said to them again, "Peace be with you. As the Father has sent me, so I send you." When he had said this, he breathed on them and said to them, "Receive the Holy Spirit. If you forgive the sins of any, they are forgiven them; if you retain the sins of any, they are retained."

- The risen Jesus penetrates the disciples' defences, overcomes their fears, and brings them joy. I ask him to pass through all my security systems and liberate me from whatever prevents me from "having life and having it in all its fullness."
- Jesus always brings peace and reconciliation. Where is there lack of peace in my life? Who do I need to make peace with? Do I make space to experience God's forgiveness and gift of peace?

Monday 8th April,
Annunciation of the Lord **Luke 1:26–33**

In the sixth month the angel Gabriel was sent by God to a town in Galilee called Nazareth, to a virgin whose name was Mary. And he came to her and said, "Greetings, favored one! The Lord is with you." But she was much perplexed by his words and pondered what sort of greeting this might be. The angel said to her, "Do not be afraid, Mary, for you have found favour with God. And now, you will conceive in your womb and bear a son, and you will name him Jesus. He will be great, and will be called the Son of the Most High, and the Lord God will give to him the throne of his ancestor David. He will reign over the house of Jacob forever, and of his kingdom there will be no end."

- Mary did not receive the angel's message as a total surprise; she was ready to engage in conversation with God's messenger. I turn to God and my prayer, and try to see God's finger at work in my life; I draw inspiration from Mary's disposition.

- Mary was prepared to say "Yes" to the direction God had in mind for her. How might I be as perceptive and as humble as she was, ready to notice and respond?

Tuesday 9th April **John 3:7–15**

Jesus said to Nicodemus, "Do not be astonished that I said to you, 'You must be born from above.' The wind blows where it chooses, and you hear the sound of it, but you do not know where it comes from or where it goes. So it is with everyone who is born of the Spirit." Nicodemus said to him, "How can these things be?" Jesus answered him, "Are you a teacher of Israel, and yet you do not understand these things? Very truly, I tell you, we speak of what we know and testify to what we have seen; yet you do not receive our testimony. If I have told you about earthly things and you do not believe, how can you believe if I tell you about heavenly things? No one has ascended into heaven except the one who descended from heaven, the Son of Man. And just as Moses lifted up the serpent in the wilderness, so must the Son of Man be lifted up, that whoever believes in him may have eternal life."

- The one we pray to and pray with is the Son of God, the One who has come from heaven and returned to heaven.
- Prayer is our time of bringing us into the space and ecology of everlasting love. This new strength happens in us not through our own efforts but through the love and power of God.

Wednesday 10th April **John 3:20–21**

Jesus said to Nicodemus, "For all who do evil hate the light and do not come to the light, so that their deeds may not be exposed. But those who do what is true come to the light, so that it may be clearly seen that their deeds have been done in God."

- I am called to live confidently in the light, realizing that I am fully known and loved, that there is nothing to cause me shame. I am recognized and called by God. I see the true beauty of those around me.

- Living in the dark creates suspicion, means partial recognition of myself and of others, suggests danger and risk. Could I be content with that?

Thursday 11th April **John 3:31–36**

John the Baptist said to his disciples, "The one who comes from above is above all; the one who is of the earth belongs to the earth and speaks about earthly things. The one who comes from heaven is above all. He testifies to what he has seen and heard, yet no one accepts his testimony."

- This time of prayer is an invitation to take another perspective as I am drawn to recognize the world as God sees it. I ask God to help me not to be trammelled by earthly things.
- God will help me to accept the words of Jesus, the witness of his life. He tells me that I am loved, forgiven, and cherished and trusted. I take his testimony to heart.

Friday 12th April **John 6:1–14**

After this Jesus went to the other side of the Sea of Galilee, also called the Sea of Tiberias. A large crowd kept following him, because they saw the signs that he was doing for the sick. Jesus went up the mountain and sat down there with his disciples. Now the Passover, the festival of the Jews, was near. When he looked up and saw a large crowd coming toward him, Jesus said to Philip, "Where are we to buy bread for these people to eat?" He said this to test him, for he himself knew what he was going to do. Philip answered him, "Six months' wages would not buy enough bread for each of them to get a little." One of his disciples, Andrew, Simon Peter's brother, said to him, "There is a boy here who has five barley loaves and two fish. But what are they among so many people?" Jesus said, "Make the people sit down." Now there was a great deal of grass in the place; so they sat down, about five thousand in all. Then Jesus took the loaves, and when he had given thanks, he distributed them to those who were seated; so also the fish, as much as they wanted. When they were satisfied, he told his disciples, "Gather up the fragments left over, so that nothing may be lost." So they gathered them up, and from the fragments of the five barley loaves, left by those who had eaten, they filled twelve baskets. When the people saw the sign that he had done, they began to say, "This is indeed the prophet who is to come into the world."

- It seems natural to calculate and understandable to feel that the resources available are not equal to the demands being made. I ask God to help me when I am inclined to despair, to give me heart and hope.
- The meagre rations that were available were enough. I pray for the courage I need to risk giving even the little that I have.

Saturday 13th April **John 6:16–21**

When evening came, his disciples went down to the sea, got into a boat, and started across the sea to Capernaum. It was now dark, and Jesus had not yet come to them. The sea became rough because a strong wind was blowing. When they had rowed about three or four miles, they saw Jesus walking on the sea and coming near the boat, and they were terrified. But he said to them, "It is I; do not be afraid." Then they wanted to take him into the boat, and immediately the boat reached the land toward which they were going.

- The disciples had often made this journey with Jesus. Now, travelling on their own on the agitated sea, they realized that Jesus was with them still; they experienced his care for them. I am reminded that I am never alone, especially in times of struggle or disorientation.
- Being sent by Jesus does not always mean leaving home, to go overseas as a missionary. Like the disciples who made this journey in the expectation of meeting with Jesus again, I am sent every day. My times of prayer see me telling Jesus about what I have experienced being nourished and sent out again.

Something to think and pray about each day this week:

Seeing Jesus, again

Luke's description of two disciples, travelling away from Jerusalem on the road to Emmaus, says so much about our life's journey (Luke 24:13ff). "We had high hopes just days past," they might say, "when in Jerusalem with Jesus. But then everything disintegrated. Now, there is nothing left to do, but return to the old familiar things. Our hopes are gone." Yet all at once there is someone, a seeming stranger, alongside . . . and what a change then takes place! And can it be the same with me, as I travel on my way, downcast and lifeless? Someone always alongside, who never gives up on me?

Perhaps even he is my partner on what might be called *'my dancing day'*—for, crazy as it may sound, he seems to *dance,* dance before me, so I find myself alive once more, and with vibrant movement coming back into my limbs. "He dances so that you may dance. He shows you what beauty is, his body awakens yours. He's there to be your partner and everyone's; sometimes you'll see him opposite you, sometimes not . . ." (Rowan Williams, *Open to Judgment*). That is a way of putting it.

And certainly at the breaking of the bread—the Eucharistic giving of his body and blood—for just a moment, we recognize Him (Luke 24:30, 35). Out of sight then, but always *there.* Always present, and so *alive*, for you and for me.

The Presence of God

What is present to me is what has a hold on my becoming.
I reflect on the presence of God always there in love,
amidst the many things that have a hold on me.
I pause and pray that I may let God
affect my becoming in this precise moment.

Freedom

If God were trying to tell me something, would I know?
If God were reassuring me or challenging me, would I notice?
I ask for the grace to be free of my own preoccupations
and open to what God may be saying to me.

Consciousness

Knowing that God loves me unconditionally,
I can afford to be honest about how I am.
How has the last day been, and how do I feel now?
I share my feelings openly with the Lord.

The Word

God speaks to each one of us individually. I need to listen to what he is saying to me. (Please turn to your scripture on the following pages. Inspiration points are there should you need them. When you are ready, return here to continue.)

Conversation

What is stirring in me as I pray?
Am I consoled, troubled, left cold?
I imagine Jesus himself standing or sitting at my side,
and share my feelings with him.

Conclusion

Glory be to the Father, and to the Son, and to the Holy Spirit,
As it was in the beginning, is now and ever shall be,
World without end. Amen

Sunday 14th April,
Third Sunday of Easter **John 21:1–14**

After these things Jesus showed himself again to the disciples by the Sea of Tiberias; and he showed himself in this way. Gathered there together were Simon Peter, Thomas called the Twin, Nathanael of Cana in Galilee, the sons of Zebedee, and two others of his disciples. Simon Peter said to them, "I am going fishing." They said to him, "We will go with you." They went out and got into the boat, but that night they caught nothing. Just after day break, Jesus stood on the beach; but the disciples did not know that it was Jesus. Jesus said to them, "Children, you have no fish, have you?" They answered him, "No." He said to them, "Cast the net to the right side of the boat, and you will find some." So they cast it, and now they were not able to haul it in because there were so many fish. That disciple whom Jesus loved said to Peter, "It is the Lord!" When Simon Peter heard that it was the Lord, he put on some clothes, for he was naked, and jumped into the lake. But the other disciples came in the boat, dragging the net full of fish, for they were not far from the land, only about a hundred yards off. When they had gone ashore, they saw a charcoal fire there, with fish on it, and bread. Jesus said to them, "Bring some of the fish that you have just caught." So Simon Peter went aboard and hauled the net ashore, full of large fish, a hundred and fifty-three of them; and though there were so many, the net was not torn. Jesus said to them, "Come and have breakfast." Now none of the disciples dared to ask him, "Who are you?" because they knew it was the Lord. Jesus came and took the bread and gave it to them, and did the same with the fish. This was now the third time that Jesus appeared to the disciples after he was raised from the dead.

- The disciples laboring all night and catching nothing is a little like what prayer can seem to us sometimes. Jesus encouraged them not to give up, to stay with the task. He knows there is benefit for me too, if I persevere.
- The charcoal fire might have reminded Peter of the High Priest's palace and his triple denial. Now Jesus gives him the opportunity

to experience total forgiveness. His triple confession draws him back into full friendship. Jesus is always offering me forgiveness, always seeking to reconcile me to himself, to draw me into ever fuller friendship, enabling me to share this with others.

Monday 15th April **John 6:22–27**

The next day the crowd that had stayed on the other side of the lake saw that there had been only one boat there. They also saw that Jesus had not got into the boat with his disciples, but that his disciples had gone away alone. Then some boats from Tiberias came near the place where they had eaten the bread after the Lord had given thanks. So when the crowd saw that neither Jesus nor his disciples were there, they themselves got into the boats and went to Capernaum looking for Jesus. When they found him on the other side of the lake, they said to him, "Rabbi, when did you come here?" Jesus answered them, "Very truly, I tell you, you are looking for me, not because you saw signs, but because you ate your fill of the loaves. Do not work for the food that perishes, but for the food that endures for eternal life, which the Son of Man will give you."

- As precious as the miracles of Jesus were, as much as they showed the generosity of God, Jesus does not want us to depend only on them. I pray for confidence in Jesus' promise of eternal life.
- Jesus does not separate belief and activity. Here he shows us that belief and trust are works of God. I ask God to help me to make a good act of faith.

Tuesday 16th April **John 6:30–35**

So they said to him, "What sign are you going to give us then, so that we may see it and believe you? What work are you performing? Our ancestors ate the manna in the wilderness; as it is written, 'He gave them bread from heaven to eat.'" Then Jesus said to them, "Very truly, I tell you, it was not Moses who gave you the bread from heaven, but it is my Father who gives you the true bread from heaven. For the bread of God is that which comes down from heaven and gives life to the world." They said to him, "Sir, give us this bread always." Jesus said to them, "I am the bread of life. Whoever comes to me will never be hungry, and whoever believes in me will never be thirsty."

- Jesus is for me bread of life; pleasure, nourishment, sustenance—daily food. I give thanks to God for the daily bread I receive. I pray that I may worry less about the future and try instead to recognize how God feeds me.
- The food that Jesus promises is not for selfish satisfaction but is offered for the world. I bring to my prayer the needs of the world as I know them, praying that people may accept the goodness God offers to them.

Wednesday 17th April **John 6:35–40**

Jesus said to them, "I am the bread of life. Whoever comes to me will never be hungry, and whoever believes in me will never be thirsty. But I said to you that you have seen me and yet do not believe. Everything that the Father gives me will come to me, and anyone who comes to me I will never drive away; for I have come down from heaven, not to do my own will, but the will of him who sent me. And this is the will of him who sent me, that I should lose nothing of all that he has given me, but raise it up on the last day. This is indeed the will of my Father, that all who see the Son and believe in him may have eternal life; and I will raise them up on the last day."

- The whole life of Jesus is a response to the pull, the polar attraction of the Father's will. Remaining completely faithful to the Father is what nourishes and sustains him. When we pray, we seek to find and do the Father's will ourselves, not to bring God round to doing ours.
- In Jesus' life of complete obedience to the Father, we recognize our own call and our true identity as human beings. He has come to draw each one of us to the Father. Everything he says and does is for this purpose. He never drives us away.

Thursday 18th April **John 6:44–51**

Jesus said to the people: "No one can come to me unless drawn by the Father who sent me; and I will raise that person up on the last day. It is written in the prophets: 'They will all be taught by God'; everyone who has listened to the Father and learned from him comes to me. Not that anyone has seen the Father except the one who is from God; he has seen the Father. Very truly, I tell you, whoever believes has eternal life. I am the bread of life. Your ancestors ate the manna in the wilderness, and they died. This is the bread that comes down from heaven, so that one may eat of it and not die. I am the living bread that came down from heaven. Whoever eats of this bread will live for ever; and the bread that I will give for the life of the world is my flesh."

- As blessed as the people in the desert were, even greater blessings are offered to me. I am accompanied on the pilgrimage of my life by the one who feeds me with living bread.
- I am not called to become familiar with Jesus and admire him. I am invited right in to the heart of God.

Friday 19th April **John 6:52–59**

The Jews then disputed among themselves, saying, "How can this man give us his flesh to eat?" So Jesus said to them, "Very truly, I tell you, unless you eat the flesh of the Son of Man and drink his blood, you have no life in you. Those who eat my flesh and drink my blood have eternal life, and I will raise them up on the last day; for my flesh is true food and my blood is true drink. Those who eat my flesh and drink my blood abide in me, and I in them. Just as the living Father sent me, and I live because of the Father, so whoever eats me will live because of me."

- I may recognize the reactions of Jesus' hearers as I listen to others, as I hear myself. Jesus calls me beyond my resistances, giving me not just life but his very being.
- I do not simply think, "What would Jesus do?" but accept that I Jesus lives in me, bringing his life to the world.

Saturday 20th April **John 6:66–69**

Because of his teaching many of his disciples turned back and no longer went about with him. So Jesus asked the twelve, "Do you also wish to go away?" Simon Peter answered him, "Lord, to whom can we go? You have the words of eternal life. We have come to believe and know that you are the Holy One of God."

- The gift of Jesus is the life that underpins our human life. He has become one of us so that we become like him. His words lead us into a quality of life which gives meaning, hope and love in all we do.
- Nobody else can give what Jesus gives—a full meaning of life, seen in the example of his life. Time with him is always time well spent.

Sacred Space

Something to think and pray about each day this week:

Hearing the true voice

The image of the Shepherd is one of the most heart-warming and encouraging in the Bible. Even if the appointed leaders of the people should fail, yet "I myself shall take care of my flock and look after it . . . I myself shall pasture my sheep . . . I shall look for the lost one, bring back the stray, bandage the wounded . . ." (Ezekiel 34:11–16). The Psalmist sings therefore: "The Lord is my shepherd, I shall lack nothing" (Psalm 23:1). And Jesus in the gospel looks out upon us all: "And when he saw the crowds he felt sorry for them because they were harassed and dejected, like sheep without a shepherd" (Matthew 9:36). Further, he says: "I am the Good Shepherd; I know my own and my own know me" (John 10:14).

So, harassed and dejected, or wandering aimlessly, or falling into ravines, there is someone calling out to us, through friends or community, or in the depths of our hearts, and especially in a moment of prayer. It is worthwhile, this continuing Eastertide, to look to Jesus, and see him as the Good Shepherd. Amid all the voices competing for my attention, his voice is clear and true, calling me by name, guiding me along a good way, and leading to safe pasture and to refreshing waters. "By tranquil streams he leads me to restore my spirit" (Psalm 23:2).

The Presence of God
At any time of the day or night we can call on Jesus.
He is always waiting, listening for our call.
What a wonderful blessing.
No phone needed, no emails, just a whisper.

Freedom
I need to close out the noise, to rise above the noise;
The noise that interrupts, that separates,
The noise that isolates.
I need to listen to God again.

Consciousness
Help me, Lord, to be more conscious of your presence.
Teach me to recognize your presence in others.
Fill my heart with gratitude for the times your love
has been shown to me through the care of others.

The Word
I read the Word of God slowly, a few times over, and I listen to what God is saying to me. (Please turn to your scripture on the following pages. Inspiration points are there should you need them. When you are ready, return here to continue.)

Conversation
Do I notice myself reacting as I pray with the Word of God?
Do I feel challenged, comforted, angry?
Imagining Jesus sitting or standing by me,
I speak out my feelings, as one trusted friend to another.

Conclusion
Glory be to the Father, and to the Son, and to the Holy Spirit,
As it was in the beginning, is now and ever shall be,
World without end. Amen

Sunday 21st April,
Fourth Sunday of Easter **John 10:27–30**

Jesus said, "My sheep hear my voice. I know them, and they follow me. I give them eternal life, and they will never perish. No one will snatch them out of my hand. What my Father has given me is greater than all else, and no one can snatch it out of the Father's hand. The Father and I are one."

- To hear the voice of Jesus is to be attuned to his word. We pray in order to become more and more perfectly attuned to his word.
- Jesus is drawn to those who hear him—he brings the nourishing gift of eternal life. He draws his own life from the Father. To follow him is to be drawn into the mystery of their life. This is what happens, in faith, at the heart of our prayer.

Monday 22nd April **John 10:7–10**

So Jesus again said to the Pharisees, "Very truly, I tell you, I am the gate for the sheep. All who came before me are thieves and bandits; but the sheep did not listen to them. I am the gate. Whoever enters by me will be saved, and will come in and go out and find pasture. The thief comes only to steal and kill and destroy. I came that they may have life, and have it abundantly."

- Some time of prayer for reflection is necessary for us to see the influences and attractions that are active in our lives. The "thieves" and "bandits" that would make away with our peace are many but time spent with Jesus helps us to recognize them for what they are.

Tuesday 23rd April **John 10:22–30**

At that time the festival of the Dedication took place in Jerusalem. It was winter, and Jesus was walking in the temple, in the portico of Solomon. So the Jews gathered around him and said to him, "How long will you keep us in suspense? If you are the Messiah, tell us plainly." Jesus answered, "I have told you, and you do not believe. The works that I do in my Father's name testify to me; but you do not believe, because you do not belong to my sheep. My sheep hear my voice. I know them, and they follow me. I give them eternal life, and they will never perish. No one will snatch them out of my hand. What my Father has given me is greater than all else, and no one can snatch it out of the Father's hand. The Father and I are one."

- I take time to receive the assurance that Jesus gives me, to realize that I am secure in the hands of God.
- As the sheep recognizes the voice of its shepherd, I look over these past days, listening for the word of God spoken to me through those around me, through my observations and experiences.

Wednesday 24th April **John 12:44–50**

Then Jesus cried aloud: "Whoever believes in me believes not in me but in him who sent me. And whoever sees me sees him who sent me. I have come as light into the world, so that everyone who believes in me should not remain in the darkness. I do not judge anyone who hears my words and does not keep them, for I came not to judge the world, but to save the world. The one who rejects me and does not receive my word has a judge; on the last day the word that I have spoken will serve as judge, for I have not spoken on my own, but the Father who sent me has himself given me a commandment about what to say and what to speak. And I know that his commandment is eternal life. What I speak, therefore, I speak just as the Father has told me."

- Jesus comes as light, making clear the reality of God. I let the light of Jesus reach any dark are shadowy areas in me so that I may be saved.
- Jesus knew he spoke for the Father. He trusts me, in turn, to act in his name. I pray now that I may receive light from God and that I may pass it on to the world around me.

Thursday 25th April,
St Mark, Evangelist **1 Peter 5:5–14**

And all of you must clothe yourselves with humility in your dealings with one another, for "God opposes the proud, but gives grace to the humble." Humble yourselves therefore under the mighty hand of God, so that he may exalt you in due time. Cast all your anxiety on him, because he cares for you. Discipline yourselves; keep alert. Like a roaring lion your adversary the devil prowls around, looking for someone to devour. Resist him, steadfast in your faith, for you know that your brothers and sisters throughout the world are undergoing the same kinds of suffering. And after you have suffered for a little while, the God of all grace, who has called you to his eternal glory in Christ, will himself restore, support, strengthen, and establish you. To him be the power for ever and ever. Amen. Through Silvanus, whom I consider a faithful brother, I have written this short letter to encourage you, and to testify that this is the true grace of God. Stand fast in it. Your sister church in Babylon, chosen together with you, sends you greetings; and so does my son Mark. Greet one another with a kiss of love.

- This is a powerful statement on the Christian's pastoral ministry. Let me sit quietly with it today, absorbing what it has to say to me. I pray that I may go on my way, refreshed and strengthened.

Friday 26th April **John 14:1–6**

Jesus said to his disciples, "Do not let your hearts be troubled. Believe in God, believe also in me. In my Father's house there are many dwelling places. If it were not so, would I have told you that I go to prepare a place for you? And if I go and prepare a place for you, I will come again and will take you to myself, so that where I am, there you may be also. And you know the way to the place where I am going." Thomas said to him, "Lord, we do not know where you are going. How can we know the way?" Jesus said to him, "I am the way, and the truth, and the life. No one comes to the Father except through me.

- As I listen to Jesus I hear him say, "Peace be with you", "Do not worry", and now, "Do not let your heart be troubled." I speak to Jesus confidently, describing what it is that weighs me down, listening for his answer as he calls me back to a new perspective.

- I sometimes feel like Thomas, not sure of the way I am going. Jesus reminds me that I am not setting out on my own, but travel with him who is the way.

Saturday 27th April **John 14:7–9**

Jesus said to Thomas, "If you know me, you will know my Father also. From now on you do know him and have seen him." Philip said to him, "Lord, show us the Father, and we will be satisfied." Jesus said to him, "Have I been with you all this time, Philip, and you still do not know me? Whoever has seen me has seen the Father."

- Philip wanted something more. Jesus pointed out to him that what he had been given was sufficient. He needed only to let his experience sink in.
- Jesus took time apart to be with his Father, always returning to serve the crowds, to lift spirits and bring healing. Prayer unites my heart with the heart of Jesus, draws me into the very life of God and encourages me to be God's presence in my world.

Something to think and pray about each day this week:

Looking to the Risen Christ

While Jesus describes himself as the "Good Shepherd" (John 10:14), he also says, "I am the Way, the Truth and the Life' (14:6). All these titles in fact go together, along with "I am the Bread of Life" (6:47), "I am the Light of the world" (8:12) and "I am the Resurrection" (11:25). What great stability our lives are given, therefore, by looking to him, and hearing him speak those words! We can look in many different places, for love, for goodness, truth, and beauty. If we search with earnest, discerning hearts, so much in life's experience can be enriching and a source for fulfillment. But, as Ignatius says towards the end of his *Spiritual Exercies,* all good things come "from above" (*de arriba*), from their origin in God, as waters flow from their source, and rays of light from the sun.

So, continuing this Eastertide, we can look to the source of everything in the Risen Christ, who manifests himself to us in very many different ways—in the beauty of a face, in friendship, in the blue sky, or a star-lit night, in art or poetry, or simple relaxation. And also in the heart's prayer, asking for guidance, or giving thanks and praise; God always there for us, "whose beauty is past change: Praise him" (Gerard Manley Hopkins).

The Presence of God
As I sit here, the beating of my heart,
the ebb and flow of my breathing, the movements of my mind
are all signs of God's ongoing creation of me.
I pause for a moment, and become aware
of this presence of God within me.

Freedom
I will ask God's help,
to be free from my own preoccupations,
to be open to God in this time of prayer,
to come to love and serve him more.

Consciousness
Knowing that God loves me unconditionally,
I look honestly over the last day, its events and my feelings.
Do I have something to be grateful for? Then I give thanks.
Is there something I am sorry for? Then I ask forgiveness.

The Word
I take my time to read the Word of God, slowly, a few times, allowing myself to dwell on anything that strikes me. (Please turn to your scripture on the following pages. Inspiration points are there should you need them. When you are ready, return here to continue.)

Conversation
Remembering that I am still in God's presence,
I imagine Jesus himself standing or sitting beside me,
and say whatever is on my mind, whatever is in my heart,
speaking as one friend to another.

Conclusion
Glory be to the Father, and to the Son, and to the Holy Spirit,
As it was in the beginning, is now and ever shall be,
World without end. Amen

Sunday 28th April,
Fifth Sunday of Easter **John 13:31–33, 34–35**

When Judas had gone out, Jesus said, "Now the Son of Man has been glorified, and God has been glorified in him. If God has been glorified in him, God will also glorify him in himself and will glorify him at once. Little children, I am with you only a little longer. You will look for me; and as I said to the Jews so now I say to you, 'Where I am going, you cannot come.' I give you a new commandment, that you love one another. Just as I have loved you, you also should love one another. By this everyone will know that you are my disciples, if you have love for one another."

- I ask God for a greater desire to go where Jesus has gone, to live as he lived, to love as he loved. I realize the cost, but I know that it is only in giving glory to God that I can become the person God made me to be.
- I imagine God looking on the world, with all its multitude of people who love and serve each other in so many different ways. I imagine all the Christian communities that gather to worship today and pray that they may be seen to be disciples of Jesus by the love they show.

Monday 29th April **John 14:21–26**

Jesus said to his disciples: "They who have my commandments and keep them are those who love me; and those who love me will be loved by my Father, and I will love them and reveal myself to them." Judas (not Iscariot) said to him, "Lord, how is it that you will reveal yourself to us, and not to the world?" Jesus answered him, "Those who love me will keep my word, and my Father will love them, and we will come to them and make our home with them. Whoever does not love me does not keep my words; and the word that you hear is not mine, but is from the Father who sent me. I have said these things to you while I am still with you. The Advocate, the Holy Spirit, whom the Father will send in my name, will teach you everything, and remind you of all that I have said to you."

- These Easter days recreate the waiting of the early apostles, their anticipation of the coming of God's Spirit. I think of the blessings I already enjoy and consider what enrichment God may have in mind for me this Pentecost.
- The Holy Spirit is already active in my life when I am reminded of God's word to me, when I am encouraged to act as Jesus did. I recognize that God's Spirit already moves in me as I pray that I might yield to it more.

Tuesday 30th April **John 14:27, 31**

Jesus said to his disciples, "Peace I leave with you; my peace I give to you. I do not give to you as the world gives. Do not let your hearts be troubled, and do not let them be afraid. Rise, let us be on our way."

- Jesus blesses me with his peace. It makes me feel reassured and secure. The peace that Jesus gives, however, is followed by an invitation to get up and go.

Wednesday 1st May **John 15:1–5**

Jesus said to his disciples, "I am the true vine, and my Father is the vine-grower. He removes every branch in me that bears no fruit. Every branch that bears fruit he prunes to make it bear more fruit. You have already been cleansed by the word that I have spoken to you. Abide in me as I abide in you. Just as the branch cannot bear fruit by itself unless it abides in the vine, neither can you unless you abide in me. I am the vine, you are the branches. Those who abide in me and I in them bear much fruit, because apart from me you can do nothing."

- It is easy for me to think of my prayer as my time, my effort. I take some time to dwell with what Jesus tells me, to listen to him say, "I abide in you."
- The evidence that Jesus lives in me is in the works I do, the fruit I bear. I recognize the good fruit and give thanks for the source from which it comes, through me.

Thursday 2nd May **John 15:9–11**

Jesus said to his disciples, "As the Father has loved me, so I have loved you; abide in my love. If you keep my commandments, you will abide in my love, just as I have kept my Father's commandments and abide in his love. I have said these things to you so that my joy may be in you, and that your joy may be complete."

- My relationship with Jesus is rooted in my prayer and its fruit is evident in how I act. As I abide in Jesus' love, my words and actions reflect who I know myself to be.
- I may recognize my connection with Jesus when I serve others. I am called, not just to be dutiful, to be joyful. I thank God for the joy that I find in life and ask Jesus to make that joy complete.

Friday 3rd May,
Ss Philip and James, Apostles **John 14:8–10**

Philip said to Jesus, "Lord, show us the Father, and we will be satisfied." Jesus said to him, "Have I been with you all this time, Philip, and you still do not know me? Whoever has seen me has seen the Father. How can you say, 'Show us the Father'? Do you not believe that I am in the Father and the Father is in me?"

- Can I see myself in Philip? One more thing and I will be satisfied. Jesus reminds him and me that we have enough already.
- Jesus and the Father are so united that I am drawn into the knowledge and love of God as I come to know and love Jesus. Jesus desires nothing less for me; he wishes to draw me deeply into the very life of God.

Saturday 4th May **John 15:18–20**

Jesus said to his disciples: "If the world hates you, be aware that it hated me before it hated you. If you belonged to the world, the world would love you as its own. Because you do not belong to the world, but I have chosen you out of the world—therefore the world hates you. Remember the word that I said to you, 'Servants are not greater than their master.' If they persecuted me, they will persecute you; if they kept my word, they will keep yours also."

- Jesus recognized that not all of his words were kept; he did not try to indoctrinate, coerce or to force his word. I ask God to strengthen my faith, that I may do what I can and accept that it may be the choice of others whether to heed or not.
- There is a way of being—"the world"—that is not the way of God. I consider where I need to resist being attracted by this other way.

Something to think and pray about each day this week:

Drawing towards God

The church draws closer to the celebration of Ascension Day. When Jesus ascended, beyond the disciple's sight, he did so to reinforce the gift of faith within them. The new reality of his resurrected life meant he was beyond the ordinary way we human beings interact with one another. "Do not cling to me," he said to Mary of Magdala, in the Easter garden scene (John 20:17). He could no longer be contacted and looked upon in the ways possible during the days of his earthly ministry. Now, *faith* becomes the medium of contact and relationship with him. We might wish for that bodily contact with him, which we value so much, and can have in varying degrees with the people around us. But our *faith* expands, and is enriched. Jesus, beyond our sight and contact, is *nearer* than before and yet *above* us, drawing us into the heavenly realms where he lives unceasingly. "Since you have been raised up to be with Christ, you must look for the things that are above, where Christ is, sitting at God's right hand" (Colossians 3:1).

A great world of mystery surrounds us therefore, the living world of God, intersecting with this earthly life of ours. Faith provides us now with an immense unlimited horizon, which is yet intimate and personal. For Christ, through his Holy Spirit, dwells in our hearts, every moment of every day.

The Presence of God

Dear Jesus, today I call on you in a special way.
Mostly I come asking for favors.
Today I'd like just to be in Your presence.
Let my heart respond to Your Love.

Freedom

'I am free.'
When I look at these words in writing
They seem to create in me a feeling of awe.
Yes, a wonderful feeling of freedom.
Thank You, God.

Consciousness

Lord, You gave me the night to rest in sleep.
In my waking hours may I not forget your goodness to me.
Guide me to share your blessings with others.

The Word

I read the Word of God slowly, a few times over, and I listen to what God is saying to me. (Please turn to your scripture on the following pages. Inspiration points are there should you need them. When you are ready, return here to continue.)

Conversation

Dear Jesus, I can open up my heart to you.
I can tell you everything that troubles me.
I know You care about all the concerns in my life.
Teach me to live in the knowledge
that You who care for me today,
will care for me tomorrow and all the days of my life.

Conclusion

Glory be to the Father, and to the Son, and to the Holy Spirit,
As it was in the beginning, is now and ever shall be,
World without end. Amen

Sunday 5th May,
Sixth Sunday of Easter **John 14:23–27**

Jesus answered him, "Those who love me will keep my word, and my Father will love them, and we will come to them and make our home with them. Whoever does not love me does not keep my words; and the word that you hear is not mine, but is from the Father who sent me. I have said these things to you while I am still with you. But the Advocate, the Holy Spirit, whom the Father will send in my name, will teach you everything, and remind you of all that I have said to you. Peace I leave with you; my peace I give to you. I do not give to you as the world gives. Do not let your hearts be troubled, and do not let them be afraid."

- Jesus' heart was like still, calm water that is both transparent and reflecting. He brings us to understand the wonder of God.
- I leave my troubles before Jesus and hear him say, "Peace I leave with you." I resist the temptation to carry my burdens alone as I consider what I might leave before him.

Monday 6th May **John 15:26–16:4**

Jesus said to his disciples, "When the Advocate comes, whom I will send to you from the Father, the Spirit of truth who comes from the Father, he will testify on my behalf. You also are to testify because you have been with me from the beginning. I have said these things to you to keep you from stumbling. They will put you out of the synagogues. Indeed, an hour is coming when those who kill you will think that by doing so they are offering worship to God. And they will do this because they have not known the Father or me. But I have said these things to you so that when their hour comes you may remember that I told you about them. I did not say these things to you from the beginning, because I was with you."

- God gives us gifts for ourselves but they are not private property. Jesus asks us to give witness. I think of how I might do this and ask for the help I need.
- Aware of how much being a witness to the gospel costs, I pray for the strength to remember these words of Jesus.

Tuesday 7th May **John 16:5–11**

Jesus said to his disciples, "But now I am going to him who sent me; yet none of you asks me, 'Where are you going?' But because I have said these things to you, sorrow has filled your hearts. Nevertheless I tell you the truth: it is to your advantage that I go away, for if I do not go away, the Advocate will not come to you; but if I go, I will send him to you. And when he comes, he will prove the world wrong about sin and righteousness and judgement: about sin, because they do not believe in me; about righteousness, because I am going to the Father and you will see me no longer; about judgement, because the ruler of this world has been condemned."

- Jesus answers the question that disciples did not ask. Sometimes my spoken prayers seem not to be answered as Jesus addresses the questions that may be deeper in my heart.
- Jesus has the good of the disciples at heart; his presence, his words and his departing are all for their good. Help me, Jesus, to see how you work always for my growth.

Wednesday 8th May **Acts 17:22–28**

Then Paul stood in front of the Areopagus and said, "Athenians, I see how extremely religious you are in every way. For as I went through the city and looked carefully at the objects of your worship, I found among them an altar with the inscription, 'To an unknown god.' What therefore you worship as unknown, this I proclaim to you. The God who made the world and everything in it, he who is Lord of heaven and earth, does not live in shrines made by human hands, nor is he served by human hands, as though he needed anything, since he himself gives to all mortals life and breath and all things. From one ancestor he made all nations to inhabit the whole earth, and he allotted the times of their existence and the boundaries of the places where they would live, so that they would search for God and perhaps grope for him and find him—though indeed he is not far from each one of us. For 'In him we live and move and have our being'; as even some of your own poets have said, 'For we too are his offspring.'"

- Paul is facing the most exclusive Athenian court, the Areopagus, in the most learned city in the world. Where can he find the words for his message? He starts with what he knows of their searching—for an unknown God.
- Loving God, you are no longer unknown. I know you, through Jesus. Give me the words to make you known to others.

Thursday 9th May **John 16:16–20**

Jesus said to his disciples, "A little while, and you will no longer see me, and again a little while, and you will see me." Then some of his disciples said to one another, "What does he mean by saying to us, 'A little while, and you will no longer see me, and again a little while, and you will see me'; and 'Because I am going to the Father'?" They said, "What does he mean by this 'a little while'? We do not know what he is talking about." Jesus knew that they wanted to ask him, so he said to them, "Are you discussing among yourselves what I meant when I said, 'A little while, and you will no longer see me, and again a little while, and you will see me'? Very truly, I tell you, you will weep and mourn, but the world will rejoice; you will have pain, but your pain will turn into joy."

- What Jesus said was not always understood by the disciples and, sometimes, their talking to each other seemed only to give rise to more questions.
- To be a follower of Jesus is to have feelings that seem to be at odds with the world. I pray for the patience that I may need.

Friday 10th May **John 16:20–23**

Jesus said to his disciples, "Very truly, I tell you, you will weep and mourn, but the world will rejoice; you will have pain, but your pain will turn into joy. When a woman is in labor, she has pain, because her hour has come. But when her child is born, she no longer remembers the anguish because of the joy of having brought a human being into the world. So you have pain now; but I will see you again, and your hearts will rejoice, and no one will take your joy from you. On that day you will ask nothing of me. Very truly, I tell you, if you ask anything of the Father in my name, he will give it to you."

- Perhaps I already know what it is like to ask nothing of Jesus, recognizing that there are times when I am content.
- I acknowledge any pain that may be in my life and ask God for wisdom and healing.

Saturday 11th May **John 16:23–24**

Jesus said to his disciples, "Very truly, I tell you, if you ask anything of the Father in my name, he will give it to you. Until now you have not asked for anything in my name. Ask and you will receive, so that your joy may be complete."

- If I can recall prayers that I made the past, I may be able to recognize how they were answered. I ask God to bless my recollection and perception.
- Jesus draws me right into his life, fully and generously offering me the relationship with his Father that he has.

Something to think and pray about each day this week:

Bringing all together

Again, our prayer can be nourished by the theme of the Ascension. The Acts of the Apostles tells us that Jesus *ascended*, went above his disciples, and out of their sight (Acts 1:1–11). Using that spatial image, we can realize that he is in the divine world *above* us. The seventeenth century Welsh poet Henry Vaughan wrote about all this in a mystical way, "My soul, there is a country / Far beyond the stars, / Where stands a wingèd sentry / All skilful in the wars: / There above noise and danger / Sweet Peace sits crowned with smiles, / And One born in a manger / Commands the beauteous files. / He is thy gracious friend / And—O my soul, awake!—/ Did in pure love descend / To die here for thy sake . . . Leave then thy foolish ranges / For none can thee secure, / But one who never changes, / Thy God, thy life, thy cure."

Vaughan's consoling lines are beautiful. But, to complement what he says, it is good to realize that the living world of God, even if in poetic language "far beyond the stars," is also wonderfully *entering into* this tangible and temporal world of ours. The two worlds intersect. And so Jesus, although gone from our sight, is all the more closely bound to us and *with* us, involved here and now in our living and in our prayer. Although ascended, and invisible, Jesus is intimately present among us, as "our God, our life, our cure."

The Presence of God

I remind myself that, as I sit here now,
God is gazing on me with love and holding me in being.
I pause for a moment and think of this.

Freedom

I need to close out the noise, to rise above the noise;
The noise that interrupts, that separates,
The noise that isolates.
I need to listen to God again.

Consciousness

In God's loving presence I unwind the past day,
starting from now and looking back, moment by moment.
I gather in all the goodness and light, in gratitude.
I attend to the shadows and what they say to me,
seeking healing, courage, forgiveness.

The Word

I take my time to read the Word of God, slowly, a few times, allowing myself to dwell on anything that strikes me. (Please turn to your scripture on the following pages. Inspiration points are there should you need them. When you are ready, return here to continue.)

Conversation

Do I notice myself reacting as I pray with the Word of God?
Do I feel challenged, comforted, angry?
Imagining Jesus sitting or standing by me,
I speak out my feelings, as one trusted friend to another.

Conclusion

Glory be to the Father, and to the Son, and to the Holy Spirit,
As it was in the beginning, is now and ever shall be,
World without end. Amen

Sunday 12th May,
Ascension **Luke 24:46–53**

Jesus said to the disciples: "Thus it is written, that the Messiah is to suffer and to rise from the dead on the third day, and that repentance and forgiveness of sins is to be proclaimed in his name to all nations, beginning from Jerusalem. You are witnesses of these things. And see, I am sending upon you what my Father promised; so stay here in the city until you have been clothed with power from on high." Then he led them out as far as Bethany, and, lifting up his hands, he blessed them. While he was blessing them, he withdrew from them and was carried up into heaven. And they worshipped him, and returned to Jerusalem with great joy; and they were continually in the temple blessing God.

- Even as he leaves the disciples and sends them as witnesses Jesus reminds them that he had to suffer, die and rise. As I face the world into which Jesus sends me I acknowledge that the marks of his suffering will identify me as his disciple.
- Jesus promises that his disciples will be clothed with power from on high. I think of those gifts of the Spirit that are necessary for me in my life. I pray for them and prepare to receive them.

Monday 13th May **John 16:29–33**

The disciples said to Jesus, "Yes, now you are speaking plainly, not in any figure of speech! Now we know that you know all things, and do not need to have anyone question you; by this we believe that you came from God." Jesus answered them, "Do you now believe? The hour is coming, indeed it has come, when you will be scattered, each one to his home, and you will leave me alone. Yet I am not alone because the Father is with me. I have said this to you, so that in me you may have peace. In the world you face persecution. But take courage; I have conquered the world!"

- Just as the disciples note their achievement, Jesus offers them another challenge. I take care about how I measure my progress.
- Where am I rooted? Do I stand firmly with Jesus, risking persecution, hazarding being thought odd?

Tuesday 14th May,
St Matthias, Apostle **John 15:15–17**

Jesus said to his disciples, "I do not call you servants any longer, because the servant does not know what the master is doing; but I have called you friends, because I have made known to you everything that I have heard from my Father. You did not choose me but I chose you. And I appointed you to go and bear fruit, fruit that will last, so that the Father will give you whatever you ask him in my name. I am giving you these commands so that you may love one another."

- I pray that I may accept the closeness of relationship to which Jesus invites me. I know myself unworthy to be a servant yet he calls me "friend."
- It is easy to come to think of religion and faith as being matters of accident, choice and lifestyle. I am reminded today that it is God who has chosen me. I humbly accept that I have been chosen and appointed by one who loves me.

Wednesday 15th May **John 17:11–19**

Jesus said, "And now I am no longer in the world, but they are in the world, and I am coming to you. Holy Father, protect them in your name that you have given me, so that they may be one, as we are one. While I was with them, I protected them in your name that you have given me. I guarded them, and not one of them was lost except the one destined to be lost, so that the scripture might be fulfilled. But now I am coming to you, and I speak these things in the world so that they may have my joy made complete in themselves. I have given them your word, and the world has hated them because they do not belong to the world, just as I do not belong to the world. I am not asking you to take them out of the world, but I ask you to protect them from the evil one. They do not belong to the world, just as I do not belong to the world. Sanctify them in the truth; your word is truth. As you have sent me into the world, so I have sent them into the world. And for their sakes I sanctify myself, so that they also may be sanctified in truth."

- The "world" has contradictory meanings; it points to all of the beautiful reality created by God and it describes what runs counter to the life of the Spirit. As I give thanks to God for all that I enjoy, I ask that no created thing may distract me.

- I allow myself to be drawn into a realization that Jesus brings me before the Father, that, even before I think of praying, my name is in the heart of God.

Thursday 16th May **John 17:20–21**

Jesus looked up to heaven and said, "Father, I ask not only on behalf of these, but also on behalf of those who will believe in me through their word, that they may all be one. As you, Father, are in me and I am in you, may they also be in us, so that the world may believe that you have sent me."

- What Jesus asks for us is what he sought for himself: unity with God. As I am invited into this relationship, I consider what it might cost me and I ask for the freedom I need.
- Jesus wants his disciples to live in such a way that the work of God is evident in them. Can I respond to this call today?

Friday 17th May **John 21:17–19**

Jesus said to him, "Feed my sheep. Very truly, I tell you, when you were younger, you used to fasten your own belt and to go wherever you wished. But when you grow old, you will stretch out your hands, and someone else will fasten a belt around you and take you where you do not wish to go." (He said this to indicate the kind of death by which he would glorify God.) After this he said to him, "Follow me."

- I pray for the elderly: that they may be given the grace to know when to yield to the leading of others; I think of how I need to let go graciously.
- I ask that I never be a disciple led only by habit or memory, but that I may hear often the voice of Jesus saying, "Follow me."

Saturday 18th May **John 21:20–25**

Peter turned and saw the disciple whom Jesus loved following them; he was the one who had reclined next to Jesus at the supper and had said, "Lord, who is it that is going to betray you?" When Peter saw him, he said to Jesus, "Lord, what about him?" Jesus said to him, "If it is my will that he remain until I come, what is that to you? Follow me!" So the rumor spread in the community that this disciple would not die. Yet Jesus did not say to him that he would not die, but, "If it is my will that he remain until I come, what is that to you?" This is the disciple who is testifying to these things and has written them, and we know that his testimony is true. But there are also many other things that Jesus did; if every one of them were written down, I suppose that the world itself could not contain the books that would be written.

- I listen quietly to these words which conclude St. John's Gospel, this Easter testimony from the disciple "whom Jesus loved."
- Amidst the noise and busyness of my day, can I listen again for the voice of Jesus saying to me, "Follow me."

Something to think and pray about each day this week:

Come, Holy Spirit

The completion of the Paschal Mystery, Christ's dying and rising, is celebrated at the feast of Pentecost. Historically, the disciples, while at prayer in Jerusalem, with Mary in their midst, experienced the fire and strength of the Holy Spirit coming into their hearts and lives (Acts 2:1–13). God's deepest life came within them, therefore, giving them light and courage, enabling them to go forth and testify in Christ's name to all peoples.

Traditionally, hymns such as the *Veni Sancte Spiritus* and the *Veni Creator* have expressed the desires of Christians to be filled and renewed by the Holy Spirit. And *this* Pentecost, we can pray, in whatever way we are inspired, for that divine presence to be within us now, enabling Christ to be always in our thoughts and actions. "Come, Holy Spirit, guide and strengthen us. Drive from our lives all that is false, burn out the roots of selfishness. Teach us instead to live with your best gifts of truth and care. Imprint upon our hearts the form of Christ—and raise us up, alive in him, so we can reach beyond the limits of our fearfulness. Expand our hearts and minds, to see what is divinely good throughout the world. Breathe in us, therefore—give us the courage that we need, so we are truly all God wishes us to be."

The Presence of God
'I stand at the door and knock,' says the Lord.
What a wonderful privilege
that the Lord of all creation desires to come to me.
I welcome His presence.

Freedom
Lord, grant me the grace to be free from the excesses of this life.
Let me not get caught up with the desire for wealth.
Keep my heart and mind free to love and serve you.

Consciousness
'There is a time and place for everything,' as the saying goes.
Lord, grant that I may always desire
to spend time in your presence. To hear your call.

The Word
God speaks to each one of us individually. I need to listen to what he is saying to me. (Please turn to your scripture on the following pages. Inspiration points are there should you need them. When you are ready, return here to continue.)

Conversation
The gift of speech is a wonderful gift.
May I use this gift with kindness.
May I be slow to utter harsh words,
hurtful words, and words spoken in anger.

Conclusion
Glory be to the Father, and to the Son, and to the Holy Spirit,
As it was in the beginning, is now and ever shall be,
World without end. Amen

Sunday 19th May,
Pentecost **John 14:23–26**

Jesus said to the disciples, "Those who love me will keep my word, and my Father will love them, and we will come to them and make our home with them. Whoever does not love me does not keep my words; and the word that you hear is not mine, but is from the Father who sent me. I have said these things to you while I am still with you. But the Advocate, the Holy Spirit, whom the Father will send in my name, will teach you everything, and remind you of all that I have said to you."

- When I recall the words of Jesus and am reminded of what he said, the Holy Spirit is at work.
- I pray that I may be more aware of the quiet working of God's Spirit in my life. I pray that my thoughts, inspirations and desires be open to the prompting of the Advocate.

Monday 20th May **Mark 9:17–24**

Someone from the crowd answered Jesus, "Teacher, I brought you my son; he has a spirit that makes him unable to speak; and whenever it seizes him, it dashes him down; and he foams and grinds his teeth and becomes rigid; and I asked your disciples to cast it out, but they could not do so." Jesus said: "Bring him to me." And they brought the boy to him. When the spirit saw him, immediately it convulsed the boy, and he fell on the ground and rolled about, foaming at the mouth. Jesus asked the father, "How long has this been happening to him?" And he said, "From childhood. It has often cast him into the fire and into the water, to destroy him; but if you are able to do anything, have pity on us and help us." Jesus said to him, "If you are able! All things can be done for the one who believes." Immediately the father of the child cried out, "I believe; help my unbelief!"

- There seems to be something in the spirits that recognized Jesus, realizing that a new way of living was in prospect.
- Jesus listens to the deep desires of those who come to him in their need. He recognizes faith and encourages it. I take time to express myself to Jesus and ask him to strengthen my faith.

Tuesday 21st May **Mark 9:30–37**

They went on from there and passed through Galilee. He did not want anyone to know it; for he was teaching his disciples, saying to them, "The Son of Man is to be betrayed into human hands, and they will kill him, and three days after being killed, he will rise again." But they did not understand what he was saying and were afraid to ask him. Then they came to Capernaum; and when he was in the house he asked them, "What were you arguing about on the way?" But they were silent, for on the way they had argued with one another who was the greatest. He sat down, called the twelve, and said to them, "Whoever wants to be first must be last of all and servant of all." Then he took a little child and put it among them; and taking it in his arms, he said to them, "Whoever welcomes one such child in my name welcomes me, and whoever welcomes me welcomes not me but the one who sent me."

- Maybe the disciples were afraid to ask Jesus because they didn't want to know anything more about a future which would involve death and resurrection. The trusting nature of a child may have been an invitation to them to trust in Jesus even though the future was unknown.
- In prayer we can ask for the gift of this sort of trust for our own future.

Wednesday 22nd May **Mark 9:38–40**

John said to Jesus, "Teacher, we saw someone casting out demons in your name, and we tried to stop him, because he was not following us." But Jesus said, "Do not stop him; for no one who does a deed of power in my name will be able soon afterwards to speak evil of me. Whoever is not against us is for us."

- Prayer brings us in touch with all in the human race, a sort of mystical communion with all God's children. Different people follow Christ and relate to God in different ways. Jesus looks for the committed person, and sees discipleship in many ways.

- Maybe some of our prayer time might be to pray for all who are committed to goodness, faith and justice in the world, no matter in what way they show this.

Thursday 23rd May **Mark 9:45–48**

Jesus said to his disciples, "If your foot causes you to stumble, cut it off; it is better for you to enter life lame than to have two feet and to be thrown into hell. And if your eye causes you to stumble, tear it out; it is better for you to enter the kingdom of God with one eye than to have two eyes and to be thrown into hell, where their worm never dies, and the fire is never quenched.

- These are tough sayings of Jesus about leading others astray or harming others' faith in God.
- Prayer purifies our motivation and our style of living. The fruits of prayer are seen in love, and in our commitment to helping others, not hindering them, on their path to goodness and to love. Our commitment will often be tested.

Friday 24th May **Mark 10:1–9**

Jesus left that place and went to the region of Judea and beyond the Jordan. And crowds again gathered around him; and, as was his custom, he again taught them. Some Pharisees came, and to test him they asked, "Is it lawful for a man to divorce his wife?" He answered them, "What did Moses command you?" They said, "Moses allowed a man to write a certificate of dismissal and to divorce her." But Jesus said to them, "Because of your hardness of heart he wrote this commandment for you. But from the beginning of creation, 'God made them male and female.' 'For this reason a man shall leave his father and mother and be joined to his wife, and the two shall become one flesh.' So they are no longer two, but one flesh. Therefore what God has joined together, let no one separate."

- Maybe our prayer today could be for marriage. If you are married, offer your love and your concern for your spouse to God—ask for God's help in your love.

- We might all pray for those who find their marriages difficult or are close to breakdown. We can bring to our prayer those about to be married, giving thanks for the gifts we receive through the married love of others.

Saturday 25th May **Mark 10:13–16**

People were bringing little children to Jesus in order that he might touch them; and the disciples spoke sternly to them. But when Jesus saw this, he was indignant and said to them, "Let the little children come to me; do not stop them; for it is to such as these that the kingdom of God belongs. Truly I tell you, whoever does not receive the kingdom of God as a little child will never enter it." And he took them up in his arms, laid his hands on them, and blessed them.

- I am like a child in the arms of Jesus; I want to trust him with my life; I want him to be close to me in joys and sorrows. I ask him for this, and ask it for all who are in my circle of life.
- Jesus wants closeness to each of us, as we want a close friendship with him. Let the child in me trust, ask, and simply enjoy being love by him.

Something to think and pray about each day this week:

The endless love of God

We celebrate now the feast of the Most Holy Trinity. It is a mystery, belief in which took many centuries to unfold. And we ourselves can find it a great challenge, to acquire some partial but faith-filled understanding of how our God is Trinitarian. That is, we strive to look to God as three Persons in unity, encompassed in divinely-charged and endless love, yet "emptied" out for us in humblest care and vulnerability. Ignatius of Loyola, for instance, saw the Most Holy Trinity in the form of three musical keys, producing a single harmony. There is indeed music in God, a threefold harmony, whose melody can be within our hearts.

And in Moscow, a century before, Andrei Rublev had painted the wonderful icon of the Trinity, based on the account of the three persons who came to visit Abraham and Sarah by the oak of Mamre (Genesis 18). In that great portrait, we are being invited by the three divine persons to share the table of their hospitality, which is the Eucharistic nourishment of their love, poured out for us in the Second Person, the beloved child, who came among us as Jesus.

At this moment, in our own personal moment of prayer, we are being drawn right now within the mystery of eternal and self-emptying Trinitarian love. We are being transformed there, as Father, Son and Spirit enable us to share intimately in their divine life.

The Presence of God
What is present to me is what has a hold on my becoming.
I reflect on the presence of God always there in love,
amidst the many things that have a hold on me.
I pause and pray that I may let God
affect my becoming in this precise moment.

Freedom
There are very few people
who realize what God would make of them
if they abandoned themselves into his hands,
and let themselves be formed by his grace. (St Ignatius)
I ask for the grace to trust myself totally to God's love.

Consciousness
In the presence of my loving Creator,
I look honestly at my feelings over the last day,
the highs, the lows and the level ground.
Can I see where the Lord has been present?

The Word
God speaks to each one of us individually. I need to listen to what he is saying to me. (Please turn to your scripture on the following pages. Inspiration points are there should you need them. When you are ready, return here to continue.)

Conversation
What is stirring in me as I pray?
Am I consoled, troubled, left cold?
I imagine Jesus himself standing or sitting at my side,
and share my feelings with him.

Conclusion
Glory be to the Father, and to the Son, and to the Holy Spirit,
As it was in the beginning, is now and ever shall be,
World without end. Amen

Sunday 26th May,
Trinity Sunday **John 16:12–15**

Jesus said to the disciples, "I still have many things to say to you, but you cannot bear them now. When the Spirit of truth comes, he will guide you into all the truth; for he will not speak on his own, but will speak whatever he hears, and he will declare to you the things that are to come. He will glorify me, because he will take what is mine and declare it to you. All that the Father has is mine. For this reason I said that he will take what is mine and declare it to you."

- Jesus wants to draw me into the life of God. The mystery of the Holy Trinity reminds me that God holds me in being, saves me and makes me holy.
- Jesus spoke these words at the Last Supper, as he gathered with his disciples, sharing life with them. His words and actions comforted and strengthened them in ways that only the Holy Spirit might help them to understand.

Monday 27th May **Mark 10:17–27**

As he was setting out on a journey, a man ran up and knelt before him, and asked him, "Good Teacher, what must I do to inherit eternal life?" Jesus said to him, "Why do you call me good? No one is good but God alone. You know the commandments: 'You shall not murder; You shall not commit adultery; You shall not steal; You shall not bear false witness; You shall not defraud; Honor your father and mother.'" He said to him, "Teacher, I have kept all these since my youth." Jesus, looking at him, loved him and said, "You lack one thing; go, sell what you own, and give the money to the poor, and you will have treasure in heaven; then come, follow me." When he heard this, he was shocked and went away grieving, for he had many possessions. Then Jesus looked around and said to his disciples, "How hard it will be for those who have wealth to enter the kingdom of God!"

- Have you ever been sad because you didn't do something good that you could have done? The visit to a sick or lonely person

postponed, the help not given to someone in great financial need, the prayer-time not given, the failure to listen to your children or people close to us—many ways in which we could, without too much difficulty, have said a "yes" to love.
- This is something like the feeling of the rich man when he walked away with his wealth and his sadness. Let that be part of prayer today.

Tuesday 28th May **Mark 10:28–30**

Peter began to say to him, "Look, we have left everything and followed you." Jesus said, "Truly I tell you, there is no one who has left house or brothers or sisters or mother or father or children or fields, for my sake and for the sake of the good news, who will not receive a hundredfold now in this age—houses, brothers and sisters, mothers and children, and fields, with persecutions—and in the age to come eternal life."

- What God offers to us, and what Jesus offers to his disciples, is a gift of God, not our right. Whatever place we think we have with God, is God's to give.
- Pray in thanks that all of us belong to God.

Wednesday 29th May **Mark 10:32–40**

They were on the road, going up to Jerusalem, and Jesus was walking ahead of them; they were amazed, and those who followed were afraid. He took the twelve aside again and began to tell them what was to happen to him, saying, "See, we are going up to Jerusalem, and the Son of Man will be handed over to the chief priests and the scribes, and they will condemn him to death; then they will hand him over to the Gentiles; they will mock him, and spit upon him, and flog him, and kill him; and after three days he will rise again." James and John, the sons of Zebedee, came forward to him and said to him, "Teacher, we want you to do for us whatever we ask of you." And he said to them, "What is it you want me to do for you?" And they said to him, "Grant us to sit, one at your right hand and one at your left, in your glory." But Jesus said to them, "You do not know what you are asking. Are you able to drink the cup that I drink, or be baptized with the baptism that I am baptized with?" They replied, "We are able." Then Jesus said to them, "The cup that I drink you will drink; and with the baptism with which I am baptized, you will be baptized; but to sit at my right hand or at my left is not mine to grant, but it is for those for whom it has been prepared."

- The call of Jesus is to share his life, his values and live as he does, not to have the top places, if even such there be in his service. Holiness is judged on our closeness to God, not on our rank, our job, our vocation.
- Prayer is one means of staying humble, and of being willing to be part of the serving ministry of Jesus. As he came to serve, so also we are called to be servants of faith and love in our world.

Thursday 30th May **Mark 10:46–52**

They came to Jericho. As he and his disciples and a large crowd were leaving Jericho, Bartimaeus son of Timaeus, a blind beggar, was sitting by the roadside. When he heard that it was Jesus of Nazareth, he began to shout out and say, "Jesus, Son of David, have mercy on me!" Many sternly ordered him to be quiet, but he cried out even more loudly, "Son of David, have mercy on me!" Jesus stood still and said, "Call him here." And they called the blind man, saying to him, "Take heart; get up, he is calling you." So throwing off his cloak, he sprang up and came to Jesus. Then Jesus said to him, "What do you want me to do for you?" The blind man said to him, "My teacher, let me see again." Jesus said to him, "Go; your faith has made you well." Immediately he regained his sight and followed him on the way.

- Like the people who scolded Bartimaeus, telling him to be quiet and not to bring shame on them, I may sometimes prefer to keep the less presentable parts of my life out of Jesus' sight.
- Thinking of this scene, I realize that Jesus wants to stop, to listen to my plea for help and to cure me. I allow myself to be before Jesus, seen as I am, expressing my need in trust.

Friday 31st May,
Visitation of the Virgin Mary **Luke 1:39–45**

In those days Mary set out and went with haste to a Judean town in the hill country, where she entered the house of Zechariah and greeted Elizabeth. When Elizabeth heard Mary's greeting, the child leaped in her womb. And Elizabeth was filled with the Holy Spirit and exclaimed with a loud cry, "Blessed are you among women, and blessed is the fruit of your womb. And why has this happened to me, that the mother of my Lord comes to me? For as soon as I heard the sound of your greeting, the child in my womb leaped for joy. And blessed is she who believed that there would be a fulfillment of what was spoken to her by the Lord."

- Let me stand back to gaze at this encounter of cousins, of friends, both carrying a child in the womb.
- Elizabeth has the grace of insight, an appreciation of what is really happening here; she is "tuned in" to the presence of God.
- What can I learn from this scene, and from my reflections?

Saturday 1st June **Mark 11:27–33**

Again they came to Jerusalem. As he was walking in the temple, the chief priests, the scribes, and the elders came to him and said, "By what authority are you doing these things? Who gave you this authority to do them?" Jesus said to them, "I will ask you one question; answer me, and I will tell you by what authority I do these things. Did the baptism of John come from heaven, or was it of human origin? Answer me." They argued with one another, "If we say, 'From heaven', he will say, 'Why then did you not believe him?' But shall we say, 'Of human origin'?"—they were afraid of the crowd, for all regarded John as truly a prophet. So they answered Jesus, "We do not know." And Jesus said to them, "Neither will I tell you by what authority I am doing these things."

- The Pharisees saw religion as a ground for dispute, challenge and authority. Jesus sees it as being at the service of faith and refuses to be drawn into an argument of the mind.

- Jesus knew that answering the Pharisees' question would lead only to further debate. I pray for the wisdom to know when, instead of trying to have the last word, it might be better for me to keep silent or to say less.

Sacred Space

Something to think and pray about each day this week:

The gift of Eucharist

As the Christian year unfolds beyond Easter, Pentecost and Trinity Sunday, in many of our Church traditions we are invited to commemorate at this time the gift of the Eucharist (*Corpus Christi*). For as life moves forward, and we continue our journey, the Eucharist, where the Body and Blood of the Lord is blessed and shared out for us, becomes the food giving us nourishment and strength for all the challenges coming our way. Indeed, as we saw last week when reflecting on Rublev's icon, we share in the table of hospitality to which we are invited by the Most Holy Trinity. And even if, just now, I do not actually partake in the Eucharist itself, still I am at this moment mystically present at that table. I am a guest there, or at least being invited there. So my prayer is always Eucharistic. And—drawn into Trinitarian life, nourished there by love poured out in Jesus, through his giving us his whole life in his Body and Blood—we are ourselves in some sense a Eucharistic gift, as we allow our lives to be shared out, as a blessing for others.

The Presence of God

'I stand at the door and knock,' says the Lord.
What a wonderful privilege
that the Lord of all creation desires to come to me.
I welcome His presence.

Freedom

Lord, grant me the grace to be free from the excesses of this life.
Let me not get caught up with the desire for wealth.
Keep my heart and mind free to love and serve you.

Consciousness

'There is a time and place for everything,' as the saying goes.
Lord, grant that I may always desire
to spend time in your presence. To hear your call.

The Word

God speaks to each one of us individually. I need to listen to what he is saying to me. (Please turn to your scripture on the following pages. Inspiration points are there should you need them. When you are ready, return here to continue.)

Conversation

The gift of speech is a wonderful gift.
May I use this gift with kindness.
May I be slow to utter harsh words,
hurtful words, and words spoken in anger.

Conclusion

Glory be to the Father, and to the Son, and to the Holy Spirit,
As it was in the beginning, is now and ever shall be,
World without end. Amen

Sunday 2nd June,
Feast of the Body and Blood of Christ **1 Corinthians 11:23–26**

For I received from the Lord what I also handed on to you, that the Lord Jesus on the night when he was betrayed took a loaf of bread, and when he had given thanks, he broke it and said, "This is my body that is for you. Do this in remembrance of me." In the same way he took the cup also, after supper, saying, "This cup is the new covenant in my blood. Do this, as often as you drink it, in remembrance of me." For as often as you eat this bread and drink the cup, you proclaim the Lord's death until he comes.

- Paul handed on only what he had received from the Lord. I think of how I hand on the blessings and insights that I receive from the Lord for the good of others. As I look for God's blessing, I pray that I may be a source of blessing for others.
- Even as he was betrayed, Jesus gave his life freely for others. I ask that I not be held back by discouragement or disappointment, but give freely of who I am, as Jesus did.

Monday 3rd June **Mark 12:1–12**

Then Jesus began to speak to them in parables. "A man planted a vineyard, put a fence around it, dug a pit for the wine press, and built a watchtower; then he leased it to tenants and went to another country. When the season came, he sent a slave to the tenants to collect from them his share of the produce of the vineyard. But they seized him, and beat him, and sent him away empty-handed. And again he sent another slave to them; this one they beat over the head and insulted. Then he sent another, and that one they killed. And so it was with many others; some they beat, and others they killed. He had still one other, a beloved son. Finally he sent him to them, saying, 'They will respect my son.' But those tenants said to one another, 'This is the heir; come, let us kill him, and the inheritance will be ours.' So they seized him, killed him, and threw him out of the vineyard. What then will the owner of the vineyard do? He will come and destroy the tenants and give the vineyard to others. Have you not read this scripture: 'The stone that the builders rejected has become the cornerstone; this was the Lord's doing, and it is amazing in our eyes'?" When they realized that he had told this parable against them, they wanted to arrest him, but they feared the crowd. So they left him and went away.

- Jesus reminds us that there are many ways in which the message of God arrives. We easily develop habits that enable us to dismiss or ignore these messages. I realize that I need to be more aware of how God is communicating with me and I ask for help.
- I carefully review my concerns of these times to see where God may be approaching me in ways I do not expect to or notice.

Tuesday 4th June **Mark 12:13–17**

Then they sent to Jesus some Pharisees and some Herodians to trap him in what he said. And they came and said to him, "Teacher, we know that you are sincere, and show deference to no one; for you do not regard people with partiality, but teach the way of God in accordance with truth. Is it lawful to pay taxes to the emperor, or not? Should we pay them, or should we not?" But knowing their hypocrisy, he said to them, "Why are you putting me to the test? Bring me a denarius and let me see it." And they brought one. Then he said to them, "Whose head is this, and whose title?" They answered, "The emperor's." Jesus said to them, "Give to the emperor the things that are the emperor's, and to God the things that are God's." And they were utterly amazed at him.

- Although the approach of the Pharisees was flattering and courteous, Jesus recognized that he was being tested. I pray that I may have the presence of mind not to be distracted by empty conversations.
- Jesus points to the importance of giving due attention in the various spheres of life. I ask God to help me to fulfil as well as I can the different roles that I occupy.

Wednesday 5th June **Mark 12:24–27**

Jesus said to the Sadducees, who say there is no resurrection, "Is not this the reason you are wrong, that you know neither the scriptures nor the power of God? For when they rise from the dead, they neither marry nor are given in marriage, but are like angels in heaven. And as for the dead being raised, have you not read in the book of Moses, in the story about the bush, how God said to him, 'I am the God of Abraham, the God of Isaac, and the God of Jacob'? He is God not of the dead, but of the living; you are quite wrong."

- The last line puts a very human problem in perspective. No matter who or how many we have loved in life, we look on relationships in eternity as part of the mystery of God and of eternal life.
- All we know is that God is the God of the living, and we know that God's wish now and always is that we have life and have it to the full.

Thursday 6th June **Mark 12:28–34**

One of the scribes came near and heard them disputing with one another, and seeing that Jesus answered them well, he asked him, "Which commandment is the first of all?" Jesus answered, "The first is, 'Hear, O Israel: the Lord our God, the Lord is one; you shall love the Lord your God with all your heart, and with all your soul, and with all your mind, and with all your strength.' The second is this, 'You shall love your neighbor as yourself.' There is no other commandment greater than these." Then the scribe said to him, "You are right, Teacher; you have truly said that 'he is one, and besides him there is no other'; and 'to love him with all the heart, and with all the understanding, and with all the strength,' and 'to love one's neighbor as oneself,'—this is much more important than all whole burnt offerings and sacrifices." When Jesus saw that he answered wisely, he said to him, "You are not far from the kingdom of God." After that no one dared to ask him any question.

- A constant theme of Jesus is the central place of love in real religion. The Jewish tradition of many generations is expressed in the formula quoted in this piece of the gospel.
- We can protect ourselves with the small details of religion and faith while neglecting the primacy of love. Prayer and religious practice are in the service of love.

Friday 7th June,
Feast of the Sacred Heart **Ezekiel 34:11–16**

For thus says the Lord God: I myself will search for my sheep, and will seek them out. As shepherds seek out their flocks when they are among their scattered sheep, so I will seek out my sheep. I will rescue them from all the places to which they have been scattered on a day of clouds and thick darkness. I will bring them out from the peoples and gather them from the countries, and will bring them into their own land; and I will feed them on the mountains of Israel, by the watercourses, and in all the inhabited parts of the land. I will feed them with good pasture, and the mountain heights of Israel shall be their pasture; there they shall lie down in good grazing land, and they shall feed on rich pasture on the mountains of Israel. I myself will be the shepherd of my sheep, and I will make them lie down, says the Lord God. I will seek the lost, and I will bring back the strayed, and I will bind up the injured, and I will strengthen the weak, but the fat and the strong I will destroy. I will feed them with justice.

- Just as the shepherd seeks out the sheep, so does God search for me. I recall times when I felt lost and thank God for bringing me safely to this day. I pray for those who are lost or disorientated and consider how I might offer them direction by how I live on what I might say.
- God promises to tend for the flock, looking after their every need. I consider whether I allow myself to receive what God offers, taking proper time for the nourishment and rest that brings me to wholeness.

Saturday 8th June **Mark 12:38–44**

As Jesus taught in the temple, he said, "Beware of the scribes, who like to walk around in long robes, and to be greeted with respect in the marketplaces, and to have the best seats in the synagogues and places of honor at banquets! They devour widows' houses and for the sake of appearance say long prayers. They will receive the greater condemnation." He sat down opposite the treasury, and watched the crowd putting money into the treasury. Many rich people put in large sums. A poor widow came and put in two small copper coins, which are worth a penny. Then he called his disciples and said to them, "Truly I tell you, this poor widow has put in more than all those who are contributing to the treasury. For all of them have contributed out of their abundance; but she out of her poverty has put in everything she had, all she had to live on."

- Jesus did not seem to believe in appearances. Shows of piety and religiousness did not of themselves impress him.
- Jesus saw behind the tiny amount of money to the huge generosity of the heart in the case of the poor widow. He declared often that religious appearances can be empty and hypocritical.

Sacred Space

Something to think and pray about each day this week:

Welcome to the stranger

While God meets me especially in my time of quiet and reflection, as the Bible shows, it is true to the Scriptures as well to realize how God comes also in the voice and face of the stranger. The stranger, the "sojourner," the person of different background and faith, has a special place in the Old Testament, and is to be respected and shown hospitality. Then in the New Testament, in the gospels, we see Jesus encountering the stranger or foreigner in significant ways. He heals the servant of the Roman centurion for instance, of whom he says "not even in Israel have I found faith as great as this" (Luke 7:9). And, most movingly, Jesus's own human consciousness is challenged and stretched by a complete outsider, the courageous Canaanite woman, whose little daughter is tormented by a devil. In his human consciousness, he learns from her something he had not fully grasped before—about the expansion of his ministry beyond the confines of Israel. As a result of her courage, after his initial hesitation he reaches out to her, and cures her little child. "You have great faith," he says to her in utter admiration (Matthew 15:28).

So, in my quiet prayer, let me think of the strangers, the "different" people I have encountered, who have perhaps challenged my faith perspective, and called me to look at things in a new way. Perhaps, in some of those meetings, God was especially coming to me, calling to me, expanding the horizons of my heart?

The Presence of God
I remind myself that, as I sit here now,
God is gazing on me with love and holding me in being.
I pause for a moment and think of this.

Freedom
I need to close out the noise, to rise above the noise;
The noise that interrupts, that separates,
The noise that isolates.
I need to listen to God again.

Consciousness
In God's loving presence I unwind the past day,
starting from now and looking back, moment by moment.
I gather in all the goodness and light, in gratitude.
I attend to the shadows and what they say to me,
seeking healing, courage, forgiveness.

The Word
I take my time to read the Word of God, slowly, a few times, allowing myself to dwell on anything that strikes me. (Please turn to your scripture on the following pages. Inspiration points are there should you need them. When you are ready, return here to continue.)

Conversation
Do I notice myself reacting as I pray with the Word of God?
Do I feel challenged, comforted, angry?
Imagining Jesus sitting or standing by me,
I speak out my feelings, as one trusted friend to another.

Conclusion
Glory be to the Father, and to the Son, and to the Holy Spirit,
As it was in the beginning, is now and ever shall be,
World without end. Amen

Sunday 9th June,
Tenth Sunday in Ordinary Time **Galatians 1:11–19**

For I want you to know, brothers and sisters, that the gospel that was proclaimed by me is not of human origin; for I did not receive it from a human source, nor was I taught it, but I received it through a revelation of Jesus Christ. You have heard, no doubt, of my earlier life in Judaism. I was violently persecuting the church of God and was trying to destroy it. I advanced in Judaism beyond many among my people of the same age, for I was far more zealous for the traditions of my ancestors. But when God, who had set me apart before I was born and called me through his grace, was pleased to reveal his Son to me, so that I might proclaim him among the Gentiles, I did not confer with any human being, nor did I go up to Jerusalem to those who were already apostles before me, but I went away at once into Arabia, and afterwards I returned to Damascus. Then after three years I did go up to Jerusalem to visit Cephas and stayed with him for fifteen days; but I did not see any other apostle except James the Lord's brother.

- We get a strong sense here of Paul's personality; his fervor, his insistent zeal—first for Judaism and persecution of Christians, then for the gospel received "through a revelation of Jesus Christ."
- Paul was transformed not by intellectual or moral thought but by his encounter with the Risen Jesus. How do I know the Risen Lord in my life? How do others know him through me?

Monday 10th June **Matthew 5:1–9**

When Jesus saw the crowds, he went up the mountain; and after he sat down, his disciples came to him. Then he began to speak, and taught them, saying: "Blessed are the poor in spirit, for theirs is the kingdom of heaven. Blessed are those who mourn, for they will be comforted. Blessed are the meek, for they will inherit the earth. Blessed are those who hunger and thirst for righteousness, for they will be filled. Blessed are the merciful, for they will receive mercy. Blessed are the pure in heart, for they will see God. Blessed are the peacemakers, for they will be called children of God."

- What the world sees as tragic or empty, Jesus sees as blessed: humility, mourning, gentleness, peacefulness and other virtues. Jesus lived by these qualities during his life with us on earth.
- Jesus could encourage us to live in the spirit of the Beatitudes because he himself lived them and knew that a life of integrity and honesty is indeed a blessed life.

Tuesday 11th June **Matthew 5:14–16**

Jesus said to the disciples, "You are the light of the world. A city built on a hill cannot be hidden. No one after lighting a lamp puts it under the bushel basket, but on the lampstand, and it gives light to all in the house. In the same way, let your light shine before others, so that they may see your good works and give glory to your Father in heaven."

- Goodness shines through and cannot be hidden. The goodness of Jesus came through even in the darkness of the Passion, and attracted good people to him.
- God's gifts to each person are to build up the community and thus glorify God. Anything done in love is done for the glory of God, for selfless love and the glory of God go together.

Wednesday 12th June **Matthew 5:17–19**

Jesus said to the crowds, "Do not think that I have come to abolish the law or the prophets; I have come not to abolish but to fulfill. For truly I tell you, until heaven and earth pass away, not one letter, not one stroke of a letter, will pass from the law until all is accomplished. Therefore, whoever breaks one of the least of these commandments, and teaches others to do the same, will be called least in the kingdom of heaven; but whoever does them and teaches them will be called great in the kingdom of heaven."

- Jesus teaches by word and action, by saying and doing. His example of life is our guide and our encouragement.

- There is a link between what we say and what we do, and when this link is strong, we are strong in the kingdom of God. We are "to walk it as we talk it."

Thursday 13th June,
St Anthony of Padua **Matthew 5:21–26**

Jesus said to the crowds, "You have heard that it was said to those of ancient times, 'You shall not murder'; and 'whoever murders shall be liable to judgment.' But I say to you that if you are angry with a brother or sister, you will be liable to judgment; and if you insult a brother or sister, you will be liable to the council; and if you say, 'You fool,' you will be liable to the hell of fire. So when you are offering your gift at the altar, if you remember that your brother or sister has something against you, leave your gift there before the altar and go; first be reconciled to your brother or sister, and then come and offer your gift."

- Jesus, you point me from the killing to the hatred behind it, from the deed to the heart that prompts it.
- Show me my heart, Lord, and the corners where I harbor resentment or contempt. Then help me to clean them out.

Friday 14th June **2 Corinthians 4:7–10**

But we have this treasure in clay jars, so that it may be made clear that this extraordinary power belongs to God and does not come from us. We are afflicted in every way, but not crushed; perplexed, but not driven to despair; persecuted, but not forsaken; struck down, but not destroyed; always carrying in the body the death of Jesus, so that the life of Jesus may also be made visible in our bodies.

- In this passage, often used pastorally in ministering to those who are sick, Paul reminds us that we are quite frail but within us is the indestructible power and glory of God. We may be afflicted, but we are not crushed.
- Can I sit quietly to ponder my own frailty, perhaps to recall times when the power of God may have shone through my weakness.

Saturday 15th June **Matthew 5:33–37**

Jesus said to the crowds, "Again, you have heard that it was said to those of ancient times, 'You shall not swear falsely, but carry out the vows you have made to the Lord.' But I say to you, Do not swear at all, either by heaven, for it is the throne of God, or by the earth, for it is his footstool, or by Jerusalem, for it is the city of the great King. And do not swear by your head, for you cannot make one hair white or black. Let your word be 'Yes, Yes' or 'No, No'; anything more than this comes from the evil one."

- To speak the truth in God and only in God is the concern of Jesus here. In prayer and in reflection, in conversation with others, the life and truth of God deepen in each of us.
- Our "yes" to life and in life is the "yes" of God. Nothing is worth our commitment in life but the truth of God and the meaning in life that is given to us by Jesus Christ.

june 16–22

Something to think and pray about each day this week:

The constant presence

Out of the depths of darkness and despair, which can swirl about in anyone's life, a cry can go up, for God's healing and wholeness. Ignatius of Loyola came to see, after his conversion, how even in a time of grace a desolating spirit of confusion can pull down into negativity, trying to destroy the gift of faith. This happened especially during his sojourn in the cave at Manresa, when he wanted to deepen the insights he had already gained. But eventually he saw how God's spirit never leaves us, but always works to counteract the hostile and accusing one. That good spirit is faithfully present in our hearts and consciousness, raising us up, and into a positive and clear-eyed faith, whose mark is consolation. From those experiences Ignatius formulated his little book, *The Spiritual Exercises,* intended to help people find the will and way of God in their lives, and to discern the difference between God's spirit and an opposing one at work in our hearts.

If I call out, as in the Psalm, "Out of the depths I cry to you, O Lord, / Lord, hear my voice!" (Psalm 130:1–2), my prayer is always heard. For God's way is always a life-giving one, drawing me on, even if at times challenging me. He is present to my heart, as the Good Shepherd, calling by name, leading to good pastures, and saying also, "I have come that you may have life, and have it to the full" (John 10:10).

The Presence of God
For a few moments, I think of God's veiled presence in things:
in the elements, giving them existence;
in plants, giving them life; in animals, giving them sensation;
and finally, in me, giving me all this and more,
making me a temple, a dwelling-place of the Spirit.

Freedom
God is not foreign to my freedom.
Instead the Spirit breathes life into my most intimate desires,
gently nudging me towards all that is good.
I ask for the grace to let myself be enfolded by the Spirit.

Consciousness
Knowing that God loves me unconditionally,
I can afford to be honest about how I am.
How has the last day been, and how do I feel now?
I share my feelings openly with the Lord.

The Word
I take my time to read the Word of God, slowly, a few times, allowing myself to dwell on anything that strikes me. (Please turn to your scripture on the following pages. Inspiration points are there should you need them. When you are ready, return here to continue.)

Conversation
How has God's Word moved me? Has it left me cold?
Has it consoled me or moved me to act in a new way?
I imagine Jesus standing or sitting beside me,
I turn and share my feelings with him.

Conclusion
Glory be to the Father, and to the Son, and to the Holy Spirit,
As it was in the beginning, is now and ever shall be,
World without end. Amen

Sunday 16th June,
Eleventh Sunday of the Year **Galatians 2:19–21**

I have been crucified with Christ; and it is no longer I who live, but it is Christ who lives in me. And the life I now live in the flesh I live by faith in the Son of God, who loved me and gave himself for me. I do not nullify the grace of God; for if justification comes through the law, then Christ died for nothing.

- Paul identifies his life with Jesus. This is not a boastful claim, but an acceptance of the invitation that Jesus himself gives to each of us. I think of how I might be mindful of living in Jesus today.
- I think of the place of the laws and regulations that shape my life. I lay my life before God, asking God to purify my motivations, to inspire me to live generously rather than in a narrow way.

Monday 17th June **Matthew 5:38–42**

Jesus said to the crowds, "You have heard that it was said, 'An eye for an eye and a tooth for a tooth.' But I say to you, Do not resist an evildoer. But if anyone strikes you on the right cheek, turn the other also; and if anyone wants to sue you and take your coat, give your cloak as well; and if anyone forces you to go one mile, go also the second mile. Give to everyone who begs from you, and do not refuse anyone who wants to borrow from you."

- To answer violence with violence or unreasonable demands with resistance is to do the expected thing. Jesus calls me to imagine my life differently and to prompt others to see themselves anew.
- Do I use laws and rules to protect my security or to promote justice for others?

Tuesday 18th June **Matthew 5:43–48**

Jesus said to the crowds, "You have heard that it was said, 'You shall love your neighbor and hate your enemy.' But I say to you, Love your enemies and pray for those who persecute you, so that you may be children of your Father in heaven; for he makes his sun rise on the evil and on the good, and sends rain on the righteous and on the unrighteous. For if you love those who love you, what reward do you have? Do not even the tax collectors do the same? And if you greet only your brothers and sisters, what more are you doing than others? Do not even the Gentiles do the same? Be perfect, therefore, as your heavenly Father is perfect."

- Jesus was familiar with the human habit of comparison and complaint. As I hear his call to a wider vision, I ask for help to let go of what constricts me.
- The rain that God sends is a blessing for some and a burden to others. I ask God to help me to recognize this day how I am blessed and strengthened to offer blessings to others.

Wednesday 19th June **Matthew 6:1–4**

Jesus said to the disciples, "Beware of practicing your piety before others in order to be seen by them; for then you have no reward from your Father in heaven. So whenever you give alms, do not sound a trumpet before you, as the hypocrites do in the synagogues and in the streets, so that they may be praised by others. Truly I tell you, they have received their reward. But when you give alms, do not let your left hand know what your right hand is doing, so that your alms may be done in secret; and your Father who sees in secret will reward you."

- Our world is one that often associates secrecy with what is wrong and needs to be hidden. Jesus reminds us that this is not a time for everything to be announced or made known—there will be another time for that. I draw reassurance from the fact that God recognizes the hidden, the small and the quiet things I do.
- I think of the good I might do in my present circumstances. I ask God to help me to act discreetly and quietly, by doing what I can to establish justice, to announce peace and to witness to God's love.

Thursday 20th June **Matthew 6:7–15**

Jesus said, "When you are praying, do not heap up empty phrases as the Gentiles do; for they think that they will be heard because of their many words. Do not be like them, for your Father knows what you need before you ask him. Pray then in this way: Our Father in heaven, hallowed be your name. Your kingdom come. Your will be done, on earth as it is in heaven. Give us this day our daily bread. And forgive us our debts, as we also have forgiven our debtors. And do not bring us to the time of trial, but rescue us from the evil one. For if you forgive others their trespasses, your heavenly Father will also forgive you; but if you do not forgive others, neither willyour Father forgive your trespasses."

- The phrases of the Our Father may be very familiar to me. I might let just one of them offer itself now; I take time to let it sink in again and take it with me through the day.
- Debts, evil and trespasses are all brought before God and assume their proper place. I am drawn to God, being made holy, nourished and forgiven.

Friday 21st June, St Aloysius Gonzaga Matthew 6:19–21

Jesus said to his disciples, "Do not store up for yourselves treasures on earth, where moth and rust consume and where thieves break in and steal; but store up for yourselves treasures in heaven, where neither moth nor rust consumes and where thieves do not break in and steal. For where your treasure is, there your heart will be also."

- As Jesus speaks of treasures, I might ask, "In what way was Jesus rich?" Jesus wants to share with me any wealth I recognize or value in him.
- I look on my world and circumstances as God does and pray with appreciation and compassion.

Saturday 22nd June Matthew 6:25–34

Jesus said to his disciples, "Therefore I tell you, do not worry about your life, what you will eat or what you will drink, or about your body, what you will wear. Is not life more than food, and the body more than clothing? Look at the birds of the air; they neither sow nor reap nor gather into barns, and yet your heavenly Father feeds them. Are you not of more value than they? And can any of you by worrying add a single hour to your span of life? And why do you worry about clothing? Consider the lilies of the field, how they grow; they neither toil nor spin, yet I tell you, even Solomon in all his glory was not clothed like one of these. But if God so clothes the grass of the field, which is alive today and tomorrow is thrown into the oven, will he not much more clothe you—you of little faith? Therefore do not worry, saying, 'What will we eat?' or 'What will we drink?' or 'What will we wear?' For it is the Gentiles who strive for all these things; and indeed your heavenly Father knows that you need all these things. But strive first for the kingdom of God and his righteousness, and all these things will be given to you as well. So do not worry about tomorrow, for tomorrow will bring worries of its own. Today's trouble is enough for today."

- Is Jesus so innocent, so naïve? It seems he is telling me to look at birds and flowers. Deep down I know that is not what is asking me to do; he is asking me to be wise, to discern something of the working of God, to be ready to loosen my grip.
- Jesus does not just invite me to let my worries and concerns go; he does not want to leave me empty-handed. He offers me a new priority—an eagerness to establish God's ways, a striving for the kingdom of God.

Something to think and pray about each day this week:

Come as you are

To pray, is to become childlike. When I enter into prayer, and come before the mystery of God as revealed in Jesus, I can open my heart in simple trust and receptivity. My defences can be laid aside, and I do not need any of the masks which my role in life may require that I put on. "Come to me, all you who labour and are overburdened," Jesus says, "and you will find rest" (Matthew 11:28). So in my prayer let me see him looking at me, lovingly and humbly (as St Teresa of Avila suggested). He is inviting me just now to be with him, and saying in effect, "Come as you are, and just as you are; come and be with me." And let me, on my part, simply respond, "Here I am, Lord, and just as I am." Prayer really is that simple: a matter of childlike, trusting presence. Such is the prayer of Jesus himself in the Gospel, before his Father, who for him is "Abba," "Pappa," "Dear Father." And he draws us into that prayer of his, where fear is banished, and we can trust, and say with him "Abba" (Romans 8:16; Galatians 4:6–7). Let me therefore, in my prayer, be enfolded in that mystery and that love. It is the deepest truth of my life. For in Jesus I am God's child.

The Presence of God

At any time of the day or night we can call on Jesus.
He is always waiting, listening for our call.
What a wonderful blessing.
No phone needed, no emails, just a whisper.

Freedom

Lord, grant me the grace to be free from the excesses of this life.
Let me not get caught up with the desire for wealth.
Keep my heart and mind free to love and serve you.

Consciousness

I exist in a web of relationships—links to nature, people, God.
I trace out these links, giving thanks for the life that flows through them.
Some links are twisted or broken: I may feel regret, anger, disappointment.
I pray for the gift of acceptance and forgiveness.

The Word

God speaks to each one of us individually. I need to listen to what he is saying to me. (Please turn to your scripture on the following pages. Inspiration points are there should you need them. When you are ready, return here to continue.)

Conversation

Remembering that I am still in God's presence,
I imagine Jesus himself standing or sitting beside me,
and say whatever is on my mind, whatever is in my heart,
speaking as one friend to another.

Conclusion

Glory be to the Father, and to the Son, and to the Holy Spirit,
As it was in the beginning, is now and ever shall be,
World without end. Amen

Sunday 23rd June,
Twelfth Sunday of Ordinary Time **Luke 9:18–24**

Once when Jesus was praying alone, with only the disciples near him, he asked them, "Who do the crowds say that I am?" They answered, "John the Baptist; but others, Elijah; and still others, that one of the ancient prophets has arisen." He said to them, "But who do you say that I am?" Peter answered, "The Messiah of God." He sternly ordered and commanded them not to tell anyone, saying, "The Son of Man must undergo great suffering, and be rejected by the elders, chief priests, and scribes, and be killed, and on the third day be raised." Then he said to them all, "If any want to become my followers, let them deny themselves and take up their cross daily and follow me. For those who want to save their life will lose it, and those who lose their life for my sake will save it."

- I answer the question that Jesus asks in many ways. I show who Jesus is to me by attending church, by professing my faith, by acting as Jesus did.
- Every time I deny myself I have an opportunity to express my faith in something greater than what I might enjoy here and now. I ask God's help to take up the crosses that I find, realizing that following Jesus is to live as he lived.

Monday 24th June,
Birth of St John the Baptist **Luke 1:57–64**

Now the time came for Elizabeth to give birth, and she bore a son. Her neighbors and relatives heard that the Lord had shown his great mercy to her, and they rejoiced with her. On the eighth day they came to circumcise the child, and they were going to name him Zechariah after his father. But his mother said, "No; he is to be called John." They said to her, "None of your relatives has this name." Then they began motioning to his father to find out what name he wanted to give him. He asked for a writing tablet and wrote, "His name is John." And all of them were amazed. Immediately his mouth was opened and his tongue freed, and he began to speak, praising God.

- The neighbours and relatives who gathered around Elizabeth want to do their best, relying on the best of human traditions. Elizabeth had her own insight and spoke her truth.
- Elizabeth and Zechariah held fast to the message that God had given them and were thus irresistible. This was the household in which John the Baptist grew up. He and Jesus must have heard this story and learned from it. Picture the scene; imagine what they savored.

Tuesday 25th June **Matthew 7:12–14**

Jesus said, "In everything do to others as you would have them do to you; for this is the law and the prophets. "Enter through the narrow gate; for the gate is wide and the road is easy that leads to destruction, and there are many who take it. For the gate is narrow and the road is hard that leads to life, and there are few who find it.

- Real love, day after day, can be difficult. We get upset and hurt, often by those closest to us. The narrow gate is the gate of love which leads to life. When we enter into the world of love, we find that it is a wide world, with its own strength, energy and beauty.
- God is the one who creates this world, and creates each of us each day in love and for love. In this world of love God can be trusted to care for us.

Wednesday 26th June **Matthew 7:15–20**

Jesus told the crowds, "Beware of false prophets, who come to you in sheep's clothing but inwardly are ravenous wolves. You will know them by their fruits. Are grapes gathered from thorns, or figs from thistles? In the same way, every good tree bears good fruit, but the bad tree bears bad fruit. A good tree cannot bear bad fruit, nor can a bad tree bear good fruit. Every tree that does not bear good fruit is cut down and thrown into the fire. Thus you will know them by their fruits."

- Jesus speaks richly in images: wolves, trees, sheep and fruit are brought to mind. If I were to speak to Jesus in images, to what might I compare my life?

- As I draw close to Jesus in prayer, I realize that he is the source of truth and meaning. Other leaders may inspire and encourage, but I trust Jesus as the Truth.

Thursday 27th June **Matthew 7:21–23**

Jesus said to his disciples, "Not everyone who says to me, 'Lord, Lord,' will enter the kingdom of heaven, but only the one who does the will of my Father in heaven. On that day many will say to me, 'Lord, Lord, did we not prophesy in your name, and cast out demons in your name, and do many deeds of power in your name?' Then I will declare to them, 'I never knew you; go away from me, you evildoers.'"

- I may sometimes call Jesus, "Lord"; I remember his telling me that I am not a servant but a friend. I take care that my prayer doesn't become a matter of dutiful routine but is time to be present with my companion.
- It may be difficult to know if I am doing the will of God but, as I lay my life before God now, I am open to learning more of God's desire for me. I receive the strength to work with God to change what I need to.

Friday 28th June **Matthew 8:1–4**

When Jesus had come down from the mountain, great crowds followed him; and there was a leper who came to him and knelt before him, saying, "Lord, if you choose, you can make me clean." He stretched out his hand and touched him, saying, "I do choose. Be made clean!" Immediately his leprosy was cleansed. Then Jesus said to him, "See that you say nothing to anyone; but go, show yourself to the priest, and offer the gift that Moses commanded, as a testimony to them."

- Inspired by the man who suffered with leprosy, I begin my prayer not with my demanding a request, but with the phrase. "Lord, if you choose to, you can. . ."
- Jesus sends the field man away telling him to keep the miracle to himself, bringing the wonder to God and showing his thankfulness. I think of how I may need to take more time in reflection, prayer or in acts of thanksgiving.

Saturday 29th June,
Ss Peter & Paul, Apostles **Matthew 16:13–19**

Now when Jesus came into the district of Caesarea Philippi, he asked his disciples, "Who do people say that the Son of Man is?" And they said, "Some say John the Baptist, but others Elijah, and still others Jeremiah or one of the prophets." He said to them, "But who do you say that I am?" Simon Peter answered, "You are the Messiah, the Son of the living God." And Jesus answered him, "Blessed are you, Simon son of Jonah! For flesh and blood has not revealed this to you, but my Father in heaven. And I tell you, you are Peter, and on this rock I will build my church, and the gates of Hades will not prevail against it. I will give you the keys of the kingdom of heaven, and whatever you bind on earth will be bound in heaven, and whatever you loose on earth will be loosed in heaven."

- Jesus leads the disciples to put aside external voices. The only question for me is, "Who do I say Jesus is?" as I put aside gossip and other opinions.
- I proclaim Jesus by the way I live as my words and actions; my attitudes and choices demonstrate who influences me.

Something to think and pray about each day this week:

God's presence, God's promise

God, in creating me, in breathing me into being, always stays with me along the course of my life. My prayer, therefore, is my effort to bring into consciousness the divine and blessed mystery always with me and before me. "O Lord, you search me and you know me . . . As you have always been there, since my earliest coming to be, in my mother's womb, so you are there now, intimately and continually present to me" (cf Psalm 139). Further, God's presence also contains a promise to me, a covenant made with me, namely that his promise and purpose for my life will not fail. This is a great promise, expressing God's determination for me. For his word, spoken into my life, and calling me by name, "will not return to me empty, without carrying out my will and succeeding in what it was sent to do" (Isaiah 55:11). My life therefore is sprinkled with the words of God, the seeds of God's blessing and goodness, which are destined to sprout and grow over my years (cf Matthew 13:1–23). Oh yes, sometimes I may be poor soil and stony ground for the seed . . . "But, Lord, help me to clear the ground of my life, to be the good earth for the seed of your loving purposes. Help me, here and now, to be receptive to you. And help me to know that the rest is your doing, for it is you who gives the increase."

The Presence of God

God is with me, but more,
God is within me, giving me existence.
Let me dwell for a moment on God's life-giving presence
in my body, my mind, my heart
and in the whole of my life.

Freedom

God is not foreign to my freedom.
Instead the Spirit breathes life into my most intimate desires,
gently nudging me towards all that is good.
I ask for the grace to let myself be enfolded by the Spirit.

Consciousness

How am I really feeling? Light-hearted? Heavy-hearted?
I may be very much at peace, happy to be here.
Equally, I may be frustrated, worried or angry.
I acknowledge how I really am. It is the real me that the Lord loves.

The Word

I read the Word of God slowly, a few times over, and I listen to what God is saying to me. (Please turn to your scripture on the following pages. Inspiration points are there should you need them. When you are ready, return here to continue.)

Conversation

How has God's Word moved me? Has it left me cold?
Has it consoled me or moved me to act in a new way?
I imagine Jesus standing or sitting beside me,
I turn and share my feelings with him.

Conclusion

Glory be to the Father, and to the Son, and to the Holy Spirit,
As it was in the beginning, is now and ever shall be,
World without end. Amen

Sunday 30th June,
Thirteenth Sunday in Ordinary Time **Luke 9:57–62**

As they were going along the road, someone said to him, "I will follow you wherever you go." And Jesus said to him, "Foxes have holes, and birds of the air have nests; but the Son of Man has nowhere to lay his head." To another he said, "Follow me." But he said, "Lord, first let me go and bury my father." But Jesus said to him, "Let the dead bury their own dead; but as for you, go and proclaim the kingdom of God." Another said, "I will follow you, Lord; but let me first say farewell to those at my home." Jesus said to him, "No one who puts a hand to the plough and looks back is fit for the kingdom of God."

- It is easy for me to think of how I might be a better disciple if my situation where different. I take some time to consider how this is the road along which I walk with Jesus; he does not speak to me from a distance but knows where I am and sees where he wants to go with me.
- Jesus asks me not to be distracted, not to have my attention dissipated by many concerns. I take some time today to let myself hear God calling me.

Monday 1st July **Matthew 8:18–22**

Now when Jesus saw great crowds around him, he gave orders to go over to the other side. A scribe then approached and said, "Teacher, I will follow you wherever you go." And Jesus said to him, "Foxes have holes, and birds of the air have nests; but the Son of Man has nowhere to lay his head." Another of his disciples said to him, "Lord, first let me go and bury my father." But Jesus said to him, "Follow me, and let the dead bury their own dead."

- Jesus might have seen the scribe as somebody who had a lot of understanding, a lot to leave behind. His answer caused them to question their conclusions. Are there conclusions that Jesus wants me to question now?
- Jesus always points us to life. I pray that I may recognize signs of growth and hope and follow them.

Tuesday 2nd July **Matthew 8:23–27**

And when Jesus got into the boat, his disciples followed him. A windstorm arose on the sea, so great that the boat was being swamped by the waves; but he was asleep. And they went and woke him up, saying, "Lord, save us! We are perishing!" And he said to them, "Why are you afraid, you of little faith?" Then he got up and rebuked the winds and the sea; and there was a dead calm. They were amazed, saying, "What sort of man is this, that even the winds and the sea obey him?"

- The disciples found out bit by bit "what kind of man this is." In different situations they would get to know Jesus; by hearing him and watching him with people, they would understand and appreciate and love him more.
- Mostly our knowledge will grow with our love of him, as both grow together. Our prayer leads us from love to knowledge, the knowledge of the heart that is at the heart of prayer.

Wednesday 3rd July,
St Thomas, Apostle **John 20:24–29**

Thomas (who was called the Twin), one of the twelve, was not with them when Jesus came. So the other disciples told him, "We have seen the Lord." But he said to them, "Unless I see the mark of the nails in his hands, and put my finger in the mark of the nails and my hand in his side, I will not believe." A week later his disciples were again in the house, and Thomas was with them. Although the doors were shut, Jesus came and stood among them and said, "Peace be with you." Then he said to Thomas, "Put your finger here and see my hands. Reach out your hand and put it in my side. Do not doubt but believe." Thomas answered him, "My Lord and my God!" Jesus said to him, "Have you believed because you have seen me? Blessed are those who have not seen and yet have come to believe."

- We call Thomas the patron saint of strugglers in faith. He believed enough to look for Jesus, but not yet enough to believe in him. He struggled on his own, and found faith again in the community of the believers.

- Thomas was an honest doubter. We can identify with him in our struggles of faith, and be called as he was to find the Lord in the community of his people.

Thursday 4th July **Matthew 9:1–8**

And after getting into a boat he crossed the water and came to his own town. And just then some people were carrying a paralyzed man lying on a bed. When Jesus saw their faith, he said to the paralytic, "Take heart, son; your sins are forgiven." Then some of the scribes said to themselves, "This man is blaspheming." But Jesus, perceiving their thoughts, said, "Why do you think evil in your hearts? For which is easier, to say, 'Your sins are forgiven,' or to say, 'Stand up and walk'? But so that you may know that the Son of Man has authority on earth to forgive sins"—he then said to the paralytic—"Stand up, take your bed and go to your home." And he stood up and went to his home. When the crowds saw it, they were filled with awe, and they glorified God, who had given such authority to human beings.

- It must have been uncomfortable for the Pharisees to have Jesus say out loud what they spoke quietly and believed in their hearts.
- It often seems to be the case that those who assist the poor and the sick impress Jesus. Here, again, he reacts to their faith. I am reminded that faith is not just a matter of my convictions but is expressed in how I live. I think of how I spend my time.

Friday 5th July **Matthew 9:9–13**

As Jesus was walking along, he saw a man called Matthew sitting at the tax booth; and he said to him, "Follow me." And he got up and followed him. And as he sat at dinner in the house, many tax collectors and sinners came and were sitting with him and his disciples. When the Pharisees saw this, they said to his disciples, "Why does your teacher eat with tax collectors and sinners?" But when he heard this, he said, "Those who are well have no need of a physician, but those who are sick. Go and learn what this means, 'I desire mercy, not sacrifice.' For I have come to call not the righteous but sinners."

- People did not expect the tax collectors to be called to be religious disciples. I think of my talents and aptitudes and wonder again how Jesus is calling me to life.
- As I move through this day, I quietly consider how Jesus wants to call all those around me. If I do not understand why, it is because I do not see what Jesus sees.

Saturday 6th July **Matthew 9:14–17**

Then the disciples of John came to him, saying, "Why do we and the Pharisees fast often, but your disciples do not fast?" And Jesus said to them, "The wedding guests cannot mourn as long as the bridegroom is with them, can they? The days will come when the bridegroom is taken away from them, and then they will fast. No one sews a piece of unshrunk cloth on an old cloak, for the patch pulls away from the cloak, and a worse tear is made. Neither is new wine put into old wineskins; otherwise, the skins burst, and the wine is spilled, and the skins are destroyed; but new wine is put into fresh wineskins, and so both are preserved."

- Do I sometimes hang on to things that I would be better letting go of: old, treasured and worn out ideas and attitudes can come between me and being fully in the presence of Jesus?
- If I find myself to be aware that Jesus is with me, I pray for the new heart I need to receive his spirit; if I am less aware that "the bridegroom is with me," I am invited to create a little more space—to "fast," to review my habits, to prepare a new wineskin.

Something to think and pray about each day this week:

Growing into the kingdom

It is interesting that Jesus spoke of his mission to us in terms of the reign or kingdom of God which he was bringing into our midst. "The kingdom of heaven is close at hand" (Matthew 4:17), he said, as he began his ministry. Then, in the prayer he gave us, he asked us to say, "your kingdom come" (Matthew 6:10). And this mysterious but very real sovereignty of God in our lives was then outlined by Jesus through the use of many parables (cf Matthew 13:1–52). A mysterious reality indeed, but influencing every aspect of our living, and more real than the tangible and material things taking up so much of our energies! As the parables show, the kingdom of God is intended to be a *growing* reality, just as seed sown in the ground is meant to grow of itself, and produce a crop at harvest time (Mark 4:26–29).

It really is worthwhile meditating on and marvelling at God's purpose for our lives, and where *growth* is a central theme. For "growth is the evidence of life," as John Henry Newman learned when young, at the time of his evangelical Christian conversion. And later he would write, "In a higher world it is otherwise. But here below, to live is to change, and to be perfect is to have changed often." So let me ponder how God is ceaselessly active in the midst of my being, working unto good in all things for me, bringing about change, so that the kingdom of justice and love will grow in my heart.

The Presence of God
To be present is to arrive as one is and open up to the other.
At this instant, as I arrive here, God is present waiting for me.
God always arrives before me, desiring to connect with me
even more than my most intimate friend.
I take a moment and greet my loving God.

Freedom
Everything has the potential to draw forth from me a fuller love and life.
Yet my desires are often fixed, caught, on illusions of fulfillment.
I ask that God, through my freedom, may orchestrate
my desires in a vibrant loving melody rich in harmony.

Consciousness
Knowing that God loves me unconditionally,
I can afford to be honest about how I am.
How has the last day been, and how do I feel now?
I share my feelings openly with the Lord.

The Word
I take my time to read the Word of God, slowly, a few times, allowing myself to dwell on anything that strikes me. (Please turn to your scripture on the following pages. Inspiration points are there should you need them. When you are ready, return here to continue.)

Conversation
What feelings are rising in me
as I pray and reflect on God's Word?
I imagine Jesus himself sitting or standing beside me,
and open my heart to him.

Conclusion
Glory be to the Father, and to the Son, and to the Holy Spirit,
As it was in the beginning, is now and ever shall be,
World without end. Amen

Sunday 7th July,
Fourteenth Sunday in Ordinary Time **Luke 10:1–6**

After this the Lord appointed seventy others and sent them on ahead of him in pairs to every town and place where he himself intended to go. He said to them, "The harvest is plentiful, but the laborers are few; therefore ask the Lord of the harvest to send out laborers into his harvest. Go on your way. See, I am sending you out like lambs into the midst of wolves. Carry no purse, no bag, no sandals; and greet no one on the road. Whatever house you enter, first say, 'Peace to this house!' And if anyone is there who shares in peace, your peace will rest on that person; but if not, it will return to you."

- Jesus sent the disciples out without resources: the first place they were to go was to the people near them. My first mission is to those around me, to help them to realize that the reign of God is within reach.
- I am sent as a lamb among wolves. Sometimes I prefer to fit in and be comfortable. I pray that I may learn how to be distinctive—while remaining alive!

Monday 8th July **Matthew 9:20–23**

Suddenly a woman who had been suffering from hemorrhages for twelve years came up behind him and touched the fringe of his cloak, for she said to herself, "If I only touch his cloak, I will be made well." Jesus turned, and seeing her he said, "Take heart, daughter; your faith has made you well." And instantly the woman was made well.

- I allow the faith of this woman to speak to me; her humility and trust call me to look again at how I approach Jesus.
- I listen to Jesus words and let them resonate with me. He invites me to take heart and wants me to be well. I consider what this might mean to me now.

Tuesday 9th July **Matthew 9:35–38**

Then Jesus went about all the cities and villages, teaching in their synagogues, and proclaiming the good news of the kingdom, and curing every disease and every sickness. When he saw the crowds, he had compassion for them, because they were harassed and helpless, like sheep without a shepherd. Then he said to his disciples, "The harvest is plentiful, but the laborers are few; therefore ask the Lord of the harvest to send out laborers into his harvest."

- I bring to mind those who feel harassed and helpless. I pray for the compassion that Jesus had: that I may recognize those in need around me and be a shepherd to them.
- Jesus recognized many missed opportunities as he looked at the people around him. I ask God to help me to recognize the rich harvest around me that I may use the opportunities I might otherwise miss.

Wednesday 10th July **Matthew 10:1–7**

Then Jesus summoned his twelve disciples and gave them authority over unclean spirits, to cast them out, and to cure every disease and every sickness. These are the names of the twelve apostles: first, Simon, also known as Peter, and his brother Andrew; James son of Zebedee, and his brother John; Philip and Bartholomew; Thomas and Matthew the tax collector; James son of Alphaeus, and Thaddaeus; Simon the Cananaean, and Judas Iscariot, the one who betrayed him. These twelve Jesus sent out with the following instructions: "Go nowhere among the Gentiles, and enter no town of the Samaritans, but go rather to the lost sheep of the house of Israel. As you go, proclaim the good news, 'The kingdom of heaven has come near.'"

- I take time to hear my name being called. Jesus chooses me because he knows me, trusts me and loves me.
- Jesus called people by name, recognizing their dignity and worth. As I address those around me I pray that I remain aware of the gift that each person is to the world.

Thursday 11th July **Matthew 10:7–14**

As you go, proclaim the good news, "The kingdom of heaven has come near." Cure the sick, raise the dead, cleanse the lepers, cast out demons. You received without payment; give without payment. Take no gold, or silver, or copper in your belts, no bag for your journey, or two tunics, or sandals, or a staff; for laborers deserve their food. Whatever town or village you enter, find out who in it is worthy, and stay there until you leave. As you enter the house, greet it. If the house is worthy, let your peace come upon it; but if it is not worthy, let your peace return to you. If anyone will not welcome you or listen to your words, shake off the dust from your feet as you leave that house or town.

- It costs me nothing to wish someone well. Can I afford to do otherwise?
- Jesus tells us to leave what encumbers, not to be slowed down by whatever is negative. I ask for the help I need to shake off whatever "dust" is not for my good.

Friday 12th July **Matthew 10:16–23**

"See, I am sending you out like sheep into the midst of wolves; so be wise as serpents and innocent as doves. Beware of them, for they will hand you over to councils and flog you in their synagogues; and you will be dragged before governors and kings because of me, as a testimony to them and the Gentiles. When they hand you over, do not worry about how you are to speak or what you are to say; for what you are to say will be given to you at that time; for it is not you who speak, but the Spirit of your Father speaking through you."

- How often Jesus wishes me peace and tells me not to worry! He knows that there are things that weigh me down. I think of what they might be and listen to him speak to me of them.
- The Spirit of God speaks through me: I try to keep that in mind as I accept the faith that God has in me.

Saturday 13th July **Matthew 10:24–25**

Jesus said to the Twelve: "A disciple is not above the teacher, nor a slave above the master; it is enough for the disciple to be like the teacher, and the slave like the master."

- Without neglecting our basic equality, I can realize that I have much to learn from others. I ask for the humility I need to remain a learner and disciple.
- It is enough for me to be like Jesus. I am made in the image of God. I pray that I may bear in mind how deeply I am honoured and blessed by God's love for me.

july 14–20

Something to think and pray about each day this week:

Growing into wisdom

How good it is to have the gift of wisdom! Solomon prayed for that gift, and received it from God (1 Kings 3:5–12). The psalmist prayed for it too: "Indeed you love truth in the heart; / then in the secret of my heart teach me wisdom" (Psalm 51:8). Without wisdom, I can be the plaything of all the world throws at me—with its cacophony of voices and blandishments. Without that gift, what stability can I have within, as I am tossed about by the winds and waves beating about me? Instead, I can be centred within, when I come to appreciate the unsurpassable value of the kingdom of heaven, which is like "treasure hidden in a field," and "the pearl of great price" (Matthew 13:44–46). God offers all this to me—this treasure and pearl which will not fail or disappoint. Sometimes a person can have a conversion moment, when all this becomes real, and wisdom is gained. But perhaps more usually this wisdom is received, not in a blinding flash, but through a growth in understanding over years, or over a lifetime—God working in my heart, through all events, even when I am unheeding or gone astray, but always there, seeking me out, and helping me to see and understand.

Lord, in the secret of my heart teach me wisdom. Help me to have a discerning spirit, to see what is important in life, and experience your presence. May I receive your gifts in my prayer this week, and especially your wisdom.

The Presence of God
What is present to me is what has a hold on my becoming.
I reflect on the presence of God always there in love,
amidst the many things that have a hold on me.
I pause and pray that I may let God
affect my becoming in this precise moment.

Freedom
There are very few people
who realize what God would make of them
if they abandoned themselves into his hands,
and let themselves be formed by his grace. (St Ignatius)
I ask for the grace to trust myself totally to God's love.

Consciousness
In the presence of my loving Creator,
I look honestly at my feelings over the last day,
the highs, the lows and the level ground.
Can I see where the Lord has been present?

The Word
God speaks to each one of us individually. I need to listen to what he is saying to me. (Please turn to your scripture on the following pages. Inspiration points are there should you need them. When you are ready, return here to continue.)

Conversation
What is stirring in me as I pray?
Am I consoled, troubled, left cold?
I imagine Jesus himself standing or sitting at my side,
and share my feelings with him.

Conclusion
Glory be to the Father, and to the Son, and to the Holy Spirit,
As it was in the beginning, is now and ever shall be,
World without end. Amen

Sunday 14th July, Fifteenth Sunday in Ordinary Time
Deuteronomy 30:9b–14

For the Lord will again take delight in prospering you, just as he delighted in prospering your ancestors, when you obey the Lord your God by observing his commandments and decrees that are written in this book of the law, because you turn to the Lord your God with all your heart and with all your soul. Surely, this commandment that I am commanding you today is not too hard for you, nor is it too far away. It is not in heaven, that you should say, "Who will go up to heaven for us, and get it for us so that we may hear it and observe it?" Neither is it beyond the sea, that you should say, "Who will cross to the other side of the sea for us, and get it for us so that we may hear it and observe it?" No, the word is very near to you; it is in your mouth and in your heart for you to observe.

- Before I ask of anything else from God in prayer, I give thanks to God for what I have already received. The word of God is already in my mouth and in my heart.
- God does not ask of me anything that is too difficult but asks me to begin from where I am right now at this time. I pray that I may grow in appreciation of how God "prospers" me.

Monday 15th July **Matthew 10:34–39, 11:1**

Jesus said to the Twelve, "Do not think that I have come to bring peace to the earth; I have not come to bring peace, but a sword. For I have come to set a man against his father, and a daughter against her mother, and a daughter-in-law against her mother-in-law; and one's foes will be members of one's own household. Whoever loves father or mother more than me is not worthy of me; and whoever loves son or daughter more than me is not worthy of me; and whoever does not take up the cross and follow me is not worthy of me. Those who find their life will lose it, and those who lose their life for my sake will find it." Now when Jesus had finished instructing his twelve disciples, he went on from there to teach and proclaim his message in their cities.

- These phrases of Jesus provide insights into what discipleship means. The priority of our relationship with him means not putting anything above him.
- All is enjoyed and experienced within our relationship with him. This may mean losing treasured bonds and taking up the difficulty of the cross.

Tuesday 16th July **Matthew 11:20–22**

Then Jesus began to reproach the cities in which most of his deeds of power had been done, because they did not repent. "Woe to you, Chorazin! Woe to you, Bethsaida! For if the deeds of power done in you had been done in Tyre and Sidon, they would have repented long ago in sackcloth and ashes. But I tell you, on the day of judgment it will be more tolerable for Tyre and Sidon than for you."

- Cities have always flattered themselves! It is easy to be proud of being first, biggest or best. All this counts for little in Jesus' scale of things. I let him recognize, not my achievements, but my quiet moments of discipleship, like the time I am giving to this prayer.
- The deeds of power of Jesus went unnoticed. I pray that I may not miss the ways in which Jesus is present and active in my life.

Wednesday 17th July **Matthew 11:25–27**

At that time Jesus said, "I thank you, Father, Lord of heaven and earth, because you have hidden these things from the wise and the intelligent and have revealed them to infants; yes, Father, for such was your gracious will. All things have been handed over to me by my Father; and no one knows the Son except the Father, and no one knows the Father except the Son and anyone to whom the Son chooses to reveal him."

- Degrees, qualifications and certificates can get in the way if I think they make me more able to discern and follow God's ways. God is revealed only to those who take time to listen.
- I offer this time to give honor to God. I try not to push my priorities or to force my issues, but allow God to be revealed in the quiet and simple ways that Jesus recognized.

Thursday 18th July **Matthew 11:28–30**

Jesus said, "Come to me, all you that are weary and are carrying heavy burdens, and I will give you rest. Take my yoke upon you, and learn from me; for I am gentle and humble in heart, and you will find rest for your souls. For my yoke is easy, and my burden is light."

- I realize that many people are overwhelmed by their concern and priorities, unable to find time even to pray. I bring them before God now, asking that their burdens be lightened hearing Jesus' invitation.
- Jesus offers me rest for my soul. I acknowledge the rest I already receive; I ask for God's help where my soul is troubled in any way.

Friday 19th July **Matthew 12:1–8**

At that time Jesus went through the grainfields on the sabbath; his disciples were hungry, and they began to pluck heads of grain and to eat. When the Pharisees saw it, they said to him, "Look, your disciples are doing what is not lawful to do on the sabbath." He said to them, "Have you not read what David did when he and his companions were hungry? He entered the house of God and ate the bread of the Presence, which it was not lawful for him or his companions to eat, but only for the priests. Or have you not read in the law that on the sabbath the priests in the temple break the sabbath and yet are guiltless? I tell you, something greater than the temple is here. But if you had known what this means, 'I desire mercy and not sacrifice,' you would not have condemned the guiltless. For the Son of Man is lord of the sabbath."

- The well-intentioned Pharisees could not stop themselves finding fault with others; paying careful attention to the details, they forgot the bigger picture. I look at life with the eye of Jesus, praying for a greater ability to understand and forgive the shortcomings of others—and my own.
- I think of how I may need to be aware of any fundamentalism that seeks first to condemn or criticise. I am called instead to the mercy that Jesus embodied.

Saturday 20th July **Matthew 12:14–21**

But the Pharisees went out and conspired against him, how to destroy him. When Jesus became aware of this, he departed. Many crowds followed him, and he cured all of them, and he ordered them not to make him known. This was to fulfill what had been spoken through the prophet Isaiah: "Here is my servant, whom I have chosen, my beloved, with whom my soul is well pleased. I will put my Spirit upon him, and he will proclaim justice to the Gentiles. He will not wrangle or cry aloud, nor will anyone hear his voice in the streets. He will not break a bruised reed or quench a smoldering wick until he brings justice to victory. And in his name the Gentiles will hope."

- Jesus values even what is fragile or bruised; I bring the hopes I cherish before him and ask for blessing and hope. I acknowledge my hopes for myself, my relationships; and I consider how I might work with God to bring them to life.
- The voice of Jesus is not shrill or contentious: the spirit of God speaks to our hearts in a gentle and non-dramatic way. I pray that I may hear the voice of the Lord.

Something to think and pray about each day this week:

To listen, to live

As I leave aside other preoccupations, and enter into this moment of prayer, I am in fact *responding* to an invitation. Whether I know it or not, my clearing away of the other things that fill my life, and my focusing on the Lord's presence to me, is the *response of my heart* to the One who is drawing me and inviting me. Always, God is before me, in Jesus, looking at me in love and in truth. I am at all times, to use the title of Ruth Burrows' book, *Before the Living God.* Moreover, God is actively *seeking me out*, so that I come to him and find the fulfillment of my life. "Oh, come to the water all you who are thirsty, though you have no money, come! . . . Why spend money on what is not bread, your wages on what fails to satisfy? Listen, listen to me . . . Pay attention, come to me; listen, and your soul will live" (Isaiah 55:1–3). These words of the Lord, spoken in Isaiah, are worthy of consideration all this week—and indeed during the whole of my life. There is an immense truth contained in them, about the overwhelming love of God in Christ, reaching into my heart, calling out to me, at this moment, and in every moment of every day. And my response, as we saw before, is simply "Here I am Lord; just as I am; let me hear your words spoken in my heart, for they are food and life. And give me grace to respond with all that I am. Then I shall be satisfied."

The Presence of God

Jesus waits silent and unseen to come into my heart.
I will respond to His call.
He comes with His infinite power and love
May I be filled with joy in His presence.

Freedom

A thick and shapeless tree-trunk would never believe
that it could become a statue, admired as a miracle of sculpture,
and would never submit itself to the chisel of the sculptor,
who sees by her genius what she can make of it. (St Ignatius)
I ask for the grace to let myself be shaped by my loving Creator.

Consciousness

Knowing that God loves me unconditionally,
I look honestly over the last day, its events and my feelings.
Do I have something to be grateful for? Then I give thanks.
Is there something I am sorry for? Then I ask forgiveness.

The Word

I read the Word of God slowly, a few times over, and I listen to what God is saying to me. (Please turn to your scripture on the following pages. Inspiration points are there should you need them. When you are ready, return here to continue.)

Conversation

Do I notice myself reacting as I pray with the Word of God?
Do I feel challenged, comforted, angry?
Imagining Jesus sitting or standing by me,
I speak out my feelings, as one trusted friend to another.

Conclusion

Glory be to the Father, and to the Son, and to the Holy Spirit,
As it was in the beginning, is now and ever shall be,
World without end. Amen

Sunday 21st July,
Sixteenth Sunday in Ordinary Time **Genesis 18:1–5**

The Lord appeared to Abraham by the oaks of Mamre, as he sat at the entrance of his tent in the heat of the day. He looked up and saw three men standing near him. When he saw them, he ran from the tent entrance to meet them, and bowed down to the ground. He said, "My lord, if I find favor with you, do not pass by your servant. Let a little water be brought, and wash your feet, and rest yourselves under the tree. Let me bring a little bread, that you may refresh yourselves, and after that you may pass on—since you have come to your servant." So they said, "Do as you have said."

- The early Christians would draw strength from this story, remembering how he, Abraham, had unknowingly entertained angels (Hebrews 13:2). I ask God to help me remain generous to the poor and to those in need.
- Being able to give generously and receive graciously are two sides of the same coin. I ask God to help me to keep my life in balance: humbly asking, graciously receiving, generously giving.

Monday 22nd July **Matthew 12:38–42**

Then some of the scribes and Pharisees said to him, "Teacher, we wish to see a sign from you." But he answered them, "An evil and adulterous generation asks for a sign, but no sign will be given to it except the sign of the prophet Jonah. For just as Jonah was three days and three nights in the belly of the sea monster, so for three days and three nights the Son of Man will be in the heart of the earth. The people of Nineveh will rise up at the judgment with this generation and condemn it, because they repented at the proclamation of Jonah, and see, something greater than Jonah is here! The queen of the South will rise up at the judgment with this generation and condemn it, because she came from the ends of the earth to listen to the wisdom of Solomon, and see, something greater than Solomon is here!

- Signs from God sometimes seem desirable—and perhaps are even reasonable to expect. Jesus reminds me that, if I want them, I may be looking in the wrong direction. I pray that I may see and appreciate where God is already at work in the events and relationships of my life.

- My prayer time can train the eye of my heart to recognize God at work in my life. As I become more familiar with and trusting in God's Spirit, I need less proof and am able to rely on what I have learnt. God trusts me. I learn to trust God's spirit in me.

Tuesday 23rd July **Matthew 12:46–50**

While he was still speaking to the crowds, his mother and his brothers were standing outside, wanting to speak to him. Someone told him, "Look, your mother and your brothers are standing outside, wanting to speak to you." But to the one who had told him this, Jesus replied, "Who is my mother, and who are my brothers?" And pointing to his disciples, he said, "Here are my mother and my brothers! For whoever does the will of my Father in heaven is my brother and sister and mother."

- Jesus counts me among his closest, his next-of-kin. I show that this is my identity as I do the will of God.
- I pray that I may do the will of God with joy and courage, perhaps praying the 'Our Father' as I ask that God's will be done in this world as it is in heaven.

Wednesday 24th July **Matthew 13:1–9**

Jesus told them many things in parables, saying: "Listen! A sower went out to sow. And as he sowed, some seeds fell on the path, and the birds came and ate them up. Other seeds fell on rocky ground, where they did not have much soil, and they sprang up quickly, since they had no depth of soil. But when the sun rose, they were scorched; and since they had no root, they withered away. Other seeds fell among thorns, and the thorns grew up and choked them. Other seeds fell on good soil and brought forth grain, some a hundredfold, some sixty, some thirty. Let anyone with ears listen!"

- The words of Jesus do not all bear fruit. Knowing this did not stop Jesus from speaking, but he continued to proclaim good news, truth and life to any who would listen. I take care to review the measures by which I value my actions and words.
- I pray for the strength to continue speaking and acting—even in the absence of evident encouraging results. I ask God to help me to hear Jesus' word for me and to take it to heart.

Thursday 25th July,
St James, Apostle **Matthew 20:20–23**

Then the mother of the sons of Zebedee came to him with her sons, and kneeling before him, she asked a favor of him. And he said to her, "What do you want?" She said to him, "Declare that these two sons of mine will sit, one at your right hand and one at your left, in your kingdom." But Jesus answered, "You do not know what you are asking. Are you able to drink the cup that I am about to drink?" They said to him, "We are able." He said to them, "You will indeed drink my cup, but to sit at my right hand and at my left, this is not mine to grant, but it is for those for whom it has been prepared by my Father."

- Jesus challenges what may seem to be ordinary and reasonable expectations. Closeness to Jesus is no guarantee of promotion, status or human recognition. I ask Jesus to help me to let go of small ambitions.
- The honesty of this mother's approach enabled Jesus to answer her situation directly. I follow her example, speaking to Jesus clearly and frankly, listening for his clear and frank answer.

Friday 26th July **Matthew 13:18–23**

Jesus said to his disciples, "Hear then the parable of the sower. When anyone hears the word of the kingdom and does not understand it, the evil one comes and snatches away what is sown in the heart; this is what was sown on the path. As for what was sown on rocky ground, this is the one who hears the word and immediately receives it with joy; yet such a person has no root, but endures only for a while, and when trouble or persecution arises on account of the word, that person immediately falls away. As for what was sown among thorns, this is the one who hears the word, but the cares of the world and the lure of wealth choke the word, and it yields nothing. But as for what was sown on good soil, this is the one who hears the word and understands it, who indeed bears fruit and yields, in one case a hundredfold, in another sixty, and in another thirty."

- I allow my imagination to dwell with the scene that Jesus presents, picturing the growth, identifying threats to it. I take care not to allow the weeds and barrenness to dominate but accept that God pictures a flourishing harvest and never gives up that hope for me.
- I think of how I might remain on the alert for anything that threatens the word that is given to me: the life that Jesus offers can be leached away by skeptical attitudes, cynical comments, despairing attitudes or unkind words.

Saturday 27th July **Matthew 13:24–30**

He put before them another parable: "The kingdom of heaven may be compared to someone who sowed good seed in his field; but while everybody was asleep, an enemy came and sowed weeds among the wheat, and then went away. So when the plants came up and bore grain, then the weeds appeared as well. And the slaves of the householder came and said to him, 'Master, did you not sow good seed in your field? Where, then, did these weeds come from?' He answered, 'An enemy has done this.' The slaves said to him, 'Then do you want us to go and gather them?' But he replied, 'No; for in gathering the weeds you would uproot the wheat along with them. Let both of them grow together until the harvest; and at harvest time I will tell the reapers, Collect the weeds first and bind them in bundles to be burned, but gather the wheat into my barn.'"

- Jesus does not condone or encourage what is not of God, yet he seems to be able to acknowledge that different motivations and spirits are at work. How might I let this spirit of Jesus shape my life?
- Perhaps I can look back on events in my life that seemed barren or weedy, and see now that God was at work. What does that say to me about judging, hope or perspective?

july 28–august 3

Something to think and pray about each day this week:

In the Lord's presence

Whenever I am able to pause, and allow myself a time of quiet, I can become conscious of God's presence to me. I enter into the deepest reality of my life, where I am before the living God. This has always been the experience of people of faith. "You are the Living God, who sees me!" Hagar said, for instance, out in the wilderness. She was alone, and in need, having fled away from Abraham and Sarah. But then she realized how God was close to her, and calling out to her (Genesis 16:1–16). Likewise, God comes to me and meets me where I am. I may be struggling, out of my depth, feeling I cannot cope. But there is Someone coming alongside to me. "Courage, it is I! Do not be afraid!" Jesus said to the fearful disciples out in the lake, in the middle of the night, rowing against a headwind, as he came walking towards them (Matthew 14:27).

My prayer, then, always will have something of this reality about it. There is a great Presence there, approaching me, calling me by name. Whatever else I may do in my time of quiet, whatever theme I take for reflection and meditation, still the most essential reality is the Lord's presence before me and within me. In the movement of a gentle breeze, in the colouring of the evening sky, or simply in the stillness of my heart, God is present. God utters my name, and upholds me.

The Presence of God
As I sit here, the beating of my heart,
the ebb and flow of my breathing, the movements of my mind
are all signs of God's ongoing creation of me.
I pause for a moment, and become aware
of this presence of God within me.

Freedom
I ask for the grace
to let go of my own concerns
and be open to what God is asking of me,
to let myself be guided and formed by my loving Creator.

Consciousness
How do I find myself today?
Where am I with God? With others?
Do I have something to be grateful for? Then I give thanks.
Is there something I am sorry for? Then I ask forgiveness.

The Word
I take my time to read the Word of God, slowly, a few times, allowing myself to dwell on anything that strikes me. (Please turn to your scripture on the following pages. Inspiration points are there should you need them. When you are ready, return here to continue.)

Conversation
Remembering that I am still in God's presence,
I imagine Jesus himself standing or sitting beside me,
and say whatever is on my mind, whatever is in my heart,
speaking as one friend to another.

Conclusion
Glory be to the Father, and to the Son, and to the Holy Spirit,
As it was in the beginning, is now and ever shall be,
World without end. Amen

Sunday 28th July,
Seventeenth Sunday in Ordinary Time **Luke 11:9–13**

Jesus said to his disciples, "Ask, and it will be given to you; search, and you will find; knock, and the door will be opened for you. For everyone who asks receives, and everyone who searches finds, and for everyone who knocks, the door will be opened. Is there anyone among you who, if your child asks for a fish, will give a snake instead of a fish? Or if the child asks for an egg, will give a scorpion? If you then, who are evil, know how to give good gifts to your children, how much more will the heavenly Father give the Holy Spirit to those who ask him!"

- I grow in awareness of my need and I turn to God. I ask, not for what is trivial or passing, but for what prepares me deeply to listen to God. Naming what I need challenges me to recognize my deepest desires.
- I realize that my prayer may not always have been answered in the ways I have expected. I pray that I may see and appreciate where God has heard and answered me.

Monday 29th July **Matthew 13:31–32**

He put before them another parable: "The kingdom of heaven is like a mustard seed that someone took and sowed in his field; it is the smallest of all the seeds, but when it has grown it is the greatest of shrubs and becomes a tree, so that the birds of the air come and make nests in its branches."

- Love is like the mustard seed that grows into a tree. As the love of a married couple can shelter children and family, the love of friends can reach out to others.
- Prayer is a time when we can ask the Lord that our love grows and that our concern for others and for the world reaches out beyond narrow circles of our people.

Tuesday 30th July **Matthew 13:36–43**

His disciples approached Jesus, saying, "Explain to us the parable of the weeds of the field." He answered, "The one who sows the good seed is the Son of Man; the field is the world, and the good seed are the children of the kingdom; the weeds are the children of the evil one, and the enemy who sowed them is the devil; the harvest is the end of the age, and the reapers are angels. Just as the weeds are collected and burned up with fire, so will it be at the end of the age. The Son of Man will send his angels, and they will collect out of his kingdom all causes of sin and all evildoers, and they will throw them into the furnace of fire, where there will be weeping and gnashing of teeth. Then the righteous will shine like the sun in the kingdom of their Father. Let anyone with ears listen!"

- The good seed is sown in the world as it is. There is no need to wait; I can do whatever good I can do right now.
- Like a seed growing towards the light, I allow myself to dwell in the presence of God who loves me. I still any voices that are not for my growth, to respond only to the word God speaks to me.

Wednesday 31st July,
St Ignatius Loyola **Matthew 13:44**

Jesus said to the disciples, "The kingdom of heaven is like treasure hidden in a field, which someone found and hid; then in his joy he goes and sells all that he has and buys that field."

- Hiding treasure seems to go against the inclination to share the good news. Perhaps there are times when I need to receive God's word quietly, turning it over in my heart, valuing it and considering my life in its light.
- The parable points to the importance of being able to let go. I ask God to give me the freedom I need to lay aside my plans, my preoccupations, even my hopes, so that God's way might unfold.

Thursday 1st August **Matthew 13:47–53**

Jesus said, "Again, the kingdom of heaven is like a net that was thrown into the sea and caught fish of every kind; when it was full, they drew it ashore, sat down, and put the good into baskets but threw out the bad. So it will be at the end of the age. The angels will come out and separate the evil from the righteous and throw them into the furnace of fire, where there will be weeping and gnashing of teeth. Have you understood all this?" They answered, "Yes." And he said to them, "Therefore every scribe who has been trained for the kingdom of heaven is like the master of a household who brings out of his treasure what is new and what is old."

- Many parables show us that the kingdom of heaven involves both good and bad mixed together. I pray for the patience and tolerance that I need to live with those who differ from me.
- I pray that I might be like the scribe that Jesus mentions, able to employ all my resources to their best end.

Friday 2nd August **Matthew 13:54–58**

Jesus came to his home town and began to teach the people in their synagogue, so that they were astounded and said, "Where did this man get this wisdom and these deeds of power? Is not this the carpenter's son? Is not his mother called Mary? And are not his brothers James and Joseph and Simon and Judas? And are not all his sisters with us? Where then did this man get all this?" And they took offense at him. But Jesus said to them, "Prophets are not without honor except in their own country and in their own house." And he did not do many deeds of power there, because of their unbelief.

- The people of Jesus' home town were not ready to hear wisdom from one of their own. Perhaps I tend not to hear the wisdom close to me, but pay more attention to voices from faraway.
- Jesus' neighbors knew all about him but they didn't seem to know him. So it would be that Jesus would invite people time and again to learn from him, to follow him closely, to share in his life.

Saturday 3rd August **Matthew 14:1–12**

At that time Herod the ruler heard reports about Jesus; and he said to his servants, "This is John the Baptist; he has been raised from the dead, and for this reason these powers are at work in him." For Herod had arrested John, bound him, and put him in prison on account of Herodias, his brother Philip's wife, because John had been telling him, "It is not lawful for you to have her." Though Herod wanted to put him to death, he feared the crowd, because they regarded him as a prophet. But when Herod's birthday came, the daughter of Herodias danced before the company, and she pleased Herod so much that he promised on oath to grant her whatever she might ask. Prompted by her mother, she said, "Give me the head of John the Baptist here on a platter." The king was grieved, yet out of regard for his oaths and for the guests, he commanded it to be given; he sent and had John beheaded in the prison. The head was brought on a platter and given to the girl, who brought it to her mother. His disciples came and took the body and buried it; then they went and told Jesus.

- The vanity of Herod brought him into terrible situations as he had John imprisoned and executed. I think of whether I am able to back down, to change my mind, to admit that I am wrong. I ask God for the help I need.
- The disciples of John the Baptist did what they could do and then they went to tell Jesus. I ask God for the strength I need to do what I can—and then to turn to Jesus in my prayer.

Something to think and pray about each day this week:

Called by name

Our lives are a journey, a pilgrimage. From our mysterious origins, through our childhood and growing years, we have set forth along a unique path amidst our families or the significant people close to us So, for myself, wherever I am along that journey which is mine, in light or in darkness, struggling or in relative peace and stability, still I am being drawn forward, along a pilgrimage way. Perhaps I haven't seen things from this perspective, or have forgotten it, but it is the truth of my life: I am called by name, journeying along a unique path, God with me, God before me, all along the way that is mine. "I will bless you and go before you," God said to Abraham and Sarah, the parents of our way of faith, journeying in the desert as virtual nomads, on the basis of God's promise and Covenant.

The Chosen People journeyed too, having come out of Egypt. John Henry Newman, at a crucial and lonely stage of his journey, wrote *Lead Kindly Light*, believing God would lead him on. And today, in our endlessly fluid, bewildering and challenging world, we are especially called to travel in faith, and to depend on God's word and blessing, especially coming to us in Jesus. And perhaps, like the disciples on the Mount of the Transfiguration, we might hear the words, "This is my Son, the Beloved; he enjoys my favour; listen to him" (Matthew 17:5).

The Presence of God
I pause for a moment
and reflect on God's life-giving presence
in every part of my body, in everything around me,
in the whole of my life.

Freedom
I ask for the grace to believe
in what I could be and do
if I only allowed God, my loving Creator,
to continue to create me, guide me and shape me.

Consciousness
In God's loving presence I unwind the past day,
starting from now and looking back, moment by moment.
I gather in all the goodness and light, in gratitude.
I attend to the shadows and what they say to me,
seeking healing, courage, forgiveness.

The Word
God speaks to each one of us individually. I need to listen to what he is saying to me. (Please turn to your scripture on the following pages. Inspiration points are there should you need them. When you are ready, return here to continue.)

Conversation
How has God's Word moved me? Has it left me cold?
Has it consoled me or moved me to act in a new way?
I imagine Jesus standing or sitting beside me,
I turn and share my feelings with him.

Conclusion
Glory be to the Father, and to the Son, and to the Holy Spirit,
As it was in the beginning, is now and ever shall be,
World without end. Amen

Sunday 4th August, Eighteenth Sunday in Ordinary Time **Ecclesiastes 1:2, 2:21–23**

Vanity of vanities, says the Teacher, vanity of vanities! All is vanity. because sometimes one who has toiled with wisdom and knowledge and skill must leave all to be enjoyed by another who did not toil for it. This also is vanity and a great evil. What do mortals get from all the toil and strain with which they toil under the sun? For all their days are full of pain, and their work is a vexation; even at night their minds do not rest. This also is vanity.

- It is possible to see the world as a full of vanities—passing things—and to become cynical. I pray for a humility that acknowledges how little I alone can do, and for the courage to do what I can.
- I realize that my life and my way of living depend upon other people. I give thanks for all of those whose skill and knowledge make my life better.

Monday 5th August **Matthew 14:13–21**

Now when Jesus heard of the death of John the Baptist, he withdrew from there in a boat to a deserted place by himself. But when the crowds heard it, they followed him on foot from the towns. When he went ashore, he saw a great crowd; and he had compassion for them and cured their sick. When it was evening, the disciples came to him and said, "This is a deserted place, and the hour is now late; send the crowds away so that they may go into the villages and buy food for themselves." Jesus said to them, "They need not go away; you give them something to eat." They replied, "We have nothing here but five loaves and two fish." And he said, "Bring them here to me." Then he ordered the crowds to sit down on the grass. Taking the five loaves and the two fish, he looked up to heaven, and blessed and broke the loaves, and gave them to the disciples, and the disciples gave them to the crowds. And all ate and were filled; and they took up what was left over of the broken pieces, twelve baskets full. And those who ate were about five thousand men, besides women and children.

- Jesus went away to be alone, needing some quiet time upon hearing of the death of John the Baptist. He was, however, ready to serve those who went to him.
- Jesus was able to meet the needs of the hungry crowd by sharing with them what they had among them. I pray that I may preserve my commitment to seeking time with the God and remain ready to serve the needs of God's people.

Tuesday 6th August,
Transfiguration of the Lord **2 Peter 1:16–19**

For we did not follow cleverly devised myths when we made known to you the power and coming of our Lord Jesus Christ, but we had been eyewitnesses of his majesty. For he received honour and glory from God the Father when that voice was conveyed to him by the Majestic Glory, saying, "This is my Son, my Beloved, with whom I am well pleased." We ourselves heard this voice come from heaven, while we were with him on the holy mountain. So we have the prophetic message more fully confirmed. You will do well to be attentive to this as to a lamp shining in a dark place, until the day dawns and the morning star rises in your hearts.

- When we worship we lift our hands to a God who seems totally beyond us. We may find that difficult; sometimes we may be tempted in our worship and prayer to try to direct God.
- Let us remember with today's feast that by God's own action, God is already present. Let us seek the light of God within each of us.

Wednesday 7th August **Matthew 15:21–28**

Jesus left that place and went away to the district of Tyre and Sidon. Just then a Canaanite woman from that region came out and started shouting, "Have mercy on me, Lord, Son of David; my daughter is tormented by a demon." But he did not answer her at all. And his disciples came and urged him, saying, "Send her away, for she keeps shouting after us." He answered, "I was sent only to the lost sheep of the house of Israel." But she came and knelt before him, saying, "Lord, help me." He answered, "It is not fair to take the children's food and throw it to the dogs." She said, "Yes, Lord, yet even the dogs eat the crumbs that fall from their masters' table." Then Jesus answered her, "Woman, great is your faith! Let it be done for you as you wish." And her daughter was healed instantly.

- This woman shows great persistence; she did not allow the disciples' irritation or Jesus' offhand remark to put her off. She knew what she wanted and she trusted that Jesus could help.
- Like the woman in the gospel, I come before Jesus bringing others in my prayer. As I pray for those I love, I grow an appreciation of their goodness and ask for blessings for them. I think again of how they are blessings for me and I give thanks.

Thursday 8th August **Matthew 16:13–16**

Now when Jesus came into the district of Caesarea Philippi, he asked his disciples, "Who do people say that the Son of Man is?" And they said, "Some say John the Baptist, but others Elijah, and still others Jeremiah or one of the prophets." He said to them, "But who do you say that I am?" Simon Peter answered, "You are the Messiah, the Son of the living God."

- Take Jesus' question, "Who do you say that I am?" and imagine where it might appear before you during the day. Picture it as a billboard on the street; it could be a line in the newspaper; or like a slogan on a TV commercial. Wherever you are, Jesus invites you to remember who you are and who he is to you.
- What others say about Jesus may be helpful, supportive or affirming. The real question is not what you have heard from others, what is commonly believed or what is popular but it's what Jesus asks you. Express your answer in your way of living, your actions and your attitudes.

Friday 9th August **Matthew 16:24–26**

Then Jesus told his disciples, "If any want to become my followers, let them deny themselves and take up their cross and follow me. For those who want to save their life will lose it, and those who lose their life for my sake will find it. For what will it profit them if they gain the whole world but forfeit their life? Or what will they give in return for their life?"

- We do so much to make ourselves comfortable; protecting and looking after can become priorities when we think the world is a rough place. Perhaps we need to be careful not to cushion ourselves too much, careful not to forget that the cross is always within sight of the Christian.
- I pray for the freedom I need to be able to let go, to realize that my life is not mine to save; it comes from God and its fullness lies in God.

Saturday 10th August,
St Lawrence **John 12:24–26**

"Very truly, I tell you, unless a grain of wheat falls into the earth and dies, it remains just a single grain; but if it dies, it bears much fruit. Those who love their life lose it, and those who hate their life in this world will keep it for eternal life. Whoever serves me must follow me, and where I am, there will my servant be also. Whoever serves me, the Father will honor."

- The image that Jesus presents is simple yet strong. He does not speak of "passing away" or "falling asleep" but of death and loss. Faith in Jesus strengthens me to look beyond death to the beginning of new life.
- Jesus speaks to me as friend and calls me into his family as he invites me to remain ready to follow and to serve.

Something to think and pray about each day this week:

Meeting face to face

Personal meetings with Jesus form one of the central threads in St John's gospel. Nicodemus meets Jesus by night (John 3:1ff), but the light of faith does not yet dawn for him. Much later, there is the loving encounter with doubting Thomas, who utters the most beautiful words of faith of any of the disciples (John 20:28). Many meetings occur in between. Especially, there is the encounter between the unnamed Samaritan woman and Jesus at Jacob's well (John 4: 1–42). She is seeking—although at first she hardly knows it—more than the actual water from the well. And the Stranger she meets, needing the actual drink she is happy to pour for him, has himself a greater thirst: to offer her that unsurpassed water, which will gush up into eternal life. "Sir," she says, "give me this water, so that I may never be thirsty." And now indeed her whole life is drawn into view and seen in Jesus' gaze. And eventually the longing within her for God's coming, through his Anointed One, the Messiah, is fulfilled when Jesus says to her, "I am he, the one who is speaking to you."

So it is with me. I seek and long for the refreshing grace and life of God. And, more than that, all the time there is Someone endlessly seeking me out, wishing to speak to me, and offering the fount of eternal water.

The Presence of God

The world is charged with the grandeur of God (Gerard Manley Hopkins).
I dwell for a moment on the presence of God
around me, in every part of my body,
and deep within my being.

Freedom

"In these days, God taught me
as a schoolteacher teaches a pupil" (St Ignatius).
I remind myself that there are things God has to teach me yet,
and ask for the grace to hear them and let them change me.

Consciousness

Help me, Lord, to be more conscious of your presence.
Teach me to recognize your presence in others.
Fill my heart with gratitude for the times your love
has been shown to me through the care of others.

The Word

I read the Word of God slowly, a few times over, and I listen to what God is saying to me. (Please turn to your scripture on the following pages. Inspirations points are there should you need them. When you are ready, return here to continue.)

Conversation

What feelings are rising in me
as I pray and reflect on God's Word?
I imagine Jesus himself sitting or standing beside me,
and open my heart to him.

Conclusion

Glory be to the Father, and to the Son, and to the Holy Spirit,
As it was in the beginning, is now and ever shall be,
World without end. Amen

Sunday 11th August,
Nineteenth Sunday in Ordinary Time **Luke 12:35–38**

Jesus said, "Be dressed for action and have your lamps lit; be like those who are waiting for their master to return from the wedding banquet, so that they may open the door for him as soon as he comes and knocks. Blessed are those slaves whom the master finds alert when he comes; truly I tell you, he will fasten his belt and have them sit down to eat, and he will come and serve them. If he comes during the middle of the night, or near dawn, and finds them so, blessed are those slaves."

- Jesus does not want us to wait passively or to be ready in some vague or general sense. Our attentive and active waiting marks us as servants looking for signs of the master's return.
- Sometimes I want to know more than is revealed to me; sometimes I am distracted by remote ideas. I pray that I may accept and give my energy to the place in which I find myself.

Monday 12th August **Matthew 17:24–27**

When they reached Capernaum, the collectors of the temple tax came to Peter and said, "Does your teacher not pay the temple tax?" He said, "Yes, he does." And when he came home, Jesus spoke of it first, asking, "What do you think, Simon? From whom do kings of the earth take toll or tribute? From their children or from others?" When Peter said, "From others." Jesus said to him, "Then the children are free. However, so that we do not give offence to them, go to the lake and cast a hook; take the first fish that comes up; and when you open its mouth, you will find a coin; take that and give it to them for you and me."

- The sayings and deeds of Jesus were under constant scrutiny. Living in faith I may, like Jesus, be ready for all my actions and words to be weighed and evaluated. Living in a culture in which shrill and judgemental reporting abounds, I may become like those who observe him, judging, suspicious and cynical.
- It seems that Jesus did not discuss everything freely in public but waited until he was alone with the disciples. Perhaps I need time before I speak—time to reflect and time to consider where my words might be best used.

Tuesday 13th August **Matthew 18:1–5**

At that time the disciples came to Jesus and asked, "Who is the greatest in the kingdom of heaven?" He called a child, whom he put among them, and said, "Truly I tell you, unless you change and become like children, you will never enter the kingdom of heaven. Whoever becomes humble like this child is the greatest in the kingdom of heaven. Whoever welcomes one such child in my name welcomes me.

- Jesus offers us a strong image: the humble child. I might sit in quiet prayer, and let it unfold its meaning for me now.
- The disciples were used to the competitive and comparative habits of adults. Jesus showed them that there is another way of seeing the world. I pray for the humility that I need to walk more slowly and talk more simply.

Wednesday 14th August **Matthew 18:15–17**

Jesus said, "If another member of the church sins against you, go and point out the fault when the two of you are alone. If the member listens to you, you have regained that one. But if you are not listened to, take one or two others along with you, so that every word may be confirmed by the evidence of two or three witnesses."

- I let my ideas of justice and fairness be worked on by Jesus' words. I resist engaging in an intellectual evaluation or a legal argument, and let Jesus' desire for harmony speak to my heart.
- I consider the effects of living in a culture that promotes gossip, scandal and the telling of tales. I pray that God's Spirit may lead me to right judgment.

Thursday 15th August,
Assumption of the Virgin Mary **Luke 1:46–56**

And Mary said, "My soul magnifies the Lord, and my spirit rejoices in God my Savior, for he has looked with favor on the lowliness of his servant. Surely, from now on all generations will call me blessed; for the Mighty One has done great things for me, and holy is his name. His mercy is for those who fear him from generation to generation. He has shown strength with his arm; he has scattered the proud in the thoughts of their hearts. He has brought down the powerful from their thrones, and lifted up the lowly; he has filled the hungry with good things, and sent the rich away empty. He has helped his servant Israel, in remembrance of his mercy, according to the promise he made to our ancestors, to Abraham and to his descendants forever." And Mary remained with Elizabeth about three months and then returned to her home.

- Mary realized that she was blessed, that great things had happened in her life. She saw the source of them and gave thanks to God. She inspires and helps me to appreciate goodness.
- As well as acknowledging God's goodness, I lay before God my thirsts for justice, peace and equality. I look forward to the day when God will satisfy the hungry.

Friday 16th August **Matthew 19:3–11**

Some Pharisees came to him, and to test him they asked, "Is it lawful for a man to divorce his wife for any cause?" He answered, "Have you not read that the one who made them at the beginning 'made them male and female,' and said, 'For this reason a man shall leave his father and mother and be joined to his wife, and the two shall become one flesh'? So they are no longer two, but one flesh. Therefore what God has joined together, let no one separate." They said to him, "Why then did Moses command us to give a certificate of dismissal and to divorce her?" He said to them, "It was because you were so hard-hearted that Moses allowed you to divorce your wives, but at the beginning it was not so. And I say to you, whoever divorces his wife, except for unchastity, and marries another commits adultery." His disciples said to him, "If such is the case of a man with his wife, it is better not to marry." But he said to them, "Not everyone can accept this teaching, but only those to whom it is given."

- Jesus calls us to high ideals. Whether we marry or remain single, we are called to live wholeheartedly.

- I pray with thanks for all the people I know who have been able to live out their dreams. I pray with compassion for those disappointed by the changing circumstances of their lives.

Saturday 17th August **Matthew 19:13–15**

Then little children were being brought to Jesus in order that he might lay his hands on them and pray. The disciples spoke sternly to those who brought them; but Jesus said, "Let the little children come to me, and do not stop them; for it is to such as these that the kingdom of heaven belongs." And he laid his hands on them and went on his way.

- I bring before Jesus everything in my life that is growing, delicate or even a dream for me. I allow him to bless my hopes and listen to him as he values my desires.
- I think of how I might look out more for the "children" around me. I remember that the poor and the weak had a secure place in the heart of Jesus and I see how I give them space in mine.

Something to think and pray about each day this week:

The gift of thankfulness

Thankfulness is a wonderful gift. It arises in people's hearts when they can look back and see how their lives have been enriched, by parents, or children, a spouse or faithful friend, or other good people. Thankfulness may be delayed, indeed, and can only come after much darkness and struggle, when sunbeams and rays of light have shone through—when, despite what has been painful and difficult, I can now see those sunbeams, in the eyes of kind friends who have stood by me, or in the little everyday things which are good and uplifting. As a result, often my prayer can be simply a mood and feeling of gratitude and praise. I simply want to be in that thankful space. "I thank you, Lord, with all my heart," the psalmist says, "you have heard the words of my mouth . . . I thank you for your faithfulness and love which excel all we ever knew of you. On the day I called, you answered; you increased the strength of my soul" (Psalm 138). How good these words are! And even if my mood is not thankful just now, perhaps in repeating these lines, or those in the rest of Psalm 138, the gift of thankfulness will rise in my heart.

The Presence of God

As I sit here, God is present,
breathing life into me and into everything around me.
For a few moments, I sit silently,
and become aware of God's loving presence.

Freedom

If God were trying to tell me something, would I know?
If God were reassuring me or challenging me, would I notice?
I ask for the grace to be free of my own preoccupations
and open to what God may be saying to me.

Consciousness

How am I really feeling? Light-hearted? Heavy-hearted?
I may be very much at peace, happy to be here.
Equally, I may be frustrated, worried or angry.
I acknowledge how I really am. It is the real me that the Lord loves.

The Word

I take my time to read the Word of God, slowly, a few times, allowing myself to dwell on anything that strikes me. (Please turn to your scripture on the following pages. Inspiration points are there should you need them. When you are ready, return here to continue.)

Conversation

What is stirring in me as I pray?
Am I consoled, troubled, left cold?
I imagine Jesus himself standing or sitting at my side,
and share my feelings with him.

Conclusion

Glory be to the Father, and to the Son, and to the Holy Spirit,
As it was in the beginning, is now and ever shall be,
World without end. Amen

Sunday 18th August,
Twentieth Sunday in Ordinary Time **Hebrews 12:1–4**

Therefore, since we are surrounded by so great a cloud of witnesses, let us also lay aside every weight and the sin that clings so closely, and let us run with perseverance the race that is set before us, looking to Jesus the pioneer and perfecter of our faith, who for the sake of the joy that was set before him endured the cross, disregarding its shame, and has taken his seat at the right hand of the throne of God. Consider him who endured such hostility against himself from sinners, so that you may not grow weary or lose heart. In your struggle against sin you have not yet resisted to the point of shedding your blood.

- This places me in my prayer: not alone, but in a cloud of witnesses, including parents, family, teachers, friends as well as the great and famous. I am not in an armchair but in a race, moving forward, drawing on my strength, persevering.
- If I meet obstacles and discouragement, I can look to Jesus, who faced and overcame worse.

Monday 19th August **Matthew 19:16–22**

Then someone came to Jesus and said, "Teacher, what good deed must I do to have eternal life?" And he said to him, "Why do you ask me about what is good? There is only one who is good. If you wish to enter into life, keep the commandments." He said to him, "Which ones?" And Jesus said, "You shall not murder; You shall not commit adultery; You shall not steal; You shall not bear false witness; Honor your father and mother; also, You shall love your neighbor as yourself." The young man said to him, "I have kept all these; what do I still lack?" Jesus said to him, "If you wish to be perfect, go, sell your possessions, and give the money to the poor, and you will have treasure in heaven; then come, follow me." When the young man heard this word, he went away grieving, for he had many possessions.

- The man found out through meeting Jesus that happiness is found not in keeping commandments but in giving away possessions. The attachment he had to his possession gave him grief, and kept him from the freedom of enjoying life.

- What holds me back from living life to the full? Offer that emptiness to the Lord in prayer and ask him to fill it.

Tuesday 20th August **Matthew 19:23–26**

Jesus said to his disciples, "Truly I tell you, it will be hard for a rich person to enter the kingdom of heaven. Again I tell you, it is easier for a camel to go through the eye of a needle than for someone who is rich to enter the kingdom of God." When the disciples heard this, they were greatly astounded and said, "Then who can be saved?" But Jesus looked at them and said, "For mortals it is impossible, but for God all things are possible."

- The astonishment of the disciples suggests that, even after all the time they spent with Jesus, they still did not understand just how radical his message was. I ask Jesus to help me to listen deeply and to let the message sink into my heart.
- Paul told the people of Philippi that nothing matters more than knowing Christ (Philippians 3:8). I think of what really matters to me, what makes me truly rich, and ask God's help to let everything else go.

Wednesday 21st August **Matthew 20:1–16**

Jesus said to his disciples, "For the kingdom of heaven is like a landowner who went out early in the morning to hire laborers for his vineyard. After agreeing with the laborers for the usual daily wage, he sent them into his vineyard. When he went out about nine o'clock, he saw others standing idle in the marketplace; and he said to them, 'You also go into the vineyard, and I will pay you whatever is right.' So they went. When he went out again about noon and about three o'clock, he did the same. And about five o'clock he went out and found others standing around; and he said to them, 'Why are you standing here idle all day?' They said to him, 'Because no one has hired us.' He said to them, 'You also go into the vineyard.' When evening came, the owner of the vineyard said to his manager, 'Call the laborers and give them their pay, beginning with the last and then going to the first.' When those hired about five o'clock came, each of them received the usual daily wage. Now when the first came, they thought they would receive more; but each of them also received the usual daily wage. And when they received it, they grumbled against the landowner, saying, 'These last worked only one hour, and you have made them equal to us who have borne the burden of the day and the scorching heat.' But he replied to one of them, 'Friend, I am doing you no wrong; did you not agree with me for the usual daily wage? Take what belongs to you and go; I choose to give to this last the same as I give to you. Am I not allowed to do what I choose with what belongs to me? Or are you envious because I am generous?' So the last will be first, and the first will be last."

- The landowner will always appear unfair if we compare only the amount received. Instead of coming to judgement about others or about myself, I ask God to help me to have a proper perspective.
- I pray that I may be big-hearted enough to rejoice in the generosity that God displays. Jesus tells us that graciousness and kindness is at the heart of God; I give thanks for this revelation.

Thursday 22nd August **Matthew 22:1–2, 8–14**

Once more Jesus spoke to them in parables, saying: "The kingdom of heaven may be compared to a king who gave a wedding banquet for his son. Then he said to his slaves, 'The wedding is ready. Go therefore into the main streets, and invite everyone you find to the wedding banquet.' Those slaves went out into the streets and gathered all whom they found, both good and bad; so the wedding hall was filled with guests. But when the king came in to see the guests, he noticed a man there who was not wearing a wedding robe, and he said to him, 'Friend, how did you get in here without a wedding robe?' And he was speechless. Then the king said to the attendants, 'Bind him hand and foot, and throw him into the outer darkness, where there will be weeping and gnashing of teeth.' For many are called, but few are chosen."

- As generous and open-ended as God's invitation is, it is not to be exploited or taken for granted. For my part I ask God to help me to respond as best I can, to prepare my heart to receive God's gifts.

- Like the slaves of the king, I am sent into to the streets of the everyday to offer an invitation to others to receive God's goodness. May my words, life and actions proclaim the good news. It is up to others to respond and to God to do the rest.

Friday 23rd August **Matthew 22:34–40**

When the Pharisees heard that Jesus had silenced the Sadducees, they gathered together, and one of them, a lawyer, asked him a question to test him. "Teacher, which commandment in the law is the greatest?" He said to him, "'You shall love the Lord your God with all your heart, and with all your soul, and with all your mind.' This is the greatest and first commandment. And a second is like it: 'You shall love your neighbor as yourself.' On these two commandments hang all the law and the prophets."

- If I have ever wished for a simple summary of the gospel, I give thanks that I have it here. Simple as this message seems, I know how difficult it is to live out. I ask God for the help I need to love fully and freely.
- Life in balance means loving God and loving others. I consider how I sometimes wobble and, in my prayer, seek again the path that Jesus puts before me.

Saturday 24th August,
St Bartholomew, Apostle **John 1:45–51**

Philip found Nathanael and said to him, "We have found him about whom Moses in the law and also the prophets wrote, Jesus son of Joseph from Nazareth." Nathanael said to him, "Can anything good come out of Nazareth?" Philip said to him, "Come and see." When Jesus saw Nathanael coming towards him, he said of him, "Here is truly an Israelite in whom there is no deceit!" Nathanael asked him, "Where did you come to know me?" Jesus answered, "I saw you under the fig tree before Philip called you." Nathanael replied, "Rabbi, you are the Son of God! You are the King of Israel!" Jesus answered,

"Do you believe because I told you that I saw you under the fig tree? You will see greater things than these." And he said to him, "Very truly, I tell you, you will see heaven opened and the angels of God ascending and descending upon the Son of Man."

- Nathaniel's answer seemed cynical but he was prepared to go and see, as Philip invited him. I pray for the strength I need to put up with dismissive answers and ask God to work gently in skeptical hearts.
- What might it have been that Jesus saw under the fig tree? What actions or words of Nathaniel impressed him? I think of how Jesus sees me under the fig trees of my life, of how he values what may be hidden from others.

Sacred Space

Something to think and pray about each day this week:

Allowing peace to enter

One of the lovely Taizé music-chants takes up the theme of Psalm 62, "In God alone my soul can find its rest and peace; in God my peace and joy." Over and over, we sing and pray that chant, allowing that peace to reside within. And Margaret Rizza has some wonderful music compositions around the same theme, such as "You are the centre, you are my life", and "O Lord, my heart is not proud . . . Truly I have set my soul in silence and peace; at rest, as a child in its mother's arms, so is my soul" (after Psalm 131).

There is a great secret here, a wonderful gift awaiting. But we can doubt that: "The Lord has abandoned me, the Lord has forgotten me . . . yet even if a mother forgets, I will never forget you" (Isaiah 49:14–15). And there are Jesus's words telling us not to worry, but to trust in God's providential care (Matthew 6:24–34). Yet how often we are overwhelmed with anxiety and worry, and feel abandoned. Lord, let your peace enter my soul. Or rather, let me *experience* that peace, since already you are the centre, you are already in the depths of my being. Lord, let me know I am never alone, for you envelop me.

The Presence of God

As I sit here with my book, God is here.
Around me, in my sensations, in my thoughts and deep within me.
I pause for a moment, and become aware
of God's life-giving presence.

Freedom

I need to close out the noise, to rise above the noise;
The noise that interrupts, that separates,
The noise that isolates.
I need to listen to God again.

Consciousness

Knowing that God loves me unconditionally,
I can afford to be honest about how I am.
How has the last day been, and how do I feel now?
I share my feelings openly with the Lord.

The Word

God speaks to each one of us individually. I need to listen to what he is saying to me. (Please turn to your scripture on the following pages. Inspiration points are there should you need them. When you are ready, return here to continue.)

Conversation

Do I notice myself reacting as I pray with the Word of God?
Do I feel challenged, comforted, angry?
Imagining Jesus sitting or standing by me,
I speak out my feelings, as one trusted friend to another.

Conclusion

Glory be to the Father, and to the Son, and to the Holy Spirit,
As it was in the beginning, is now and ever shall be,
World without end. Amen

Sunday 25th August,
Twenty-first Sunday in Ordinary Time — Luke 13:22–30

Jesus went through one town and village after another, teaching as he made his way to Jerusalem. Someone asked him, "Lord, will only a few be saved?" He said to them, "Strive to enter through the narrow door; for many, I tell you, will try to enter and will not be able. When once the owner of the house has got up and shut the door, and you begin to stand outside and to knock at the door, saying, 'Lord, open to us,' then in reply he will say to you, 'I do not know where you come from.' Then you will begin to say, 'We ate and drank with you, and you taught in our streets.' But he will say, 'I do not know where you come from; go away from me, all you evildoers!' There will be weeping and gnashing of teeth when you see Abraham and Isaac and Jacob and all the prophets in the kingdom of God, and you yourselves thrown out. Then people will come from east and west, from north and south, and will eat in the kingdom of God. Indeed, some are last who will be first, and some are first who will be last."

- Sometimes we like to picture Jesus as gentle and forgiving, not because of what it says about him but because it seems to allow us to relax. I accept that Jesus places a challenge before me in telling me about the narrow door. I acknowledge that there are choices I must make and I ask Jesus' help.
- I speak to Jesus about my joys and hopes, my anxieties and difficulties, listening for his voice as I come to know my own life better.

Monday 26th August — Matthew 23:13–17

Jesus said to the people, "But woe to you, scribes and Pharisees, hypocrites! For you lock people out of the kingdom of heaven. For you do not go in yourselves, and when others are going in, you stop them. Woe to you, scribes and Pharisees, hypocrites! For you cross sea and land to make a single convert, and you make the new convert twice as much a child of hell as yourselves. Woe to you, blind guides, who say, 'Whoever swears by the sanctuary is bound by nothing, but whoever swears by the gold of the sanctuary is bound by the oath.' You blind fools! For which is greater, the gold or the sanctuary that has made the gold sacred?"

- Jesus keeps the strongest language to condemn those who confuse the externals of religion with what might be at its heart. I let God lead me in my time of prayer, prepared even to let go of habits and rituals so that I may better hear the voice of God.
- I pray for the community with which I worship; may we never confuse the beautiful things we have or do with their source, but may we grown together in humble service of God.

Tuesday 27th August **Matthew 23:23–24**

Jesus said, "Woe to you, scribes and Pharisees, hypocrites! For you tithe mint, dill, and cummin, and have neglected the weightier matters of the law: justice and mercy and faith. It is these you ought to have practiced without neglecting the others. You blind guides! You strain out a gnat but swallow a camel!

- The Pharisees were caught up in the detail, but had lost sight of the bigger picture. Their desire for precision had made them critical and judgemental.
- As I see Jesus engage with the self-important and scrupulous Pharisees, I pray for the wisdom I need. I ask God to direct me to know when to speak out against injustice and the oppression of the poor.

Wednesday 28th August **Matthew 23:27–28**

Jesus said to the people, "Woe to you, scribes and Pharisees, hypocrites! For you are like whitewashed tombs, which on the outside look beautiful, but inside they are full of the bones of the dead and of all kinds of filth. So you also on the outside look righteous to others, but inside you are full of hypocrisy and lawlessness."

- God sees the inside. God sees our efforts at doing good, and is not fooled by empty prayer and worship.

- Jesus is harsh on hypocrisy, on the pretence that a life is more religious than another's. He invites us to sincerity, humility and trust in him.

Thursday 29th August **Matthew 24:42–44**

Jesus said to his disciples, "Keep awake therefore, for you do not know on what day your Lord is coming. But understand this: if the owner of the house had known in what part of the night the thief was coming, he would have stayed awake and would not have let his house be broken into. Therefore you also must be ready, for the Son of Man is coming at an unexpected hour."

- I ask for help to keep awake as I bring my life in prayer before God. I need to remain alert to notice, appreciate and give thanks to God as I see where the Spirit has been at work.
- Recognizing where God's Spirit has been, I am encouraged to see that the Spirit still moves. Taking to heart what Jesus says about the unexpected hour, I look at my life again lest I become blind to God's presence.

Friday 30th August **Matthew 25:1–13**

Jesus said to his disciples, "Then the kingdom of heaven will be like this. Ten bridesmaids took their lamps and went to meet the bridegroom. Five of them were foolish, and five were wise. When the foolish took their lamps, they took no oil with them; but the wise took flasks of oil with their lamps. As the bridegroom was delayed, all of them became drowsy and slept. But at midnight there was a shout, 'Look! Here is the bridegroom! Come out to meet him.' Then all those bridesmaids got up and trimmed their lamps. The foolish said to the wise, 'Give us some of your oil, for our lamps are going out.' But the wise replied, 'No! there will not be enough for you and for us; you had better go to the dealers and buy some for yourselves.' And while they went to buy it, the bridegroom came, and those who were ready went with him into the wedding banquet; and the door was shut. Later the other bridesmaids came also, saying, 'Lord, lord, open to us.' But he replied, 'Truly I tell you, I do not know you.' Keep awake therefore, for you know neither the day nor the hour."

- I pray for all who have given up hope, for those for whom the waiting seemed too much to ask.
- Jesus suggests that there is a proper time to prepare. I look to the "oil and lamps" of my life and ask God to replenish and restock my reserves.

Saturday 31st August **Matthew 25:14–28**

Jesus told his disciples this parable, "For it is as if a man, going on a journey, summoned his slaves and entrusted his property to them; to one he gave five talents, to another two, to another one, to each according to his ability. Then he went away. The one who had received the five talents went off at once and traded with them, and made five more talents. In the same way, the one who had the two talents made two more talents. But the one who had received the one talent went off and dug a hole in the ground and hid his master's money. After a long time the master of those slaves came and settled accounts with them. Then the one who had received the five talents came forward, bringing five more talents, saying, 'Master, you handed over to me five talents; see, I have made five more talents.' His master said to him, 'Well done, good and trustworthy slave; you have been trustworthy in a few things, I will put you in charge of many things; enter into the joy of your master.' And the one with the two talents also came forward, saying, 'Master, you handed over to me two talents; see, I have made two more talents.' His master said to him, 'Well done, good and trustworthy slave; you have been trustworthy in a few things, I will put you in charge of many things; enter into the joy of your master.' Then the one who had received the one talent also came forward, saying, 'Master, I knew that you were a harsh man, reaping where you did not sow, and gathering where you did not scatter seed; so I was afraid, and I went and hid your talent in the ground. Here you have what is yours.' But his master replied, 'You wicked and lazy slave! You knew, did you, that I reap where I did not sow, and gather where I did not scatter? Then you ought to have invested my money with the bankers, and on my return I would have received what was my own with interest. So take the talent from him, and give it to the one with the ten talents.'"

- Before I think of what my talents might be and count them out, I turn to the One from whom all blessings come. Help me, God, to appreciate how I make a difference in the world. Refine me so that who I am may give glory to you.
- The servants did not judge one another's results nor did they look to the markets. Each stood honestly before the master, as I do now.

Sacred Space

september 1–7

Something to think and pray about each day this week:

Sharing in the Cross

The mystery of the Cross will overshadow every Christian's life. Much as we may consider the gift of peace the mark of strong faith, and be tempted to think that such peace will render us impervious to "the slings and arrows of fortune," yet the following of Christ will bring us inevitably to share in some manner in his Passion. "If any of you wish to be my disciples," Jesus said, "let them deny themselves and take up their cross and follow me" (Matthew 16:24). Naturally, we can recoil at such a prospect. And Peter, who had confessed his faith in Jesus, nevertheless was taken aback when Jesus subsequently spoke about his future suffering in Jerusalem. But, to continue to accompany someone on their journey, and stay with them in their troubles, is the mark of love. And the sufferings that come our way in life, leading to anguish and darkness, will not be in vain if we appreciate that through those sufferings we are sharing in the Cross of the Lord. For the Cross is also the mystery of divine love, poured out to the end, for the world's redeeming. In our own tribulations, small or great, we are mysteriously joined to that great love, and are part of it for the healing and uplifting of humanity. In the Cross is our own redemption and eternal hope, and also that of the whole world. Nothing we suffer is in vain, therefore, but is made fruitful, in the fruitfulness of Christ's offering and eternal love.

The Presence of God
I pause for a moment, aware that God is here.
I think of how everything around me,
the air I breathe, my whole body,
is tingling with the presence of God.

Freedom
I will ask God's help,
to be free from my own preoccupations,
to be open to God in this time of prayer,
to come to love and serve him more.

Consciousness
In the presence of my loving Creator,
I look honestly at my feelings over the last day,
the highs, the lows and the level ground.
Can I see where the Lord has been present?

The Word
I read the Word of God slowly, a few times over, and I listen to what God is saying to me. (Please turn to your scripture on the following pages. Inspiration points are there should you need them. When you are ready, return here to continue.)

Conversation
Remembering that I am still in God's presence,
I imagine Jesus himself standing or sitting beside me,
and say whatever is on my mind, whatever is in my heart,
speaking as one friend to another.

Conclusion
Glory be to the Father, and to the Son, and to the Holy Spirit,
As it was in the beginning, is now and ever shall be,
World without end. Amen

Sunday 1st September,
Twenty-second Sunday in Ordinary Time Luke 14:1, 7–11

On one occasion when Jesus was going to the house of a leader of the Pharisees to eat a meal on the sabbath, they were watching him closely. When he noticed how the guests chose the places of honor, he told them a parable. 'When you are invited by someone to a wedding banquet, do not sit down at the place of honor, in case someone more distinguished than you has been invited by your host; and the host who invited both of you may come and say to you, "Give this person your place", and then in disgrace you would start to take the lowest place. But when you are invited, go and sit down at the lowest place, so that when your host comes, he may say to you, "Friend, move up higher"; then you will be honored in the presence of all who sit at the table with you. For all who exalt themselves will be humbled, and those who humble themselves will be exalted.'

- As I come to pray, I take care to seat myself properly. I choose a lowly place because I am aware of my status; God invites me closer because of love.
- I realize that I sometimes want to earn God's love or feel that I deserve it, and I ask forgiveness.
- I think of how appreciation or recognition have encouraged me and consider how I might raise someone up with my words.

Monday 2nd September Luke 4:16–22

When he came to Nazareth, where he had been brought up, he went to the synagogue on the sabbath day, as was his custom. He stood up to read, and the scroll of the prophet Isaiah was given to him. He unrolled the scroll and found the place where it was written: "The Spirit of the Lord is upon me, because he has anointed me to bring good news to the poor. He has sent me to proclaim release to the captives and recovery of sight to the blind, to let the oppressed go free, to proclaim the year of the Lord's favor." And he rolled up the scroll, gave it back to the attendant, and sat down. The eyes of all in the synagogue were fixed on him. Then he began to say to them,

"Today this scripture has been fulfilled in your hearing." All spoke well of him and were amazed at the gracious words that came from his mouth.

- Jesus lists his priorities: all who are restricted or confined are invited to freedom. I realize that I am included, called to new liberty and life. What does Jesus have in mind for me? Where is he calling me to freedom, to life?
- Jesus lived among people whose vision was narrow and who found it difficult to accept his inspired words—they were ready even to kill him. Yet he remained part of them, going to pray with them "as was his custom."

Tuesday 3rd September **Luke 4:31–37**

He went down to Capernaum, a city in Galilee, and was teaching them on the sabbath. They were astounded at his teaching, because he spoke with authority. In the synagogue there was a man who had the spirit of an unclean demon, and he cried out with a loud voice, "Let us alone! What have you to do with us, Jesus of Nazareth? Have you come to destroy us? I know who you are, the Holy One of God." But Jesus rebuked him, saying, "Be silent, and come out of him!" When the demon had thrown him down before them, he came out of him without having done him any harm. They were all amazed and kept saying to one another, "What kind of utterance is this? For with authority and power he commands the unclean spirits, and out they come!" And a report about him began to reach every place in the region.

- The spirit that was not of God cried out, "Let us alone." The message of Jesus may often disturb and unsettle. I pray that I may receive more fully now, in this time of prayer, strength from the Spirit of Jesus and not settle for other meaner spirits that promise me comfort.
- The authority of Jesus is unlike any other; it is not coercive or forceful but calls to my heart. This time of prayer is the time for my heart to speak to his heart, and for me to acknowledge the authority I give him.

Wednesday 4th September **Luke 4:40–44**

As the sun was setting, all those who had any who were sick with various kinds of diseases brought them to Jesus; and he laid his hands on each of them and cured them. Demons also came out of many, shouting, "You are the Son of God!" But he rebuked them and would not allow them to speak, because they knew that he was the Messiah. At daybreak he departed and went into a deserted place. And the crowds were looking for him; and when they reached him, they wanted to prevent him from leaving them. But he said to them, "I must proclaim the good news of the kingdom of God to the other cities also; for I was sent for this purpose." So he continued proclaiming the message in the synagogues of Judea.

- The people wanted to stay where they were and to keep Jesus with them. He saw his mission ahead, however, and spoke to them about how he must move on. Jesus doesn't want me to settle where I am but calls me to go with him.
- Jesus went to a deserted place so that he might find time to be alone with God. Inspired by him I do the same, creating this moment of quiet so that I might meet with God.

Thursday 5th September **Luke 5:4–11**

When Jesus had finished speaking, he said to Simon, "Put out into the deep water and let down your nets for a catch." Simon answered, "Master, we have worked all night long but have caught nothing. Yet if you say so, I will let down the nets." When they had done this, they caught so many fish that their nets were beginning to break. So they signaled their partners in the other boat to come and help them. And they came and filled both boats, so that they began to sink. But when Simon Peter saw it, he fell down at Jesus' knees, saying, "Go away from me, Lord, for I am a sinful man!" For he and all who were with him were amazed at the catch of fish that they had taken; and so also were James and John, sons of Zebedee, who were partners with Simon. Then Jesus said to Simon, "Do not be afraid; from now on you will be catching people." When they had brought their boats to shore, they left everything and followed him.

- Peter knew his unworthiness; to follow Jesus closely seemed too much to ask. He forgot that his discipleship was not his own idea—it was Jesus who called him as friend.
- I try to shift my focus from what I believe, what I think so that I might appreciate more just how lovingly God looks on me, knows me, loves me and call speak to draw closer.

Friday 6th September **Luke 5:33–39**

Then the Pharisees and the scribes said to Jesus, "John's disciples, like the disciples of the Pharisees, frequently fast and pray, but your disciples eat and drink." Jesus said to them, "You cannot make wedding guests fast while the bridegroom is with them, can you? The days will come when the bridegroom will be taken away from them, and then they will fast in those days." He also told them a parable: "No one tears a piece from a new garment and sews it on an old garment; otherwise the new will be torn, and the piece from the new will not match the old. And no one puts new wine into old wineskins; otherwise the new wine will burst the skins and will be spilled, and the skins will be destroyed. But new wine must be put into fresh wineskins.'"

- The Pharisees saw different ways of living and made comparisons; Jesus simply sought life.
- Jesus saw the ordinary things of the world—torn clothes, spilt wine—and recognized how God is at work in us. How might I look more closely at the bits and pieces of my everyday?

Saturday 7th September **Psalm 53(54):1–2, 4, 6**

Save me, O God, by your name, and vindicate me by your might. Hear my prayer, O God; give ear to the words of my mouth. But surely God is my helper; the Lord is the upholder of my life. I will give thanks to your name, O Lord, for it is good.

- The Psalms express so much to us about prayer in all its simplicity, and its complexity. With the psalmist we acknowledge God's power and protection which bring stability and hope each day, even when life presses down on us.
- With the psalmist, we give thanks as we pray to our God who loves us, who saves us, and who listens to us—to each and every word we utter.

Sacred Space

september 8–14

Something to think and pray about each day this week:

Embracing humanity

The holiness of God is purifying. "The Living One who sees me," as Hagar realized (Genesis 16:13), is also the Purifying One experienced by the prophet Isaiah (Isaiah 6:1–7). And the great Psalm on God's presence, "O Lord, you search me and you know me" (Psalm 139), expresses in unforgettable words how God is always with me and before me. God seeks me out, with burning love, so that I am purified and transformed in that love. In all of my life, I will somehow encounter that love, no matter how I try to hide from it. God will not let me go. For I must be brought into that divine love, and in turn display it to others in my life. "You must therefore be perfect, as your heavenly Father is perfect," Jesus says (Matthew 5:48). Especially, this perfection is meant to be a mirror of God's own love, which reaches out to all humanity.

Such a universal love can seem impossible to us—particularly when it includes a spirit of forgiveness towards those who offend us (cf Matthew 6:12–17; and 18:21–35). How can this be possible? How can I, in my frail and limited humanity, reach out in such a way? How can one forgive, particularly when there has been hurt and injustice, and no acknowledgement of the wrong perpetrated? "Lord, reach deeply into my heart with your redeeming, purifying love. Gift me with your love. And then I know your love will reach out from me, despite my weakness, and in the ways you know best. Amen."

The Presence of God

For a few moments, I think of God's veiled presence in things:
in the elements, giving them existence;
in plants, giving them life; in animals, giving them sensation;
and finally, in me, giving me all this and more,
making me a temple, a dwelling-place of the Spirit.

Freedom

God is not foreign to my freedom.
Instead the Spirit breathes life into my most intimate desires,
gently nudging me towards all that is good.
I ask for the grace to let myself be enfolded by the Spirit.

Consciousness

Knowing that God loves me unconditionally,
I look honestly over the last day, its events and my feelings.
Do I have something to be grateful for? Then I give thanks.
Is there something I am sorry for? Then I ask forgiveness.

The Word

I take my time to read the Word of God, slowly, a few times, allowing myself to dwell on anything that strikes me. (Please turn to your scripture on the following pages. Inspiration points are there should you need them. When you are ready, return here to continue.)

Conversation

How has God's Word moved me? Has it left me cold?
Has it consoled me or moved me to act in a new way?
I imagine Jesus standing or sitting beside me,
I turn and share my feelings with him.

Conclusion

Glory be to the Father, and to the Son, and to the Holy Spirit,
As it was in the beginning, is now and ever shall be,
World without end. Amen

Sunday 8th September,
Twenty-third Sunday in Ordinary Time Wisdom 9:13–18

For who can learn the counsel of God? Or who can discern what the Lord wills? For the reasoning of mortals is worthless, and our designs are likely to fail; for a perishable body weighs down the soul, and this earthy tent burdens the thoughtful mind. We can hardly guess at what is on earth, and what is at hand we find with labor; but who has traced out what is in the heavens? Who has learned your counsel, unless you have given wisdom and sent your holy spirit from on high? And thus the paths of those on earth were set right, and people were taught what pleases you, and were saved by wisdom.

- Certainty sometimes appeals to me, but too much caution may still my hands and keep me inactive. I pray for trust in what God reveals to me and for the courage I need to follow God.
- Science continues to probe the mysteries of the world even as some come to conclusions about the workings of God. I pray that I may preserve an attitude of wonder and awe at God's ways.

Monday 9th September Luke 6:6–11

On another sabbath Jesus entered the synagogue and taught, and there was a man there whose right hand was withered. The scribes and the Pharisees watched him to see whether he would cure on the sabbath, so that they might find an accusation against him. Even though he knew what they were thinking, he said to the man who had the withered hand, "Come and stand here." He got up and stood there. Then Jesus said to them, "I ask you, is it lawful to do good or to do harm on the sabbath, to save life or to destroy it?" After looking around at all of them, he said to him, "Stretch out your hand." He did so, and his hand was restored. But they were filled with fury and discussed with one another what they might do to Jesus.

- The Pharisees watch, alert to any transgression. Jesus looks around and recognizes where there is a need. As I perceive the world around me, I pray that I may be blessed to see as Jesus does, and to respond by bringing life.

- As I am here in prayer, I am asked to stretch out my hand in confidence and hope, trusting that I will be healed and blessed.

Tuesday 10th September **Luke 6:12–16**

Now during those days he went out to the mountain to pray; and he spent the night in prayer to God. And when day came, he called his disciples and chose twelve of them, whom he also named apostles: Simon, whom he named Peter, and his brother Andrew, and James, and John, and Philip, and Bartholomew, and Matthew, and Thomas, and James son of Alphaeus, and Simon, who was called the Zealot, and Judas son of James, and Judas Iscariot, who became a traitor.

- Each time I consider Jesus calling the disciples, I think of my name among them. Jesus sees and values what I can bring to the task; I pray for a deeper appreciation of myself as I acknowledge that Jesus calls me to growth.
- Jesus' decision about the disciples was preceded by a time in prayer. My regular prayer helps me to grow into understanding the ways of God, allowing my everyday choices and my bigger decisions to be shaped and changed.

Wednesday 11th September **Luke 6:20–21**

Then Jesus looked up at his disciples and said: "Blessed are you who are poor, for yours is the kingdom of God. Blessed are you who are hungry now, for you will be filled. Blessed are you who weep now, for you will laugh."

- The disciples sometimes asked, "What about us?", worried about their future prospects. Jesus drew their attention instead to the present, to "now." He still calls us to be aware of our needs—not to fill them—but to realize our dependency and so that we might hope for what God offers.
- God, whose heart is full of compassion, does not ignore what is overlooked, poor or neglected. I acknowledge and name my needs and wait on God with patience and trust.

Thursday 12th September **Luke 6:27, 32–36**

"But I say to you that listen, if you love those who love you, what credit is that to you? For even sinners love those who love them. If you do good to those who do good to you, what credit is that to you? For even sinners do the same. If you lend to those from whom you hope to receive, what credit is that to you? Even sinners lend to sinners, to receive as much again. But love your enemies, do good, and lend, expecting nothing in return. Your reward will be great, and you will be children of the Most High; for he is kind to the ungrateful and the wicked. Be merciful, just as your Father is merciful."

- I pray for all of those who might be thought of as "enemy" or despicable, calling to mind all hopeless cases, those who are overlooked and neglected. I pray that they may experience kindness and love and that any who describe them negatively may be given the vision that Jesus had.
- Those I love are in my prayer. As I think of them, I allow feelings of gratitude and appreciation to come to the fore and allow myself to be blessed again.

Friday 13th September **Luke 6:39–42**

He also told them a parable: "Can a blind person guide a blind person? Will not both fall into a pit? A disciple is not above the teacher, but everyone who is fully qualified will be like the teacher. Why do you see the speck in your neighbor's eye, but do not notice the log in your own eye? Or how can you say to your neighbor, 'Friend, let me take out the speck in your eye,' when you yourself do not see the log in your own eye? You hypocrite, first take the log out of your own eye, and then you will see clearly to take the speck out of your neighbor's eye.

- I bring myself before Jesus and allow myself some time to be regarded by his loving look. I ask him to remove any speck or plank that may be in my eye. I pray for the clarity of vision that he had.
- My perspective may not be the best one; my view of myself and of the world may need correction. I pray for humility and for a deeper capacity to perceive God's presence and action around me.

Saturday 14th September,
Triumph of the Holy Cross **John 3:13–17**

Jesus said, "And just as Moses lifted up the serpent in the wilderness, so must the Son of Man be lifted up, that whoever believes in him may have eternal life. For God so loved the world that he gave his only Son, so that everyone who believes in him may not perish but may have eternal life. Indeed, God did not send the Son into the world to condemn the world, but in order that the world might be saved through him."

- It is so common for people to associate self-examination and guilt with religion but here we are drawn to the core: God loves us and calls us to life.
- The cross is full of contradictions as we speak of it in terms of life, freedom and hope. I ask God to allow the contradictory message of the Gospel to have sway in my life.

Something to think and pray about each day this week:

Meeting the mystery of God

God is mystery—the nameless One I cannot grasp or comprehend. Sometimes that mystery seems never-ending, and no matter how I try to penetrate it, I am left simply in a kind of dark unknowing. This may be so, even though I find myself still drawn to long for God, to desire what is totally beyond me, and say "you" in the face of the ever-greater mystery. That chasm, that abyss, between me and the One to whom I am drawn, is perhaps expressed best in the words the prophet heard, "For my thoughts are not your thoughts, my ways not your ways—it is the Lord who speaks. Yes, the heavens are as high above earth as my ways are above your ways, my thoughts above your thoughts" (Isaiah 55:8–9). And yet, despite that great distancing, there is, most wonderfully, the greatest nearness—God close to me, approaching me in the person of Jesus, and entering into the house of my heart. For what is ungraspable and utter mystery is also coming close in Christ, speaking my name, whispering wordless words of truth and love into my being. I have said "you" into the darkness, because already I have been approached and addressed myself as "you." Within the deepest mystery, there is a meeting, an encounter, a conversation, a prayer. As Saint Augustine wrote, "God is nearer to me than I am to myself, more intimate to me than my inmost being."

The Presence of God
Jesus waits silent and unseen to come into my heart.
I will respond to His call.
He comes with His infinite power and love
May I be filled with joy in His presence.

Freedom
Everything has the potential to draw forth from me a fuller love and life.
Yet my desires are often fixed, caught, on illusions of fulfillment.
I ask that God, through my freedom, may orchestrate
my desires in a vibrant loving melody rich in harmony.

Consciousness
How do I find myself today?
Where am I with God? With others?
Do I have something to be grateful for? Then I give thanks.
Is there something I am sorry for? Then I ask forgiveness.

The Word
God speaks to each one of us individually. I need to listen to what he is saying to me. (Please turn to your scripture on the following pages. Inspiration points are there should you need them. When you are ready, return here to continue.)

Conversation
What feelings are rising in me
as I pray and reflect on God's Word?
I imagine Jesus himself sitting or standing beside me,
and open my heart to him.

Conclusion
Glory be to the Father, and to the Son, and to the Holy Spirit,
As it was in the beginning, is now and ever shall be,
World without end. Amen

Sunday 15th September,
Twenty-fourth Sunday in Ordinary Time **Luke 15:1–7**

Now all the tax-collectors and sinners were coming near to listen to Jesus. And the Pharisees and the scribes were grumbling and saying, "This fellow welcomes sinners and eats with them." So he told them this parable: "Which one of you, having a hundred sheep and losing one of them, does not leave the ninety-nine in the wilderness and go after the one that is lost until he finds it? When he has found it, he lays it on his shoulders and rejoices. And when he comes home, he calls together his friends and neighbors, saying to them, 'Rejoice with me, for I have found my sheep that was lost.' Just so, I tell you, there will be more joy in heaven over one sinner who repents than over ninety-nine righteous people who need no repentance."

- The joy of the shepherd did not end in the discovery of the sheep that was lost; he wanted to share his joy at by celebrating with others. I give thanks to God for the opportunities I have had to share with others what really matters to me. I give thanks to God for those who share their lives with me.
- I may be downcast and disheartened when I know myself to be a sinner. Let me listen today for the voice of God who rejoices at my repentance.

Monday 16th September **Luke 7:1–10**

After Jesus had finished all his sayings in the hearing of the people, he entered Capernaum. A centurion there had a slave whom he valued highly, and who was ill and close to death. When he heard about Jesus, he sent some Jewish elders to him, asking him to come and heal his slave. When they came to Jesus, they appealed to him earnestly, saying, "He is worthy of having you do this for him, for he loves our people, and it is he who built our synagogue for us." And Jesus went with them, but when he was not far from the house, the centurion sent friends to say to him, "Lord, do not trouble yourself, for I am not worthy to have you come under my roof; therefore I did not presume to come to you. But only speak the word, and let my servant be healed. For I also am a man set under authority, with soldiers under me; and I say to one, 'Go,' and he goes, and to another, 'Come,' and he comes, and to my slave, 'Do this,' and the slave does it." When Jesus heard this he was amazed at him, and turning to the crowd that followed him, he said, "I tell you, not even in Israel have I found such faith." When those who had been sent returned to the house, they found the slave in good health.

- The humility of the centurion prompted him not to trouble Jesus but his faith allowed him to profess his trust. It is easy to imitate him in the first quality without being like him in the second. God, give me something of this man's modesty and belief.
- Familiarity with power had not corrupted the centurion, but had brought him an awareness of others. I pray that I not mistake the privileges I enjoy for rights, and that I not allow them to cut me off from others.

Tuesday 17th September,
St Robert Bellarmine **Luke 7:11–17**

Soon afterwards he went to a town called Nain, and his disciples and a large crowd went with him. As he approached the gate of the town, a man who had died was being carried out. He was his mother's only son, and she was a widow; and with her was a large crowd from the town. When the Lord saw her, he had compassion for her and said to her, "Do not weep." Then he came forward and touched the bier, and the bearers stood still. And he said, "Young man, I say to you, rise!" The dead man sat up and began to speak, and Jesus gave him to his mother. Fear seized all of them; and they glorified God, saying, "A great prophet has risen among us!" and "God has looked favourably on his people!" This word about him spread throughout Judea and all the surrounding country.

- Jesus looked at the widow with compassion—just as he looks at me now. I allow time to acknowledge who or what I mourn, to let Jesus behold me, and to receive his blessing of hope.

- Jesus says, "Do not weep" as he sees a bigger and more hopeful picture than the one that is hidden from the bereft mother. I pray for all who feel alone, abandoned or bereaved. May they be given hope through the presence and prayer of people like me.

Wednesday 18th September **Luke 7:31–35**

Jesus said to the people, "To what then will I compare the people of this generation, and what are they like? They are like children sitting in the market-place and calling to one another, 'We played the flute for you, and you did not dance; we wailed, and you did not weep.' For John the Baptist has come eating no bread and drinking no wine, and you say, 'He has a demon;' the Son of Man has come eating and drinking, and you say, 'Look, a glutton and a drunkard, a friend of tax-collectors and sinners!' Nevertheless, wisdom is vindicated by all her children."

- Jesus' frustration with his hearers is behind this short group of sayings. He could never please everyone. He knows that he will be accepted in faith by some, and that his way of life will make sense to faithful followers.
- In prayer we often wonder what Jesus means by some sayings and stories. We are led in the words of Jesus into the mystery of God's communication with us.

Thursday 19th September **Luke 7:36–38**

One of the Pharisees asked Jesus to eat with him, and he went into the Pharisee's house and took his place at the table. And a woman in the city, who was a sinner, having learned that he was eating in the Pharisee's house, brought an alabaster jar of ointment. She stood behind him at his feet, weeping, and began to bathe his feet with her tears and to dry them with her hair. Then she continued kissing his feet and anointing them with the ointment.

- Jesus had awoken something in this woman that enabled her to be courageous, humble and generous in her action. I allow Jesus to call me freely to life as I respond to his message.
- We may often picture Jesus as he served and taught the people around him. He also had a capacity to allow people to serve him, letting them be gracious to him in return.

Friday 20th September **Luke 8:1–3**

Soon afterwards he went on through cities and villages, proclaiming and bringing the good news of the kingdom of God. The twelve were with him, as well as some women who had been cured of evil spirits and infirmities: Mary, called Magdalene, from whom seven demons had gone out, and Joanna, the wife of Herod's steward Chuza, and Susanna, and many others, who provided for them out of their resources.

- The generous women who cared for Jesus are usually out of sight, like so many women who give of themselves for others. I pray for all who enrich my life by their discreet service.
- Jesus did not just proclaim the good news—he was the good news. Saint Francis' advice about preaching the gospel—using words, if necessary—comes to mind. As I receive the word of God, I pray that I may embody it and proclaim it.

Saturday 21st September,
St Matthew, Apostle and Evangelist **Matthew 9:9–13**

As Jesus was walking along, he saw a man called Matthew sitting at the tax booth; and he said to him, "Follow me." And he got up and followed him. And as he sat at dinner in the house, many tax collectors and sinners came and were sitting with him and his disciples. When the Pharisees saw this, they said to his disciples, "Why does your teacher eat with tax collectors and sinners?" But when he heard this, he said, "Those who are well have no need of a physician, but those who are sick. Go and learn what this means, 'I desire mercy, not sacrifice.' For I have come to call not the righteous but sinners."

- Despite being concerned with his balances and rates, Matthew was ready to hear a deeper message. How might I preserve a readiness to hear the promptings of Jesus when I am in the midst of my daily occupation?
- We are challenged when we see that Jesus was tolerant of sinners so we sometimes relax and imagine that he was tolerant of sin. I allow my time of prayer to draw me into understanding Jesus more fully.

Something to think and pray about each day this week:

Open in prayer

It has been said that the truest prayer is when I am utterly open to God, unprotected, defenseless, trusting. The best and simplest prayer is summed up when I say, "Here I am, O Lord, and just as I am." It is the prayer where I open my heart, my whole being, in childlike trust, in simplicity. I simply entrust myself to Christ, who is always there for me. And I can do that, because I know I will be received in love. But such a prayer is in fact a *response* to what is being done towards me. First and foremost, there is the whole mystery of *God's* openness to me, *God's* vulnerability before me, in the self-giving of Jesus. This is the amazing thing. The greatest reality in my prayer is *God's* openness towards me, *God's* childlike giving of himself into my hands in Jesus. The truth is expressed by Paul's hymn in the Letter to the Philippians which tells us that Jesus "emptied himself" and also "humbled himself" for us (Philippians 2:7,8).

God's innermost heart is opened to me in love, through the person of Jesus. In my moment of stillness, therefore, Jesus is looking on me in love—and, further, becomes poor and vulnerable for me.

And so my prayer becomes none other than a loving response in simplicity and childlike trust. Someone is saying to me, "Here I am for you," and so I can say in turn, "And here I am, O Lord, and as I am, for you."

The Presence of God
'I stand at the door and knock,' says the Lord.
What a wonderful privilege
that the Lord of all creation desires to come to me.
I welcome His presence.

Freedom
Lord, grant me the grace to be free from the excesses of this life.
Let me not get caught up with the desire for wealth.
Keep my heart and mind free to love and serve you.

Consciousness
'There is a time and place for everything,' as the saying goes.
Lord, grant that I may always desire
to spend time in your presence. To hear your call.

The Word
God speaks to each one of us individually. I need to listen to what he is saying to me. (Please turn to your scripture on the following pages. Inspiration points are there should you need them. When you are ready, return here to continue.)

Conversation
The gift of speech is a wonderful gift.
May I use this gift with kindness.
May I be slow to utter harsh words,
hurtful words, and words spoken in anger.

Conclusion
Glory be to the Father, and to the Son, and to the Holy Spirit,
As it was in the beginning, is now and ever shall be,
World without end. Amen

Sunday 22nd September,
Twenty-fifth Sunday in Ordinary Time Luke 16:10–13

Then Jesus said to the disciples, "Whoever is faithful in a very little is faithful also in much; and whoever is dishonest in a very little is dishonest also in much. If then you have not been faithful with the dishonest wealth, who will entrust to you the true riches? And if you have not been faithful with what belongs to another, who will give you what is your own? No slave can serve two masters; for a slave will either hate the one and love the other, or be devoted to the one and despise the other. You cannot serve God and wealth."

- It may be that my bigger faults draw my attention—and the attention of others. God sees not just my failures but also recognizes my efforts and intentions to do good. I offer to God the small ways in which I am already faithful, give thanks and ask for God's strength to do more.
- If I am called into the service of God and of other people. I recognize that there are times when I turn aside to serve other masters. I prepare myself now to resist these voices, seeking from God the help I will need.

Monday 23rd September Luke 8:16–18

Jesus said to his disciples, "No one after lighting a lamp hides it under a jar, or puts it under a bed, but puts it on a lampstand, so that those who enter may see the light. For nothing is hidden that will not be disclosed, nor is anything secret that will not become known and come to light. Then pay attention to how you listen; for to those who have, more will be given; and from those who do not have, even what they seem to have will be taken away."

- The lamp is lit for a purpose; the light it gives shows it at its fullest potential. When loving others we express our love of God. Our acts of kindness, thoughtfulness or thanks are ways in which we can be lamps that are lit.
- "Secret" revelations sounds like the stuff of modern journalism; here it assures us that our every deed, our quiet gestures, our

forbearance and patient tolerance are all valued and build up God's presence in our midst.

Tuesday 24th September **Luke 8:19–21**

Then his mother and his brothers came to him, but they could not reach him because of the crowd. And he was told, "Your mother and your brothers are standing outside, wanting to see you." But he said to them, "My mother and my brothers are those who hear the word of God and do it."

- The compass of God's family is not limited by blood or heritage, but is thrown open to include all who receive and enact the word of God. I review any boundaries I tolerate and look beyond them in response to Jesus' words.
- "Hear" and "do"; this is my time for listening closely, for attending to where God is speaking in my life. Later I will move into the "doing" when I express my responses to what this time of prayer brings me to understand. I ask God now to help me later.

Wednesday 25th September **Luke 9:1–6**

Jesus called the twelve together and gave them power and authority over all demons and to cure diseases, and he sent them out to proclaim the kingdom of God and to heal. He said to them, "Take nothing for your journey, no staff, nor bag, nor bread, nor money—not even an extra tunic. Whatever house you enter, stay there, and leave from there. Wherever they do not welcome you, as you are leaving that town shake the dust off your feet as a testimony against them." They departed and went through the villages, bringing the good news and curing diseases everywhere.

- Most of us would like to bring good news wherever we go. We know people whose lives light up the lives of others. We know the opposite too!
- Daily prayer calms the soul, gives joy and peace; it brings a new perspective on worries and anxieties. It is our time of relaxing into the mystery of being loved by God.

Thursday 26th September **Haggai 1:5–6**

Now therefore, thus says the Lord of hosts: "Consider how you have fared. You have sown much, and harvested little; you eat, but you never have enough; you drink, but you never have your fill; you clothe yourselves, but no one is warm; and you that earn wages earn wages to put them into a bag with holes."

- Human endeavour and toil are brought into perspective in my prayer. All my busyness and all my concerns are distractions if I lose sight of what really matters.
- What would it be like for me to be satisfied with less? What difference would it make to me? To others? I ask God to help me to let go a little more, to trust.

Friday 27th September **Luke 9:18–22**

Once when Jesus was praying alone, with only the disciples near him, he asked them, "Who do the crowds say that I am?" They answered, "John the Baptist; but others, Elijah; and still others, that one of the ancient prophets has arisen." He said to them, "But who do you say that I am?" Peter answered, "The Messiah of God." He sternly ordered and commanded them not to tell anyone, saying, "The Son of Man must undergo great suffering, and be rejected by the elders, chief priests, and scribes, and be killed, and on the third day be raised."

- I answer Jesus' question, "Who do you say that I am?" every day. I take that time I need now to put it in words, expressing myself as honestly as I can, listening for Jesus' response.
- Jesus often tells the disciples not to tell others about him. A time of reflection and consideration is needed before proclamation. I ask God's help to know where I might speak and when I might remain silent.

Saturday 28th September **Luke 9:43–45**

And all were astounded at the greatness of God. While everyone was amazed at all that he was doing, he said to his disciples, "Let these words sink into your ears: The Son of Man is going to be betrayed into human hands." But they did not understand this saying; its meaning was concealed from them, so that they could not perceive it. And they were afraid to ask him about this saying.

- This starts as a moment of triumph. Everyone was amazed at all that Jesus was doing. Jesus calms the disciples down with a solemn warning that he would be betrayed.
- "Let these words sink into your ears." He constantly calls us out of our comfort zone, asks us to open our eyes compassionately to human misery.

Something to think and pray about each day this week:

Filling our minds and hearts

Towards the end of his Letter to the Philippians, St Paul has words on which we can often ponder. He had written earlier in the letter about his own following of Christ, which is everything for him and which he proposes for each one of us (Phil :7–16). But then he adds: "Finally, brothers and sisters fill your minds with everything that is true, everything that is honourable, everything that is upright and pure, everything that we love and admire" (4:8). These are indeed significant additions. Paul is saying that, as we are captivated by Christ and transformed in him, then also every good thing displayed in this world should fill our hearts and minds.

He means especially whatever is True, and Good, and Beautiful. The manifestations of these are worthy of our admiration and interest. They are in fact supremely given us in Christ, so we are invited to have a care for them. Sometimes in life, indeed, we feel overwhelmed by their opposites—when so much that is unjust, and untrue, and ugly, seems to predominate in the world around us. But all the more then are we called to discern and uphold what is true, and good, and upright. "Lord, help me always to revere and uphold all that is true, and good, and supremely beautiful in this world."

The Presence of God

I remind myself that, as I sit here now,
God is gazing on me with love and holding me in being.
I pause for a moment and think of this.

Freedom

Lord, grant me the grace to be free from the excesses of this life.
Let me not get caught up with the desire for wealth.
Keep my heart and mind free to love and serve you.

Consciousness

How am I really feeling? Light-hearted? Heavy-hearted?
I may be very much at peace, happy to be here.
Equally, I may be frustrated, worried or angry.
I acknowledge how I really am. It is the real me that the Lord loves.

The Word

I take my time to read the Word of God, slowly, a few times, allowing myself to dwell on anything that strikes me. (Please turn to your scripture on the following pages. Inspiration points are there should you need them. When you are ready, return here to continue.)

Conversation

Do I notice myself reacting as I pray with the Word of God?
Do I feel challenged, comforted, angry?
Imagining Jesus sitting or standing by me,
I speak out my feelings, as one trusted friend to another.

Conclusion

Glory be to the Father, and to the Son, and to the Holy Spirit,
As it was in the beginning, is now and ever shall be,
World without end. Amen

Sunday 29th September,
Twenty-sixth Sunday in Ordinary Time **Amos 6:1, 4–7**

Alas for those who are at ease in Zion, and for those who feel secure on Mount Samaria, the notables of the first of the nations, to whom the house of Israel resorts! Alas for those who lie on beds of ivory, and lounge on their couches, and eat lambs from the flock, and calves from the stall; who sing idle songs to the sound of the harp, and like David improvise on instruments of music; who drink wine from bowls, and anoint themselves with the finest oils, but are not grieved over the ruin of Joseph! Therefore they shall now be the first to go into exile, and the revelry of the loungers shall pass away.

- Amos saw that too much concern with security and pleasure made people complacent and careless about the needs of the poor. I bring to mind all those people whose work provides the comforts I enjoy.
- I pray in gratitude for them and in appreciation of the good things I enjoy. I ask for the detachment I need to enjoy them without becoming enslaved by them.

Monday 30th September **Luke 9:46–50**

An argument arose among them as to which one of them was the greatest. But Jesus, aware of their inner thoughts, took a little child and put it by his side, and said to them, "Whoever welcomes this child in my name welcomes me, and whoever welcomes me welcomes the one who sent me; for the least among all of you is the greatest." John answered, "Master, we saw someone casting out demons in your name, and we tried to stop him, because he does not follow with us." But Jesus said to him, "Do not stop him; for whoever is not against you is for you."

- Children were not the focus of attention in Jesus' time that they often are now. Who are the overlooked, ignored or patronised in your place? How might you welcome them more?
- Human arrangements often exclude and promote; Jesus speaks of inclusion and equality. I consider how I may drift away from Jesus

when I am judgemental or feel superior and ask for the blessing of humility.

Tuesday 1st October **Luke 9:51–56**

When the days drew near for him to be taken up, Jesus set his face to go to Jerusalem. And he sent messengers ahead of him. On their way they entered a village of the Samaritans to make ready for him; but they did not receive him, because his face was set toward Jerusalem. When his disciples James and John saw it, they said, Lord, do you want us to command fire to come down from heaven and consume them?" But he turned and rebuked them. Then they went on to another village.

- We may sometimes feel disappointed when others don't see the world as we do. Jesus did not surrender to the "logical" view of the disciples; he simply turned and went on his way.
- Jesus had his heart set and thus was not deflected by the lack of welcome or tempted to punish. I think of what my heart is set on and ask God to purify my desires and seek the strength I need to persevere.

Wednesday 2nd October **Luke 9:57–62**

As they were going along the road, someone said to him, "I will follow you wherever you go." And Jesus said to him, "Foxes have holes, and birds of the air have nests; but the Son of Man has nowhere to lay his head." To another he said, "Follow me." But he said, "Lord, first let me go and bury my father." But Jesus said to him, "Let the dead bury their own dead; but as for you, go and proclaim the kingdom of God." Another said, "I will follow you, Lord; but let me first say farewell to those at my home." Jesus said to him, "No one who puts a hand to the plow and looks back is fit for the kingdom of God."

- Following Jesus does not necessarily mean perpetual self-denial and poverty—but we need to remain ready to travel lightly. Jesus calls us to lay aside our own priorities and expectations so that we might live and follow freely.

- The people who approach Jesus are brought to see how they are tied down. I ask Jesus to show me how I might be more free.

Thursday 3rd October **Luke 10:1–7**

After this the Lord appointed seventy others and sent them on ahead of him in pairs to every town and place where he himself intended to go. He said to them, "The harvest is plentiful, but the laborers are few; therefore ask the Lord of the harvest to send out laborers into his harvest. Go on your way. See, I am sending you out like lambs into the midst of wolves. Carry no purse, no bag, no sandals; and greet no one on the road. Whatever house you enter, first say, 'Peace to this house!' And if anyone is there who shares in peace, your peace will rest on that person; but if not, it will return to you. Remain in the same house, eating and drinking whatever they provide, for the laborer deserves to be paid."

- There is an encouragement here from Jesus to place trust only in him as we work for the kingdom of God. We are to carry little for the journey.
- Often what we do in faith and love seems to bear little fruit. Offered to the work of Jesus in the world, we never know when it may bear fruit. We are people who work hard for the Lord and leave the results to him.

Friday 4th October,
St Francis of Assisi **Luke 10:13–16**

"Woe to you, Chorazin! Woe to you, Bethsaida! For if the deeds of power done in you had been done in Tyre and Sidon, they would have repented long ago, sitting in sackcloth and ashes. But at the judgment it will be more tolerable for Tyre and Sidon than for you. And you, Capernaum, will you be exalted to heaven? No, you will be brought down to Hades." "Whoever listens to you listens to me, and whoever rejects you rejects me, and whoever rejects me rejects the one who sent me."

- I take some time to let these words of Jesus sink in; they may challenge as I realize how I am given responsibility and console considering the trust in me that Jesus expresses.
- I do not have to feel personally affronted when others do not hear the Gospel as I do. I pray for those who do not realize the truth that God offers them.

Saturday 5th October **Luke 10:21–24**

Jesus rejoiced in the Holy Spirit and said, "I thank you, Father, Lord of heaven and earth, because you have hidden these things from the wise and the intelligent and have revealed them to infants; yes, Father, for such was your gracious will. All things have been handed over to me by my Father; and no one knows who the Son is except the Father, or who the Father is except the Son and anyone to whom the Son chooses to reveal him." Then turning to the disciples, Jesus said to them privately, "Blessed are the eyes that see what you see! For I tell you that many prophets and kings desired to see what you see, but did not see it, and to hear what you hear, but did not hear it."

- The truth is at hand, Jesus tells me. I don't have to wait for an authority to proclaim, for a teacher to explain or for a leader to pronounce.
- The gracious will of God is revealed to the simple and humble. When the will of God seems hidden from me, could it be that I am making things too complicated? Do I need instead to be called back to simplicity of life?

Something to think and pray about each day this week:

God's banquet

Already, here and now in our lives, the kingdom of God surrounds us and is in our midst. One of the best scriptural images for the kingdom is that of a banquet to which we are invited. We arrive as cherished guests, to partake of the richest of foods and good wines (cf Isaiah 25:6–10; Psalm 23:5; and Matthew 22:1–14). Moreover, this banquet is a wedding feast, for deep down we are beginning to celebrate the wedding of the Lamb (Christ) with his people. The people of God have already been redeemed and cleansed (cf Rev 19:7–10), and have in that sense passed beyond the upheavals and tragedies of history.

So as I pause for reflection and prayer, let me realize how I am already being drawn into that banquet, and am being nourished in that celebration. I perhaps experience in some way how certain words of scripture are nourishing for me, and satisfying. These then are a foretaste of the food and wine of the eternal banquet. Perhaps I am drawn into the banquet like the Prodigal—the wayward son who has tramped back along the dusty road, to be embraced by his waiting Father who exclaims, "We will celebrate by having a feast, because this child of mine was lost and is found!" (Luke 15:23–24).

The Presence of God
In the silence of my innermost being,
in the fragments of my yearned-for wholeness,
can I hear the whispers of God's presence?
Can I remember when I felt God's nearness?
When we walked together and I let myself be embraced by God's love.

Freedom
I ask for the grace
to let go of my own concerns
and be open to what God is asking of me,
to let myself be guided and formed by my loving Creator.

Consciousness
I exist in a web of relationships—links to nature, people, God.
I trace out these links, giving thanks for the life that flows through them.
Some links are twisted or broken: I may feel regret, anger, disappointment.
I pray for the gift of acceptance and forgiveness.

The Word
The word of God comes down to us through the scriptures. May the Holy Spirit enlighten my mind and my heart to respond to the gospel teachings. (Please turn to your scripture on the following pages. Inspiration points are there should you need them. When you are ready, return here to continue.)

Conversation
Remembering that I am still in God's presence,
I imagine Jesus himself standing or sitting beside me,
and say whatever is on my mind, whatever is in my heart,
speaking as one friend to another.

Conclusion
Glory be to the Father, and to the Son, and to the Holy Spirit,
As it was in the beginning, is now and ever shall be,
World without end. Amen

Sunday 6th October,
Twenty-seventh Sunday in Ordinary Time Luke 17:5–10

The apostles said to the Lord, "Increase our faith!" The Lord replied, "If you had faith the size of a mustard seed, you could say to this mulberry tree, 'Be uprooted and planted in the sea', and it would obey you. Who among you would say to your slave who has just come in from ploughing or tending sheep in the field, 'Come here at once and take your place at the table'? Would you not rather say to him, 'Prepare supper for me, put on your apron and serve me while I eat and drink; later you may eat and drink'? Do you thank the slave for doing what was commanded? So you also, when you have done all that you were ordered to do, say, 'We are worthless slaves; we have done only what we ought to have done!'"

- Jesus warns us against the seeking credit for our good deeds. Saying, "I have done only what I ought to have done" tests our humility.
- As I spend time in prayer, God draws my attention to my life and hopes and my faith becomes stronger as I learn to trust in God and in myself.

Monday 7th October Luke 10:25–37

Just then a lawyer stood up to test Jesus. "Teacher," he said, "what must I do to inherit eternal life?" He said to him, "What is written in the law? What do you read there?" He answered, "You shall love the Lord your God with all your heart, and with all your soul, and with all your strength, and with all your mind; and your neighbour as yourself." And he said to him, "You have given the right answer; do this, and you will live." But wanting to justify himself, he asked Jesus, "And who is my neighbour?" Jesus replied, "A man was going down from Jerusalem to Jericho, and fell into the hands of robbers, who stripped him, beat him, and went away, leaving him half dead. Now by chance a priest was going down that road; and when he saw him, he passed by on the other side. So likewise a Levite, when he came to the place and saw him, passed by on the other side. But a Samaritan while travelling came near him; and when he saw him, he was moved with pity. He went to him and bandaged his wounds, having poured oil and wine on them. Then he put him on his own animal, brought him to an inn, and took care of him. The next day he took out two denarii, gave them to the innkeeper, and said, 'Take care of him; and when I come back, I will repay you whatever more you spend'; Which of these three, do you think, was a neighbor to the man who fell into the hands of the robbers?" He said, "The one who showed him mercy." Jesus said to him, "Go and do likewise."

- Often I am unable to help, but I do help when I can, and I ask God to make me alert to the needs of others and to keep them in my prayer.
- Jesus here reversed the expectations of people about priests, Levites and Samaritans. He challenged their ideas, he valued the outcast. Am I ready to have my values challenged?

Tuesday 8th October **Luke 10:38–42**

Now as they went on their way, Jesus entered a certain village, where a woman named Martha welcomed him into her home. She had a sister named Mary, who sat at the Lord's feet and listened to what he was saying. But Martha was distracted by her many tasks; so she came to him and asked, "Lord, do you not care that my sister has left me to do all the work by myself? Tell her then to help me." But the Lord answered her, "Martha, Martha, you are worried and distracted by many things; there is need of only one thing. Mary has chosen the better part, which will not be taken away from her."

- I think of myself in this scene and hear Jesus' words addressed to myself. He calls me away from over-busyness and reminds me of what is central.
- When there are many things to be done and time seems short, I pray that I might remember what Jesus says; that I might think like Mary even when I have to act like Martha.

Wednesday 9th October **Luke 11:1–4**

Jesus was praying in a certain place, and after he had finished, one of his disciples said to him, "Lord, teach us to pray, as John taught his disciples." He said to them, "When you pray, say: Father, hallowed be your name. Your kingdom come. Give us each day our daily bread. And forgive us our sins, for we ourselves forgive everyone indebted to us. And do not bring us to the time 0f trial."

- I am in the presence of God right now. I have begun my prayer by my willingness to offer God this time.
- The Lord's prayer is my prayer. Sometimes what I ask is granted. At other times I must pray for God's grace, especially to have a forgiving heart.

Thursday 10th October **Luke 11:9–13**

Jesus said, "I say to you, Ask, and it will be given to you; search, and you will find; knock, and the door will be opened for you. For everyone who asks receives, and everyone who searches finds, and for everyone who knocks, the door will be opened. Is there anyone among you who, if your child asks for a fish, will give a snake instead of a fish? Or if the child asks for an egg, will give a scorpion? If you then, who are evil, know how to give good gifts to your children, how much more will the heavenly Father give the Holy Spirit to those who ask him!"

- I bring different intentions to my prayer as my priorities shift. I review what is really important to me and see what I might let go.
- I ask God for the faith I need. My prayer may be less in the waiting for the answer than in approaching God with a child's confident trust.

Friday 11th October **Luke 11:15–20**

Some of the crowd said of Jesus, "He casts out demons by Beelzebul, the ruler of the demons." Others, to test him, kept demanding from him a sign from heaven. But he knew what they were thinking and said to them, "Every kingdom divided against itself becomes a desert, and house falls on house. If Satan also is divided against himself, how will his kingdom stand?—for you say that I cast out the demons by Beelzebul. Now if I cast out the demons by Beelzebul, by whom do your exorcists cast them out? Therefore they will be your judges. But if it is by the finger of God that I cast out the demons, then the kingdom of God has come to you."

- Am I divided within myself, or do I try to be fully made over to Jesus as his disciple?
- When I notice a bad spirit in my heart toward someone, I need to ask Jesus to free me.

Saturday 12th October **Luke 11:27–28**

While Jesus was speaking, a woman in the crowd raised her voice and said to him, "Blessed is the womb that bore you and the breasts that nursed you!" But he said, "Blessed rather are those who hear the word of God and obey it!"

- Jesus' answer does not diminish his mother Mary, but embraces her and all others who hear and obey the word of God. Do I accept that I am included too in his blessing?
- Prayer of praise is a beautiful, ancient, tradition. Do I give praise?

october 13–19

Something to think and pray about each day this week:

The panorama of prayer

Prayer is not selfish! Whenever I stop and try to pray, I enter into my own heart. But also in some mysterious way I touch the lives of all who yearn for goodness and truth, and who lift up their hearts in prayer as I do. Through my prayer and theirs, the wide expanse of the world is lifted up before God. Some people's whole lives are spent in this way—for instance, the Carthusian contemplatives portrayed in the 2005 film, *Into Great Silence*. These ordinary people who have been called to silence and prayer are devoted day and night to the mystery of the living God, and continually raise up the world and its needs before Him.

We each have our part in that great panorama of prayer—for when we stop to pray in the midst of our practical concerns, we enter *Sacred Space* and are joined to a multitude of praying hearts across the world. In the film the text from Jeremiah 20:7 appears from time to time: "You have seduced me, Lord, and I have let myself be seduced." Such strong language has a particular meaning when applied to the extraordinary vocation of a Carthusian monk. But the words can also be applied to myself. When I feel drawn into quiet and prayer, I am being "seduced" by God! Coming before Him, as best I can, with all my poor heart, the whole world and its needs are present as well.

The Presence of God
God is with me, but more,
God is within me, giving me existence.
Let me dwell for a moment on God's life-giving presence
in my body, my mind, my heart
and in the whole of my life.

Freedom
I ask for the grace to believe
in what I could be and do
if I only allowed God, my loving Creator,
to continue to create me, guide me and shape me.

Consciousness
Knowing that God loves me unconditionally,
I can afford to be honest about how I am.
How has the last day been, and how do I feel now?
I share my feelings openly with the Lord.

The Word
I read the Word of God slowly, a few times over, and I listen to what God is saying to me. (Please turn to your scripture on the following pages. Inspiration points are there should you need them. When you are ready, return here to continue.)

Conversation
How has God's Word moved me? Has it left me cold?
Has it consoled me or moved me to act in a new way?
I imagine Jesus standing or sitting beside me,
I turn and share my feelings with him.

Conclusion
Glory be to the Father, and to the Son, and to the Holy Spirit,
As it was in the beginning, is now and ever shall be,
World without end. Amen

Sunday 13th October,
Twenty-eighth Sunday in Ordinary Time **Luke 17:11–19**

On the way to Jerusalem Jesus was going through the region between Samaria and Galilee. As he entered a village, ten lepers approached him. Keeping their distance, they called out, saying, "Jesus, Master, have mercy on us!" When he saw them, he said to them, "Go and show yourselves to the priests." And as they went, they were made clean. Then one of them, when he saw that he was healed, turned back, praising God with a loud voice. He prostrated himself at Jesus' feet and thanked him. And he was a Samaritan. Then Jesus asked, "Were not ten made clean? But the other nine, where are they? Was none of them found to return and give praise to God except this foreigner?" Then he said to him, "Get up and go on your way; your faith has made you well."

- The men who were healed all realized their good fortune and rejoiced in it, recognizing where it came from. Only one took time to address himself to Jesus. Something is missing when it does not involve a humble return to Jesus to give thanks.
- We come back to Jesus not just to give thanks, but ready to receive our mission. Jesus' healing is a gift in itself but may be given to us for others. We listen in prayer to hear his plans for us.

Monday 14th October **Luke 11:29–32**

When the crowds were increasing, Jesus began to say, "This generation is an evil generation; it asks for a sign, but no sign will be given to it except the sign of Jonah. For just as Jonah became a sign to the people of Nineveh, so the Son of Man will be to this generation. The queen of the South will rise at the judgment with the people of this generation and condemn them, because she came from the ends of the earth to listen to the wisdom of Solomon, and see, something greater than Solomon is here! The people of Nineveh will rise up at the judgment with this generation and condemn it, because they repented at the proclamation of Jonah, and see, something greater than Jonah is here!"

- Jesus is the only sign I need to chart my life well. I ask to be brought close to Jesus, so that I may read this divine sign well.
- "Something greater" hints at the profound mystery of Jesus. How privileged I am to be his companion!

Tuesday 15th October,
St Teresa of Avila **Luke 11:37–41**

While Jesus was speaking, a Pharisee invited him to dine with him; so he went in and took his place at the table. The Pharisee was amazed to see that he did not first wash before dinner. Then the Lord said to him, "Now you Pharisees clean the outside of the cup and of the dish, but inside you are full of greed and wickedness. You fools! Did not the one who made the outside make the inside also? So give for alms those things that are within; and see, everything will be clean for you."

- Jesus tells us that holiness lies in wholeness and integrity; we are invited to be "of one piece," without deep contradictions.
- I bring my life before God fully and openly, asking that any divisions in me be healed—that I be made whole.

Wednesday 16th October **Luke 11:42–46**

"But woe to you Pharisees! For you tithe mint and rue and herbs of all kinds, and neglect justice and the love of God; it is these you ought to have practiced, without neglecting the others. Woe to you Pharisees! For you love to have the seat of honour in the synagogues and to be greeted with respect in the market-places. Woe to you! For you are like unmarked graves, and people walk over them without realizing it." One of the lawyers answered him, "Teacher, when you say these things, you insult us too." And he said, "Woe also to you lawyers! For you load people with burdens hard to bear, and you yourselves do not lift a finger to ease them."

- Does Jesus perhaps need to shock me into living my life more from the inside than from outward appearances?
- "Justice and the love of God" are what matter. I beg that I may ease the burdens of others and be compassionate to those at the bottom of the social scale.

Thursday 17th October **Luke 11:47–51**

Jesus said to the lawyers, "Woe to you! For you build the tombs of the prophets whom your ancestors killed. So you are witnesses and approve of the deeds of your ancestors; for they killed them, and you build their tombs. Therefore also the Wisdom of God said, 'I will send them prophets and apostles, some of whom they will kill and persecute,' so that this generation may be charged with the blood of all the prophets shed since the foundation of the world, from the blood of Abel to the blood of Zechariah, who perished between the altar and the sanctuary. Yes, I tell you, it will be charged against this generation."

- To be prophetic is a risky business! It means to speak and do as God would wish.
- What is God trying to say to me? Do I notice the promptings of the Holy Spirit, so that I can be the Spirit's spokesperson?

Friday 18th October,
St Luke, Evangelist **Luke 10:1–9**

After this the Lord appointed seventy others and sent them on ahead of him in pairs to every town and place where he himself intended to go. He said to them, "The harvest is plentiful, but the laborers are few; therefore ask the Lord of the harvest to send out laborers into his harvest. Go on your way. See, I am sending you out like lambs into the midst of wolves. Carry no purse, no bag, no sandals; and greet no one on the road. Whatever house you enter, first say, 'Peace to this house!' And if anyone is there who shares in peace, your peace will rest on that person; but if not, it will return to you. Remain in the same house, eating and drinking whatever they provide, for the laborer deserves to be paid. Do not move about from house to house. Whenever you enter a town and its people welcome you, eat what is set before you; cure the sick who are there, and say to them, 'The kingdom of God has come near to you.'"

- The Lord sends me out as his ambassador! When people see me coming, do they think of me as bringing Good News?

- "The kingdom of God" means that God's ways of relating to people are to prevail. I ask that all my interactions with others may be life-giving and liberating rather than unhelpful.

Saturday 19th October **Luke 12:8–12**

Jesus said to the disciples, "And I tell you, everyone who acknowledges me before others, the Son of Man also will acknowledge before the angels of God; but whoever denies me before others will be denied before the angels of God. And everyone who speaks a word against the Son of Man will be forgiven; but whoever blasphemes against the Holy Spirit will not be forgiven. When they bring you before the synagogues, the rulers, and the authorities, do not worry about how you are to defend yourselves or what you are to say; for the Holy Spirit will teach you at that very hour what you ought to say."

- In the Acts of the Apostles we see the openness and courage of the first Christians. Do I stand up for what is true and right?
- The Holy Spirit works by gently prompting us to live and act as Jesus did. The time I give to *Sacred Space* pleases the Spirit. The Spirit then invites me to put into action what I learn in prayer.

Something to think and pray about each day this week:

Creating love

In times of prayer we can be helped by others who have tried to put words on what is going on. Take the prayers of the Bengali Hindu poet mystic, Rabindranath Tagore. His little collection, *Gitanjali, Song Offerings to the Creator*, has inspired many people and his songs have become Christian hymns in India. He celebrates the immense creating love of God: "You have made me endless, Lord, such is your pleasure. This frail vessel you empty out again and again, and fill it ever with fresh life. Your infinite gifts come to me only on these very small hands of mine. Ages pass, and still you pour, and still there is room to fill."

Elsewhere he prays: "Give me the strength, Lord, lightly to bear my joys and sorrows. Give me the strength to make my love fruitful in service. Give me the strength never to disown the poor or bend my knees before insolent might."

The Presence of God

To be present is to arrive as one is and open up to the other.
At this instant, as I arrive here, God is present waiting for me.
God always arrives before me, desiring to connect with me
even more than my most intimate friend.
I take a moment and greet my loving God.

Freedom

"In these days, God taught me
as a schoolteacher teaches a pupil" (St Ignatius).
I remind myself that there are things God has to teach me yet,
and ask for the grace to hear them and let them change me.

Consciousness

In the presence of my loving Creator,
I look honestly at my feelings over the last day,
the highs, the lows and the level ground.
Can I see where the Lord has been present?

The Word

I take my time to read the Word of God, slowly, a few times, allowing myself to dwell on anything that strikes me. (Please turn to your scripture on the following pages. Inspiration points are there should you need them. When you are ready, return here to continue.)

Conversation

What feelings are rising in me
as I pray and reflect on God's Word?
I imagine Jesus himself sitting or standing beside me,
and open my heart to him.

Conclusion

Glory be to the Father, and to the Son, and to the Holy Spirit,
As it was in the beginning, is now and ever shall be,
World without end. Amen

Sunday 20th October,
Twenty-ninth Sunday in Ordinary Time Luke 18:1–8

Then Jesus told them a parable about their need to pray always and not to lose heart. He said, "In a certain city there was a judge who neither feared God nor had respect for people. In that city there was a widow who kept coming to him and saying, 'Grant me justice against my opponent.' For a while he refused; but later he said to himself, 'Though I have no fear of God and no respect for anyone, yet because this widow keeps bothering me, I will grant her justice, so that she may not wear me out by continually coming.'" And the Lord said, "Listen to what the unjust judge says. And will not God grant justice to his chosen ones who cry to him day and night? Will he delay long in helping them? I tell you, he will quickly grant justice to them. And yet, when the Son of Man comes, will he find faith on earth?"

- Jesus tells us of the persistence of the woman in the parable and helps us to recognize that whether this quality is present in our prayer. As I pray, I listen for the deeper note that may underlie what I say and hear how God responds to me.
- Jesus tells the parable so we may not lose heart. I listen for the voice of Jesus is speaking to me, urging me to persist.

Monday 21st October Luke 12:13–21

Someone in the crowd said to Jesus, "Teacher, tell my brother to divide the family inheritance with me." But he said to him, "Friend, who set me to be a judge or arbitrator over you?" And he said to them, "Take care! Be on your guard against all kinds of greed; for one's life does not consist in the abundance of possessions." Then he told them a parable: "The land of a rich man produced abundantly. And he thought to himself, 'What should I do, for I have no place to store my crops?' Then he said, 'I will do this: I will pull down my barns and build larger ones, and there I will store all my grain and my goods.' And I will say to my soul, 'Soul, you have ample goods laid up for many years; relax, eat, drink, be merry.' But God said to him, 'You fool! This very night your life is being demanded of you. And the things you have prepared, whose will they be?' So it is with those who store up treasures for themselves but are not rich toward God."

- Am I "greedy" about anything? Possessions, self-care, food, drink, entertainment and so on are good things but they can trap me. I see easily how others get caught, and so I ask Jesus that I may live in the truth which alone sets me free.
- St Ignatius invites us "to keep God always before our eyes." In the big and small choices I make do I keep an eye on what God would wish me to do?

Tuesday 22nd October **Luke 12:36–38**

Jesus said to his disciples, "Be dressed for action and have your lamps lit; be like those who are waiting for their master to return from the wedding banquet, so that they may open the door for him as soon as he comes and knocks. Blessed are those slaves whom the master finds alert when he comes; truly I tell you, he will fasten his belt and have them sit down to eat, and he will come and serve them. If he comes during the middle of the night, or near dawn, and finds them so, blessed are those slaves."

- Here we have another picture of Jesus the servant, the master who would serve the slaves. This image turns cultural customs upside down, as Jesus later would wash the feet of the disciples.
- This is how he visits us; the one who stands at our door and knocks, and then brings the meal for us to eat. The meal of the word of God, of the Eucharist, the gift of God's love. This is his gift in the time of prayer.

Wednesday 23rd October **Luke 12:39–48**

Jesus said to the people, "But know this: if the owner of the house had known at what hour the thief was coming, he would not have let his house be broken into. You also must be ready, for the Son of Man is coming at an unexpected hour." Peter said, "Lord, are you telling this parable for us or for everyone?" And the Lord said, "Who then is the faithful and prudent manager whom his master will put in charge of his slaves, to give them their allowance of food at the proper time? Blessed is that slave whom his master will find at work when he arrives. Truly I tell you, he will put that one in charge of all his possessions. But if that slave says to himself, 'My master is delayed in coming', and if he begins to beat the other slaves, men and women, and to eat and drink and get drunk, the master of that slave will come on a day when he does not expect him and at an hour that he does not know, and will cut him in pieces, and put him with the unfaithful. That slave who knew what his master wanted, but did not prepare himself or do what was wanted, will receive a severe beating. But one who did not know and did what deserved a beating will receive a light beating. From everyone to whom much has been given, much will be required; and from one to whom much has been entrusted, even more will be demanded."

- "Being ready" means that I try to respond to the ways God is working in my life and around me. I ask that I may not slow down the advance of the kingdom of God.
- The kingdom of God is all about fostering good relationships and helping to repair damaged ones. Whatever truly builds up the community of God will receive God's reward.
- I pray that I may serve others well.

Thursday 24th October **Luke 12:49–53**

Jesus said to the crowds, "I came to bring fire to the earth, and how I wish it were already kindled! I have a baptism with which to be baptized, and what stress I am under until it is completed! Do you think that I have come to bring peace to the earth? No, I tell you, but rather division! From now on five in one household will be divided, three against two and two against three; they will be divided: father against son and son against father, mother against daughter and daughter against mother, mother-in-law against her daughter-in-law and daughter-in-law against mother-in-law."

- Living out your life as a companion of Jesus is anything but dull! Christians are meant to be "on fire" with God's love, and be moved by the Holy Spirit.
- Jesus does not try to cause divisions, but he does insist that we must put God first. In him the new age of God has dawned, and I ask to be part of it. I want to live a fruitful life that will be a blessing to everyone, especially the oppressed and excluded.

Friday 25th October **Luke 12:54–59**

Jesus also said to the crowds, "When you see a cloud rising in the west, you immediately say, 'It is going to rain'; and so it happens. And when you see the south wind blowing, you say, 'There will be scorching heat'; and it happens. You hypocrites! You know how to interpret the appearance of earth and sky, but why do you not know how to interpret the present time? And why do you not judge for yourselves what is right? Thus, when you go with your accuser before a magistrate, on the way make an effort to settle the case, or you may be dragged before the judge, and the judge hand you over to the officer, and the officer throw you in prison. I tell you, you will never get out until you have paid the very last penny."

- We are asked to interpret our present times rightly. This involves standing up against injustice and domination. I cannot do this alone, so daily I beg for God's strength, as Jesus did in his prayer.
- Jesus tells me to judge for myself what is right. Do I allow the Spirit to speak to me in my conscience, so that I no longer go with the trends of the day, but follow instead the inspiration of God?

Saturday 26th October **Luke 13:1–9**

At that very time there were some present who told him about the Galileans whose blood Pilate had mingled with their sacrifices. He asked them, "Do you think that because these Galileans suffered in this way they were worse sinners than all other Galileans? No, I tell you; but unless you repent, you will all perish as they did. Or those eighteen who were killed when the tower of Siloam fell on them—do you think that they were worse offenders than all the others living in Jerusalem? No, I tell you; but unless you repent, you will all perish just as they did." Then he told this parable: "A man had a fig tree planted in his vineyard; and he came looking for fruit on it and found none. So he said to the gardener, 'See here! For three years I have come looking for fruit on this fig tree, and still I find none. Cut it down! Why should it be wasting the soil?' He replied, 'Sir, let it alone for one more year, until I dig round it and put manure on it. If it bears fruit next year, well and good; but if not, you can cut it down.'"

- Like the fig tree, I can feel that my life is sterile. But I ask God for a little more time to bear fruit. What nourishment do I need to become a fruitful tree that gives itself generously?
- Jesus often speaks of the need to repent. This means turning away from anything that is not of God. I ask to be brought more and more into the world of goodness and love, of light and of truth. I want to be a genuine disciple.

Sacred Space

october 27–november 2

Something to think and pray about each day this week:

Remembering

Across the world, the month of November brings people to church to remember their departed ones in rite and in symbol. All Souls' Day evokes expressions of love and concern, whether through participation in the Eucharist or personal prayer. In Ireland, Cemetery Sunday, with its blessing of graves, can be a major pastoral event. Why is it popular? Because it is a rich expression of Christian community. Families and friends gather, often despite cold and rain, expressing care for those they loved. People are helped by doing practical things—preparing the grave, bringing flowers and lighting candles, engaging in liturgy and private prayer. Graves are blessed with holy water; then comes the sharing of a meal and story-telling which brings both laughter and tears. All this is Christian community.

Such concrete ways of remembering departed ones is healthy, because we are enfleshed spirit, and we want to keep bonded with relatives and friends with whom we have shared life, with its joy and tears. They are no farther from us than God, and God is very near. Human and divine join hands across the void that is death, and the longing we feel for final and open reunion brings a mysterious peace to our hearts. All will be well in God's time.

Presence of God
What is present to me is what has a hold on my becoming.
I reflect on the presence of God always there in love,
amidst the many things that have a hold on me.
I pause and pray that I may let God
affect my becoming in this precise moment.

Freedom
If God were trying to tell me something, would I know?
If God were reassuring me or challenging me, would I notice?
I ask for the grace to be free of my own preoccupations
and open to what God may be saying to me.

Consciousness
Knowing that God loves me unconditionally,
I look honestly over the last day, its events and my feelings.
Do I have something to be grateful for? Then I give thanks.
Is there something I am sorry for? Then I ask forgiveness.

The Word
God speaks to each one of us individually. I need to listen to what he is saying to me. (Please turn to your scripture on the following pages. Inspiration points are there should you need them. When you are ready, return here to continue.)

Conversation
What is stirring in me as I pray?
Am I consoled, troubled, left cold?
I imagine Jesus himself standing or sitting at my side,
and share my feelings with him.

Conclusion
Glory be to the Father, and to the Son, and to the Holy Spirit,
As it was in the beginning, is now and ever shall be,
World without end. Amen

Sunday 27th October,
Thirtieth Sunday in Ordinary Time **Luke 18:9–14**

Jesus also told this parable to some who trusted in themselves that they were righteous and regarded others with contempt: "Two men went up to the temple to pray, one a Pharisee and the other a tax collector. The Pharisee, standing by himself, was praying thus, 'God, I thank you that I am not like other people: thieves, rogues, adulterers, or even like this tax collector. I fast twice a week; I give a tenth of all my income.' But the tax collector, standing far off, would not even look up to heaven, but was beating his breast and saying, 'God, be merciful to me, a sinner!' I tell you, this man went down to his home justified rather than the other; for all who exalt themselves will be humbled, but all who humble themselves will be exalted."

- I allow my prayer to be, "God be merciful to me, a sinner." I identify myself without excuses and I address myself to God, confident of being met with love and mercy.
- Jesus cautions me against anything that elevates me or sets me apart from others. I ask God to help me to be aware of any attitudes or words that demean other people.

Monday 28th October,
Ss Simon & Jude **Ephesians 2:19–22**

So then you are no longer strangers and aliens, but you are citizens with the saints and also members of the household of God, built upon the foundation of the apostles and prophets, with Christ Jesus himself as the cornerstone. In him the whole structure is joined together and grows into a holy temple in the Lord; in whom you also are built together spiritually into a dwelling-place for God.

- Although I pray alone, I am linked in *Sacred Space* with so many others. I am connected, not just with those who pray now, but with the generations of apostles, saints and prophets built on the corner stone that is Christ Jesus himself.
- I pray that I may remember that I am a dwelling-place for God. I cannot make myself worthy, but try to reflect God's generosity by how I live, by what I say and do.

Tuesday 29th October **Luke 13:18–21**

Jesus said to the crowds, "What is the kingdom of God like? And to what should I compare it? It is like a mustard seed that someone took and sowed in the garden; it grew and became a tree, and the birds of the air made nests in its branches." And again he said, "To what should I compare the kingdom of God? It is like yeast that a woman took and mixed in with three measures of flour until all of it was leavened."

- Our attention is naturally drawn to what is biggest and best; it is easy to overlook things that are small, frail and humble. I may be able to trace the "yeast" of a vision, a desire, a dream and see how it has inspired me and others.
- Jesus compared the kingdom of God to common ingredients; to what might I compare God's reign in the ordinary things of my life?

Wednesday 30th October **Luke 13:22–30**

Jesus went through one town and village after another, teaching as he made his way to Jerusalem. Someone asked him, "Lord, will only a few be saved?" He said to them, "Strive to enter through the narrow door; for many, I tell you, will try to enter and will not be able. When once the owner of the house has got up and shut the door, and you begin to stand outside and to knock at the door, saying, 'Lord, open to us', then in reply he will say to you, 'I do not know where you come from.' Then you will begin to say, 'We ate and drank with you, and you taught in our streets.' But he will say, 'I do not know where you come from; go away from me, all you evildoers!' There will be weeping and gnashing of teeth when you see Abraham and Isaac and Jacob and all the prophets in the kingdom of God, and you yourselves thrown out. Then people will come from east and west, from north and south, and will eat in the kingdom of God. Indeed, some are last who will be first, and some are first who will be last."

- Jesus' message is a warning for those who think themselves secure. I am here, praying, seeking signs of God's presence in my life. God already looks on me with love and I already respond.

- My time of prayer draws me into a relationship that shapes how I see myself and how I see the world. I show who God is to me by my words and actions.

Thursday 31st October **Luke 13:31–35**

At that very hour some Pharisees came and said to him, "Get away from here, for Herod wants to kill you." He said to them, "Go and tell that fox for me, 'Listen, I am casting out demons and performing cures today and tomorrow, and on the third day I finish my work. Yet today, tomorrow, and the next day I must be on my way, because it is impossible for a prophet to be killed outside of Jerusalem.' Jerusalem, Jerusalem, the city that kills the prophets and stones those who are sent to it! How often have I desired to gather your children together as a hen gathers her brood under her wings, and you were not willing! See, your house is left to you. And I tell you, you will not see me until the time comes when you say, 'Blessed is the one who comes in the name of the Lord.'"

- When Saint Ignatius suggests that we look on the world as God does, we might have this image of Jesus in mind as he looked on Jerusalem. I think of the cities and towns around me, of all the occupations and busyness of people and consider how God's heart yearns for them all.
- Jesus accepted the cross not only in his crucifixion but in the many small choices that led him to Jerusalem. I pray that I may be ready to embrace God's will not only in the dramatic moments but also in the smaller and painful ones.

Friday 1st November,
Feast of All Saints **Matthew 5:1–12**

When Jesus saw the crowds, he went up the mountain; and after he sat down, his disciples came to him. Then he began to speak, and taught them, saying: "Blessed are the poor in spirit, for theirs is the kingdom of heaven. Blessed are those who mourn, for they will be comforted. Blessed are the meek, for they will inherit the earth. Blessed are those who hunger and thirst for righteousness, for they will be filled. Blessed are the merciful, for they will receive mercy. Blessed are the pure in heart, for they will see God. Blessed are the peacemakers, for they will be called children of God. Blessed are those who are persecuted for righteousness' sake, for theirs is the kingdom of heaven. Blessed are you when people revile you and persecute you and utter all kinds of evil against you falsely on my account. Rejoice and be glad, for your reward is great in heaven, for in the same way they persecuted the prophets who were before you."

- Can I sit before Jesus and listen to him, as if I had never heard these words, these Beatitudes before? What effect do they have on my heart? Joy, tears, confusion, longing?
- Where do I fit in the Beatitudes? Perhaps there is something especially difficult going on in my life right now, such as sickness, or the challenge to be a good carer, or loss of faith and hope. I ask Jesus to make my difficulty into a blessing.

Saturday 2nd November,
Feast of All Souls **Matthew 11:25–30**

At that time Jesus said, "I thank you, Father, Lord of heaven and earth, because you have hidden these things from the wise and the intelligent and have revealed them to infants; yes, Father, for such was your gracious will. All things have been handed over to me by my Father; and no one knows the Son except the Father, and no one knows the Father except the Son and anyone to whom the Son chooses to reveal him. Come to me, all you that are weary and are carrying heavy burdens, and I will give you rest. Take my yoke upon you, and learn from me; for I am gentle and humble in heart, and you will find rest for your souls. For my yoke is easy, and my burden is light."

- Let me spend some moments in quiet gratitude that God cares about me, even though I am not very wise and intelligent! What matters is that I love God, just like an infant who loves a parent.
- I reflect on the burdens I am carrying. I bring them to Jesus. What difference does it make when he takes my burdens on his shoulders? Do I find rest? I ask for the grace to be aware that I am never alone in my weariness, for he is there.

Something to think and pray about each day this week:

Communion with the saints

Can there be communication between the living and those who have died? I mean an awareness of a sensitive if not a dramatic kind, which has nothing to do with mediums and their messages. The Oxford writer C. S. Lewis expressed what went on in him, unbidden and unexpected, after the death of his beloved wife, Joy. This has awakened many of his readers to a sensitivity towards the unobtrusive but solid presence of a deceased beloved. "The sound of a chuckle in the darkness . . . so business-like . . . yet there was a cheerful intimacy . . . solid, utterly reliable, firm. There is no nonsense about the dead . . ."

Such intimate and humble revelations are in line with what many of us may dimly experience. Those with exceptional awareness can encourage us to tune into this new frequency. Human solidarity and the doctrine of the Communion of Saints offer an understanding, in terms of relationships, of the widespread experience of connectedness with those we cared for and who cared for us. They still care.

The Presence of God
God is with me, but more, God is within me.
Let me dwell for a moment on God's life-giving presence
in my body, in my mind, in my heart,
as I sit here, right now.

Freedom
I need to close out the noise, to rise above the noise;
The noise that interrupts, that separates,
The noise that isolates.
I need to listen to God again.

Consciousness
I remind myself that I am in the presence of the Lord.
I will take refuge in His loving heart.
He is my strength in times of weakness.
He is my comforter in times of sorrow.

The Word
I read the Word of God slowly, a few times over, and I listen to what God is saying to me. (Please turn to your scripture on the following pages. Inspiration points are there should you need them. When you are ready, return here to continue.)

Conversation
Do I notice myself reacting as I pray with the Word of God?
Do I feel challenged, comforted, angry?
Imagining Jesus sitting or standing by me,
I speak out my feelings, as one trusted friend to another.

Conclusion
Glory be to the Father, and to the Son, and to the Holy Spirit,
As it was in the beginning, is now and ever shall be,
World without end. Amen

Sunday 3rd November,
Thirty-first Sunday in Ordinary Time **Luke 19:1–10**

Jesus entered Jericho and was passing through it. A man was there named Zacchaeus; he was a chief tax collector and was rich. He was trying to see who Jesus was, but on account of the crowd he could not, because he was short in stature. So he ran ahead and climbed a sycamore tree to see him, because he was going to pass that way. When Jesus came to the place, he looked up and said to him, "Zacchaeus, hurry and come down; for I must stay at your house today." So he hurried down and was happy to welcome him. All who saw it began to grumble and said, "He has gone to be the guest of one who is a sinner." Zacchaeus stood there and said to the Lord, "Look, half of my possessions, Lord, I will give to the poor; and if I have defrauded anyone of anything, I will pay back four times as much." Then Jesus said to him, "Today salvation has come to this house, because he too is a son of Abraham. For the Son of Man came to seek out and to save the lost."

- Zacchaeus was used to getting the best for himself—he even ran ahead of Jesus to get a good vantage point. When Jesus caught up with him, Zacchaeus put his imagination to use in seeing his life differently. I let Jesus find me where I am, hear him recognize my talents, and consider how I might put them to their best use in Jesus' service.
- The people grumbled at Jesus recognition of Zacchaeus—as they were probably used to grumbling at his diligent tax-collecting. I take care that no grumbling habit blind me to the presence of God's grace.

Monday 4th November **Luke 14:12–14**

Jesus said also to the one who had invited him, "When you give a luncheon or a dinner, do not invite your friends or your brothers or your relatives or rich neighbors, in case they may invite you in return, and you would be repaid. But when you give a banquet, invite the poor, the crippled, the lame, and the blind. And you will be blessed, because they cannot repay you, for you will be repaid at the resurrection of the righteous."

- Jesus' words reveal his generous heart. I try again to accept that I am here in prayer not because I am worthy but so that I might become more open to accept the gifts that God offers to me.
- I call to mind those who are without the advantages I enjoy: Jesus wishes such blessings for them too. How can I wish anything less for them? What might I do to express my gratitude to God for being so good to me?

Tuesday 5th November **Romans 12:9–16**

Let love be genuine; hate what is evil, hold fast to what is good; love one another with mutual affection; outdo one another in showing honor. Do not lag in zeal, be ardent in spirit, serve the Lord. Rejoice in hope, be patient in suffering, persevere in prayer. Contribute to the needs of the saints; extend hospitality to strangers. Bless those who persecute you; bless and do not curse them. Rejoice with those who rejoice, weep with those who weep. Live in harmony with one another; do not be haughty, but associate with the lowly; do not claim to be wiser than you are.

- Paul provides us with practical instruction about how to act. We must live positively and with energy in our service—"rejoice", "contribute", "extend", "bless", "live in harmony."
- Are we joyful Christians? Do we show genuine love in energetic service of others?

Wednesday 6th November **Luke 14:25–27**

Now large crowds were travelling with him; and he turned and said to them, "Whoever comes to me and does not hate father and mother, wife and children, brothers and sisters, yes, and even life itself, cannot be my disciple. Whoever does not carry the cross and follow me cannot be my disciple."

- "Carry the cross" reminds us of Good Friday, and Jesus stumbling under the weight of his cross. For most of us, the cross is not inflicted from outside us, but part of our make-up: the body's and mind's infirmities, the addictions, temptations and recurrent desires that rob us of our freedom.
- "Carrying my cross" means that we do not so much solve these problems, as learn to live with them, unsurprisable and humble.

Thursday 7th November **Luke 15:1–10**

Now all the tax-collectors and sinners were coming near to listen to him. And the Pharisees and the scribes were grumbling and saying, "This fellow welcomes sinners and eats with them." So he told them this parable: "Which one of you, having a hundred sheep and losing one of them, does not leave the ninety-nine in the wilderness and go after the one that is lost until he finds it? When he has found it, he lays it on his shoulders and rejoices. And when he comes home, he calls together his friends and neighbours, saying to them, 'Rejoice with me, for I have found my sheep that was lost.' Just so, I tell you, there will be more joy in heaven over one sinner who repents than over ninety-nine righteous people who need no repentance. "Or what woman having ten silver coins, if she loses one of them, does not light a lamp, sweep the house, and search carefully until she finds it? When she has found it, she calls together her friends and neighbours, saying, 'Rejoice with me, for I have found the coin that I had lost.' Just so, I tell you, there is joy in the presence of the angels of God over one sinner who repents."

- Would I join in with the present-day tax-collectors and sinners as they flock to Jesus? Or would I want a private audience? I talk with Jesus about this.
- This passage reveals the heart of God, who searches out for the lost. Can I admit that I often get lost and forget where my true home is? How does it feel to imagine Jesus going in search of me and finding me?

Friday 8th November **Luke 16:1–8**

Then Jesus said to the disciples, "There was a rich man who had a manager, and charges were brought to him that this man was squandering his property. So he summoned him and said to him, 'What is this that I hear about you? Give me an accounting of your management, because you cannot be my manager any longer.' Then the manager said to himself, 'What will I do, now that my master is taking the position away from me? I am not strong enough to dig, and I am ashamed to beg. I have decided what to do so that, when I am dismissed as manager, people may welcome me into their homes.' So, summoning his master's debtors one by one, he asked the first, 'How much do you owe my master?' He answered, 'A hundred jugs of olive oil.' He said to him, 'Take your bill, sit down quickly, and make it fifty.' Then he asked another, 'And how much do you owe?' He replied, 'A hundred containers of wheat.' He said to him, 'Take your bill and make it eighty.' And his master commended the dishonest manager because he had acted shrewdly; for the children of this age are more shrewd in dealing with their own generation than are the children of light."

- The master's commendation may seem strange until I realize that he values the imagination, energy and commitment displayed by the steward. I think of how I bring my imagination to the service of others in the name of the Gospel.
- I may hear criticism of "the children of this age." I think about what example they might offer to me as I endeavour to live in Jesus' way.

Saturday 9th November,
Dedication of the Lateran Basilica **John 2:13–22**

The Passover of the Jews was near, and Jesus went up to Jerusalem. In the temple he found people selling cattle, sheep, and doves, and the money changers seated at their tables. Making a whip of cords, he drove all of them out of the temple, both the sheep and the cattle. He also poured out the coins of the money changers and overturned their tables. He told those who were selling the doves, "Take these things out of here! Stop making my Father's house a marketplace!" His disciples remembered that it was written, "Zeal for your house will consume me." The Jews then said to him, "What sign can you show us for doing this?" Jesus answered them, "Destroy this temple, and in three days I will raise it up." The Jews then said, "This temple has been under construction for forty-six years, and will you raise it up in three days?" But he was speaking of the temple of his body. After he was raised from the dead, his disciples remembered that he had said this; and they believed the scripture and the word that Jesus had spoken.

- I pray: "Jesus, you got really angry in the temple! Are there things about me that make you angry? My heart is your temple: do I clutter it up so much that there is little space for you?"
- When I see things going on which are wrong, do I do anything about it? I need to ask Jesus for some of his courage to stand up for the truth and not to give in to those who threaten me.

Sacred Space

november 10–16

Something to think and pray about each day this week:

Filling emptiness
One song of the Bengali Hindu poet mystic, Rabindranath Tagore, could stay with us in our prayer, celebrating the mysterious and endless coming of God into our empty hearts: "Have you not heard his silent steps? He comes, comes, ever comes. Every moment and every age, every day and every night, he comes, comes, ever comes. In the fragrant days of sunny April through the forest path he comes, comes, ever comes. In sorrow after sorrow it is his steps that press upon my heart, and it is the golden touch of his feet that makes my joy to shine."

The Presence of God
As I sit here, the beating of my heart,
the ebb and flow of my breathing, the movements of my mind
are all signs of God's ongoing creation of me.
I pause for a moment, and become aware
of this presence of God within me.

Freedom
Lord, grant me the grace to be free from the excesses of this life.
Let me not get caught up with the desire for wealth.
Keep my heart and mind free to love and serve you.

Consciousness
In God's loving presence I unwind the past day,
starting from now and looking back, moment by moment.
I gather in all the goodness and light, in gratitude.
I attend to the shadows and what they say to me,
seeking healing, courage, forgiveness.

The Word
I take my time to read the Word of God, slowly, a few times, allowing myself to dwell on anything that strikes me. (Please turn to your scripture on the following pages. Inspiration points are there should you need them. When you are ready, return here to continue.)

Conversation
Remembering that I am still in God's presence,
I imagine Jesus himself standing or sitting beside me,
and say whatever is on my mind, whatever is in my heart,
speaking as one friend to another.

Conclusion
Glory be to the Father, and to the Son, and to the Holy Spirit,
As it was in the beginning, is now and ever shall be,
World without end. Amen

Sunday 10th November,
Thirty-second Sunday in Ordinary Time Luke 20:27–38

Some Sadducees, those who say there is no resurrection, came to Jesus and asked him a question, "Teacher, Moses wrote for us that if a man's brother dies, leaving a wife but no children, the man shall marry the widow and raise up children for his brother. Now there were seven brothers; the first married, and died childless; then the second and the third married her, and so in the same way all seven died childless. Finally the woman also died. In the resurrection, therefore, whose wife will the woman be? For the seven had married her." Jesus said to them, "Those who belong to this age marry and are given in marriage; but those who are considered worthy of a place in that age and in the resurrection from the dead neither marry nor are given in marriage. Indeed they cannot die any more, because they are like angels and are children of God, being children of the resurrection. And the fact that the dead are raised Moses himself showed, in the story about the bush, where he speaks of the Lord as the God of Abraham, the God of Isaac, and the God of Jacob. Now he is God not of the dead, but of the living; for to him all of them are alive."

- It may be that the conundrum of the Sadducees was offered more to confound Jesus than to seek illumination. I consider whether my conversations with others help to bring light and meaning.
- I pray with compassion for all those whose reason and intelligence is missing the humility to accept the truths that faith uncovers, I give thanks for the intuitions and insights that have been given to me.

Monday 11th November Luke 17:1–6

Jesus said to his disciples, "Occasions for stumbling are bound to come, but woe to anyone by whom they come! It would be better for you if a millstone were hung around your neck and you were thrown into the sea than for you to cause one of these little ones to stumble. Be on your guard! If another disciple sins, you must rebuke the offender, and if there is repentance, you must forgive. And if the same person sins against you seven times a day, and turns back to you seven times and says, 'I repent,' you must forgive." The apostles said to the Lord, "Increase our faith!" The Lord replied, "If you had faith the size of a mustard seed, you could say to this mulberry tree, 'Be uprooted and planted in the sea,' and it would obey you."

- "Little ones" means vulnerable people who cannot defend themselves. Have I ever hurt or diminished someone weaker than myself? Am I a bully? If so I beg forgiveness of God and pray for those whose happiness I have taken away.
- Do people think of me as someone who forgives easily? Jesus never holds grudges against anyone, and I must become like him to be a true disciple.

Tuesday 12th November **Luke 17:7–10**

Jesus said to his disciples, "Who among you would say to your slave who has just come in from plowing or tending sheep in the field, 'Come here at once and take your place at the table'? Would you not rather say to him, 'Prepare supper for me, put on your apron and serve me while I eat and drink; later you may eat and drink'? Do you thank the slave for doing what was commanded? So you also, when you have done all that you were ordered to do, say, 'We are worthless slaves; we have done only what we ought to have done!'"

- If I feel a bit deflated by this Gospel, I have got its message! I can easily focus on my virtue, my good deeds, my generosity in forgiving others, my care for the vulnerable, and so on. Instead I must see that God gives me the ability to do all these things. There is absolutely nothing for me to boast about.
- I pray: "Dear Lord, you didn't spend your time boasting about all you did and all you suffered. You were like a slave, serving us all, washing our feet, dying for us. Make me a bit more like you in your humility and self-forgetfulness."

Wednesday 13th November **Luke 17:11–19**

On the way to Jerusalem Jesus was going through the region between Samaria and Galilee. As he entered a village, ten lepers approached him. Keeping their distance, they called out, saying, "Jesus, Master, have mercy on us!" When he saw them, he said to them, "Go and show yourselves to the priests." And as they went, they were made clean. Then one of them, when he saw that he was healed, turned back, praising God with a loud voice. He prostrated himself at Jesus' feet and thanked him. And he was a Samaritan. Then Jesus asked, "Were not ten made clean? But the other nine, where are they? Was none of them found to return and give praise to God except this foreigner?" Then he said to him, "Get up and go on your way; your faith has made you well."

- The healed man finds it in his heart to praise God. His first words had been words of trustful petition: petition and thanks are fundamental movements of prayer. We engage one or the other, sometimes both.
- Asking for what we want, giving praise for what we are grateful for—these are the essentials of prayer.

Thursday 14th November **Luke 17:20–25**

Once Jesus was asked by the Pharisees when the kingdom of God was coming, and he answered, "The kingdom of God is not coming with things that can be observed; nor will they say, 'Look, here it is!' or 'There it is!' For, in fact, the kingdom of God is among you." Then he said to the disciples, "The days are coming when you will long to see one of the days of the Son of Man, and you will not see it. They will say to you, 'Look there!' or 'Look here!' Do not go, do not set off in pursuit. For as the lightning flashes and lights up the sky from one side to the other, so will the Son of Man be in his day. But first he must endure much suffering and be rejected by this generation."

- The kingdom of God is quiet and unobtrusive, not a big show. One way to understand it is as a domination-free society in which people are liberated to become what God means them to be. I ask that I may not dominate anyone but respect everyone's freedom to be themselves.

- I pray: "Jesus, you often speak about having to suffer. May I have the courage to bear patiently the crosses that life sends me. May I believe that unavoidable suffering, patiently endured, brings good to the world, as your death did."

Friday 15th November **Luke 17:26–37**

Just as it was in the days of Noah, so too it will be in the days of the Son of Man. They were eating and drinking, and marrying and being given in marriage, until the day Noah entered the ark, and the flood came and destroyed all of them. Likewise, just as it was in the days of Lot: they were eating and drinking, buying and selling, planting and building, but on the day that Lot left Sodom, it rained fire and sulfur from heaven and destroyed all of them—it will be like that on the day that the Son of Man is revealed. On that day, anyone on the housetop who has belongings in the house must not come down to take them away; and likewise anyone in the field must not turn back. Remember Lot's wife. Those who try to make their life secure will lose it, but those who lose their life will keep it. I tell you, on that night there will be two in one bed; one will be taken and the other left. There will be two women grinding meal together; one will be taken and the other left.

- The preacher asked his congregation: "You all want to go to heaven. Isn't that right?" "Yes," they responded. The preacher went on: "Good. Who wants to go to heaven right now?" There was silence! I ask not to be so caught up in my affairs that I am no longer focussed on God.
- I pray: "Lord, I can be like Lot's wife. She spent her time looking back at her possessions instead of looking forward to what God would provide for her. Teach me to look forward to your coming."

Saturday 16th November **Luke 18:1–8**

Then Jesus told them a parable about their need to pray always and not to lose heart. He said, "In a certain city there was a judge who neither feared God nor had respect for people. In that city there was a widow who kept coming to him and saying, 'Grant me justice against my opponent.' For a while he refused; but later he said to himself, 'Though I have no fear of God and no respect for anyone, yet because this widow keeps bothering me, I will grant her justice, so that she may not wear me out by continually coming.'" And the Lord said, "Listen to what the unjust judge says. And will not God grant justice to his chosen ones who cry to him day and night? Will he delay long in helping them? I tell you, he will quickly grant justice to them. And yet, when the Son of Man comes, will he find faith on earth?"

- St Luke shows that Jesus prayed consistently during his public life and his Passion. I am Jesus' disciple, and he needs me to be a person of prayer also. Prayer is like a rope that keeps us close to God. If I let the rope go, I drift away from God.
- I pray: "Jesus, when you search my heart, do you find any faith inside it? Stretch my small heart so that I may take the risk of entrusting myself more to you."

Sacred Space

Something to think and pray about each day this week:

The question

"What happens after death?" This question won't go away, even though it is rarely asked in public. In the confusion of our times, many believers have adopted a "wait and see" attitude. Some believe in God, but not in a life to come. Others believe in an after-life, but not in God! For one parent, the issue of the afterlife never arose until her child asked while a funeral was passing, "Mam, what's in that nice brown box with the flowers on it?" Then, "Mam, will you die too?" And then, "Where will you go? Can I come too?"

Christianity opens out a vast vision of the life to come. You don't have to be a practicing Christian to enter the next life, but if you are a Christian, certain things follow. To be a Christian certainly means membership of a particular Church and adherence to the Golden Rule which is common to many religions, "Treat others as you would wish them to treat you." But Christianity is much more than that: it is strongly future-oriented. It claims that God in Jesus Christ intervened creatively in our history, so that our lives now have not only present but ultimate meaning. It teaches that our destiny lies beyond this present world; that we are in fact made to be in joy with God eternally. To be truly a Christian, then, is to commit yourself to hope in the life of the world to come. Eternal life is our inheritance, held safe for us by a loving God. This is the great promise of Jesus.

The Presence of God
As I sit here, the beating of my heart,
the ebb and flow of my breathing, the movements of my mind
are all signs of God's ongoing creation of me.
I pause for a moment, and become aware
of this presence of God within me.

Freedom
I will ask God's help,
to be free from my own preoccupations,
to be open to God in this time of prayer,
to come to love and serve him more.

Consciousness
Help me, Lord, to be more conscious of your presence.
Teach me to recognize your presence in others.
Fill my heart with gratitude for the times your love
has been shown to me through the care of others.

The Word
I take my time to read the Word of God, slowly, a few times, allowing myself to dwell on anything that strikes me. (Please turn to your scripture on the following pages. Inspiration points are there should you need them. When you are ready, return here to continue.)

Conversation
Remembering that I am still in God's presence,
I imagine Jesus himself standing or sitting beside me,
and say whatever is on my mind, whatever is in my heart,
speaking as one friend to another.

Conclusion
Glory be to the Father, and to the Son, and to the Holy Spirit,
As it was in the beginning, is now and ever shall be,
World without end. Amen

Sunday 17th November,
Thirty-third Sunday in Ordinary Time — Luke 21:5–8

When some were speaking about the temple, how it was adorned with beautiful stones and gifts dedicated to God, Jesus said, "As for these things that you see, the day will come when not one stone will be left upon another; all will be thrown down." They asked him, "Teacher, when will this be, and what will be the sign that this is about to take place?" And he said, "Beware that you are not led astray; for many will come in my name and say, 'I am he' and, 'The time is near!' Do not go after them."

- Jesus reminds us not to become too proud of our achievements or set in unnecessary convictions.
- There are many who speak in extreme words, telling the news in alarming and unsettling ways. Unlike Jesus, they do not offer truth or life. I listen to him now and hear how he speaks to me of the voices that are not for my good.

Monday 18th November — Luke 18:35–43

As he approached Jericho, a blind man was sitting by the roadside begging. When he heard a crowd going by, he asked what was happening. They told him, "Jesus of Nazareth is passing by." Then he shouted, "Jesus, Son of David, have mercy on me!" Those who were in front sternly ordered him to be quiet; but he shouted even more loudly, "Son of David, have mercy on me!" Jesus stood still and ordered the man to be brought to him; and when he came near, he asked him, "What do you want me to do for you?" He said, "Lord, let me see again." Jesus said to him, "Receive your sight; your faith has saved you." Immediately he regained his sight and followed him, glorifying God; and all the people, when they saw it, praised God.

- The poor can be a nuisance because they disturb our comfortable lives. I talk with Jesus about my attitude to the needy. I see that Jesus reverses human values and puts this blind beggar first. I ask for grace to do the same.

- I pray: "Jesus, I am the blind beggar. I just don't see the things that are truly important. Have mercy on me! Heal me, so that I may glorify you and follow you more closely."

Tuesday 19th November **Luke 19:1–10**

Jesus entered Jericho and was passing through it. A man was there named Zacchaeus; he was a chief tax-collector and was rich. He was trying to see who Jesus was, but on account of the crowd he could not, because he was short in stature. So he ran ahead and climbed a sycamore tree to see him, because he was going to pass that way. When Jesus came to the place, he looked up and said to him, "Zacchaeus, hurry and come down; for I must stay at your house today." So he hurried down and was happy to welcome him. All who saw it began to grumble and said, "He has gone to be the guest of one who is a sinner." Zacchaeus stood there and said to the Lord, "Look, half of my possessions, Lord, I will give to the poor; and if I have defrauded anyone of anything, I will pay back four times as much." Then Jesus said to him, "Today salvation has come to this house, because he too is a son of Abraham. For the Son of Man came to seek out and to save the lost."

- I am small, so I ask Jesus to lift me up onto his shoulders, so that I may see the world as he sees it. This is what prayer is like.
- I pray: "Jesus, you became the guest of a sinner that day. Please be my guest every day, though I am a sinner too."

Wednesday 20th November **Luke 19:11–28**

As they were listening to this, he went on to tell a parable, because he was near Jerusalem, and because they supposed that the kingdom of God was to appear immediately. So he said, 'A nobleman went to a distant country to get royal power for himself and then return. He summoned ten of his slaves, and gave them ten pounds, and said to them, "Do business with these until I come back." But the citizens of his country hated him and sent a delegation after him, saying, "We do not want this man to rule over us." When he returned, having received royal power, he ordered these slaves, to whom he had given the money, to be summoned so that he might find out what they had gained by trading. The first came forward and said, "Lord, your pound has made ten more pounds." He said to him, "Well done, good slave! Because you have been trustworthy in a very small thing, take charge of ten cities." Then the second came, saying, "Lord, your pound has made five pounds." He said to him, "And you, rule over five cities." Then the other came, saying, "Lord, here is your pound. I wrapped it up in a piece of cloth, for I was afraid of you, because you are a harsh man; you take what you did not deposit, and reap what you did not sow." He said to him, "I will judge you by your own words, you wicked slave! You knew, did you, that I was a harsh man, taking what I did not deposit and reaping what I did not sow? Why then did you not put my money into the bank? Then when I returned, I could have collected it with interest." He said to the bystanders, "Take the pound from him and give it to the one who has ten pounds." (And they said to him, "Lord, he has ten pounds!") "I tell you, to all those who have, more will be given; but from those who have nothing, even what they have will be taken away. But as for these enemies of mine who did not want me to be king over them—bring them here and slaughter them in my presence."

- I pray: "Jesus, you are near Jerusalem, the place where you will be put to death. I travel with you, though I am afraid. I ask you to travel with me when my path is difficult and leads to the cross."
- God gives me my daily tasks, some of them easy, some laborious. Each morning I ask that I may work with a generous heart, and each evening I bring the fruits to God and receive God's thanks and blessing.

Thursday 21st November,
Presentation of the Blessed Virgin Mary — Luke 19:41–44

As Jesus came near and saw the city, he wept over it, saying, "If you, even you, had only recognized on this day the things that make for peace! But now they are hidden from your eyes. Indeed, the days will come upon you, when your enemies will set up ramparts around you and surround you, and hem you in on every side. They will crush you to the ground, you and your children within you, and they will not leave within you one stone upon another; because you did not recognize the time of your visitation from God."

- I sit with Jesus as he weeps, and put my arm around his shoulders. I ask to be moved, even to tears, for the state of the world. Then I ask him to comfort me when things get to be too much for me.
- I pray: "Jesus, you come to visit me all the time. You come in this prayer time now, and when it ends you will visit me in the disguise of all those I meet. You work with me in my daily tasks, enabling me to do what pleases you. And you visit me in my sorrows, taking my burdens on yourself. Thank you!"

Friday 22nd November **Luke 19:45–48**

Then Jesus entered the temple and began to drive out those who were selling things there; and he said, "It is written, 'My house shall be a house of prayer'; but you have made it a den of robbers." Every day he was teaching in the temple. The chief priests, the scribes, and the leaders of the people kept looking for a way to kill him; but they did not find anything they could do, for all the people were spellbound by what they heard.

- The house I live in can be a house of prayer, a place where God feels welcome and at home. I say to God: "Make yourself at home: you're always welcome!"
- "The people were spellbound by what they heard." When I listen to the Word of God or read it for myself I need to do so as if I had never heard it before. It comes to me fresh, original, every day. It's like bread just taken from the oven, ready to nourish me for the day.

Saturday 23rd November **Luke 20:27–40**

Some Sadducees, those who say there is no resurrection, came to him and asked him a question, "Teacher, Moses wrote for us that if a man's brother dies, leaving a wife but no children, the man shall marry the widow and raise up children for his brother. Now there were seven brothers; the first married, and died childless; then the second and the third married her, and so in the same way all seven died childless. Finally the woman also died. In the resurrection, therefore, whose wife will the woman be? For the seven had married her." Jesus said to them, "Those who belong to this age marry and are given in marriage; but those who are considered worthy of a place in that age and in the resurrection from the dead neither marry nor are given in marriage. Indeed they cannot die any more, because they are like angels and are children of God, being children of the resurrection. And the fact that the dead are raised Moses himself showed, in the story about the bush, where he speaks of the Lord as the God of Abraham, the God of Isaac, and the God of Jacob. Now he is God not of the dead, but of the living; for to him all of them are alive." Then some of the scribes answered, "Teacher, you have spoken well." For they no longer dared to ask him another question.

- I watch as Jesus tries to raise the minds of his questioners to a higher level, to the level from which God sees. I ask him to share his vision, so that I may see something of the wonderful plans God has for us all.
- I pray: "Dear God, you are God of the living. In death you meet us and make us live eternally. Help me to believe that there are no 'dead' people, only people who have passed through death and are now fully alive, children of the resurrection."

Sacred Space

Something to think and pray about each day this week:

Freedom with God

What is God planning as our final destiny? Many fear that in the next life God will somehow take us over and remove from us our freedom to be ourselves. But what God is about is not our submission but our freedom, a gift we rightly value so much. God is free, and invites us to be free. Parents, at their best, want their children to mature into fully free persons; likewise God desires this for us.

Freedom is not simply the capacity to do nothing, or to be selfish. To be truly free is to be able to express our potential fully and appropriately. And that is the freedom that Jesus brings. The New Testament is full of it. Jesus proclaims freedom for captives and the oppressed (Luke 4:18). Paul asserts: "For freedom Christ has set us free!" (Galatians 5:1). The story of salvation is all about liberation from the various traps of political slavery, sin, law and death which inhibit God's people from living life to the full. "Where the Spirit of the Lord is, there is freedom" (2 Corinthians 3:17). Freedom is God's goal for us. One great theologian, Balthasar, remarks that when God says, "Be holy as I am holy" (1 Peter 1:16) this means *"Be free as I am free."*

This can help to dispel our fear that God is out to limit our autonomy. God is not a dominating God, but rather wants to make us "fully alive" as St Irenaeus said long ago, in loving friendship with God and with one another.

The Presence of God

I pause for a moment
and reflect on God's life-giving presence
in every part of my body, in everything around me,
in the whole of my life.

Freedom

God is not foreign to my freedom.
Instead the Spirit breathes life into my most intimate desires,
gently nudging me towards all that is good.
I ask for the grace to let myself be enfolded by the Spirit.

Consciousness

I exist in a web of relationships—links to nature, people, God.
I trace out these links, giving thanks for the life that flows through them.
Some links are twisted or broken: I may feel regret, anger, disappointment.
I pray for the gift of acceptance and forgiveness.

The Word

God speaks to each one of us individually. I need to listen to what he is saying to me. (Please turn to your scripture on the following pages. Inspiration points are there should you need them. When you are ready, return here to continue.)

Conversation

How has God's Word moved me? Has it left me cold?
Has it consoled me or moved me to act in a new way?
I imagine Jesus standing or sitting beside me,
I turn and share my feelings with him.

Conclusion

Glory be to the Father, and to the Son, and to the Holy Spirit,
As it was in the beginning, is now and ever shall be,
World without end. Amen

Sunday 24th November,
Feast of Christ the King **Luke 23:35–43**

And the people stood by, watching; but the leaders scoffed at Jesus, saying, "He saved others; let him save himself if he is the Messiah of God, his chosen one!" The soldiers also mocked him, coming up and offering him sour wine, and saying, "If you are the King of the Jews, save yourself!" There was also an inscription over him, "This is the King of the Jews." One of the criminals who were hanged there kept deriding him and saying, "Are you not the Messiah? Save yourself and us!" But the other rebuked him, saying, "Do you not fear God, since you are under the same sentence of condemnation? And we indeed have been condemned justly, for we are getting what we deserve for our deeds, but this man has done nothing wrong." Then he said, "Jesus, remember me when you come into your kingdom." He replied, "Truly I tell you, today you will be with me in Paradise."

- Glamour and splendor mark the presence of earthly royalty. Jesus is not recognizable as King to those expecting power or glory. We need to train ourselves to look for signs of Jesus' reign. His real identity can be seen only by the humble.
- The "good thief" saw things as they were: he knew his own sinfulness; he recognized Jesus' character; he asked for little yet was rewarded for his honesty. Humility brings a true perspective and is the ground for meeting God. I pray for humility.

Monday 25th November **Luke 21:1–4**

Jesus looked up and saw rich people putting their gifts into the treasury; he also saw a poor widow put in two small copper coins. He said, "Truly I tell you, this poor widow has put in more than all of them; for all of them have contributed out of their abundance, but she out of her poverty has put in all she had to live on."

- Years of talk and the experience of financial crises, downturns and recession have made many of us cautious. Generosity can be a sign of the goodness of God. In times of constraint and financial stress for many people it may be all the more necessary.

Tuesday 26th November **Luke 21:5–11**

When some were speaking about the temple, how it was adorned with beautiful stones and gifts dedicated to God, Jesus said, "As for these things that you see, the days will come when not one stone will be left upon another; all will be thrown down." They asked him, "Teacher, when will this be, and what will be the sign that this is about to take place?" And he said, "Beware that you are not led astray; for many will come in my name and say, 'I am he!' and, 'The time is near!' Do not go after them. When you hear of wars and insurrections, do not be terrified; for these things must take place first, but the end will not follow immediately." Then he said to them, "Nation will rise against nation, and kingdom against kingdom; there will be great earthquakes, and in various places famines and plagues; and there will be dreadful portents and great signs from heaven."

- The readings from today until Advent are full of warnings about the end times. But I am not to be terrified, because God's providence will see me through whatever evils may beset our world.
- I pray: "Jesus, you care about the whole world. Even though the human story seems to be full of disasters, you are labouring so that it may end in triumph. Give me courage and energy to play my small part, so that at the end I may rejoice with you."

Wednesday 27th November **Luke 21:12–19**

Jesus said to his disciples, "But before all this occurs, they will arrest you and persecute you; they will hand you over to synagogues and prisons, and you will be brought before kings and governors because of my name. This will give you an opportunity to testify. So make up your minds not to prepare your defense in advance; for I will give you words and a wisdom that none of your opponents will be able to withstand or contradict. You will be betrayed even by parents and brothers, by relatives and friends; and they will put some of you to death. You will be hated by all because of my name. But not a hair of your head will perish. By your endurance you will gain your souls."

- Jesus does not promise that life will be easy for his disciples. What he does promise is that he will give us words and wisdom to hold fast to the Good News. This Good News includes the promise of our resurrection.
- I pray: "Jesus, I admire your endurance. You put up with so much frustration and opposition; you were betrayed and put to death. Give me a share of that endurance, so that I may not crumble when things get tough!"

Thursday 28th November **Luke 21:20–28**

Jesus said to the disciples, "When you see Jerusalem surrounded by armies, then know that its desolation has come near. Then those in Judea must flee to the mountains, and those inside the city must leave it, and those out in the country must not enter it; for these are days of vengeance, as a fulfillment of all that is written. Woe to those who are pregnant and to those who are nursing infants in those days! For there will be great distress on the earth and wrath against this people; they will fall by the edge of the sword and be taken away as captives among all nations; and Jerusalem will be trampled on by the Gentiles, until the times of the Gentiles are fulfilled. There will be signs in the sun, the moon, and the stars, and on the earth distress among nations confused by the roaring of the sea and the waves. People will faint from fear and foreboding of what is coming upon the world, for the powers of the heavens will be shaken. Then they will see 'the Son of Man coming in a cloud' with power and great glory. Now when these things begin to take place, stand up and raise your heads, because your redemption is drawing near."

- Day after day in these Gospel passages Jesus is speaking with his disciples, bracing them against disasters. If he were preaching now he would speak of wars, nuclear and ecological disasters, terrorist attacks. "Don't lose heart," he says to us, "God still directs human history and will bring good out of it—your redemption."
- I pray: "Jesus, when the evil and suffering of the world tempt me to lose faith, let the words of St Thomas Aquinas calm me. He writes that God is so powerful and good that he would allow no evil in any of his works unless he could bring good out of it."

Friday 29th November **Luke 21:29–33**

Then Jesus told them a parable: "Look at the fig tree and all the trees; as soon as they sprout leaves you can see for yourselves and know that summer is already near. So also, when you see these things taking place, you know that the kingdom of God is near. Truly I tell you, this generation will not pass away until all things have taken place. Heaven and earth will pass away, but my words will not pass away."

- Nature can be a great teacher. As the seasons change they can reveal much to me about the ways of God. Jesus learnt from birds and foxes, lilies and fig trees. By becoming a more reflective person, I can do the same.
- While everything else may change and pass away, the Good News remains, because it is beyond history: it comes from God. I thank Jesus for bringing the Good News of hope for our world, and I ask as a disciple to share it with those willing to listen.

Saturday 30th November,
St Andrew, Apostle **Matthew 4:18–22**

As he walked by the Sea of Galilee, he saw two brothers, Simon, who is called Peter, and Andrew his brother, casting a net into the sea—for they were fishermen. And he said to them, "Follow me, and I will make you fish for people." Immediately they left their nets and followed him. As he went from there, he saw two other brothers, James son of Zebedee and his brother John, in the boat with their father Zebedee, mending their nets, and he called them. Immediately they left the boat and their father, and followed him.

- Jesus recognizes our skills: he takes them and redirects them to a higher cause, so that we can serve others through them. I ask to see that I have my personal mission, given me by Jesus. I am part of the *Sacred Space* network—good people who try to be Good News wherever they may be.
- I pray: "Jesus, show me what I need to leave behind in order to be a good disciple. Do not let me fall far behind you and lose sight of you. Keep me close. Thank you for these times of prayer, and for inviting me to share a meal with you in the Eucharist."

Sacred Space Prayer

Dear Lord
The music of our lives is meant to be a symphony of love.

Endlessly and lovingly you sustain us
and we learn to respond as best we can.

You gaze on us and you smile, and we smile back.

You speak your life-giving Word in our hearts
and refresh us constantly through our daily prayer.

Grant that we, the Sacred Space Community, may become the 'Good News in the present tense' to a needy world.